Bodies Under Siege
How the Far-Right Attack on Reproductive Rights Went Global

SIAN NORRIS

UNCORRECTED PAGE PROOFS
Please do not reprint without publisher's prior approval

VERSO

Contact: Michelle Betters
michelle@versobooks.com

ISBN 9781839764738
304 pages · Hardcover • $29.95
On s   · 2023

D1409113

Bodies Under Siege
How the Far-Right Attack on Reproductive Rights Went Global

SIAN NORRIS

UNCORRECTED PAGE PROOF
Please do not quote without checking against the finished book

Contact Michelle Bernard
michelle@versobooks.com

ISBN 978-1-83976-473-8
307 pp · Hardback · $29.95
Publication date: 2023

Bodies Under Siege

How the Far-Right Attack on Reproductive Rights Went Global

Siân Norris

VERSO

London • New York

First published by Verso 2023
© Siân Norris 2023

1 3 5 7 9 10 8 6 4 2

Verso
UK: 6 Meard Street, London W1F 0EG
US: 388 Atlantic Avenue, Brooklyn, NY 11217
versobooks.com

Verso is the imprint of New Left Books

ISBN-13: 978-1-83976-473-8
ISBN-13: 978-1-83976-478-3 (UK EBK)
ISBN-13: 978-1-83976-479-0 (US EBK)

British Library Cataloguing in Publication Data
A catalogue record for this book is available from the British Library

Library of Congress Cataloging-in-Publication Data
A catalog record for this book is available from the Library of Congress

Typeset in Sabon by MJ & N Gavan, Truro, Cornwall
Printed and bound by CPI Group (UK) Ltd, Croydon CR0 4YY

By denying women control over their bodies, the states deprived them of the most fundamental condition for physical and psychological integrity and degraded maternity to the status of forced labour.

Silvia Federici

The truth will set you free. But first of all it will piss you off.

Gloria Steinem

The Catholic hierarchy in Ireland in the 1980s was the far-right. And it remained the far-right for a very long time. Until we started smashing it.

Ailbhe Smyth

Contents

A Note on Language

In this book, I refer to reproductive rights to mean access to abortion and contraception, as well as maternal healthcare. I refer to sexual rights to mean the freedom to love and have consensual physical relationships with the person we choose. I refer to 'black and global majority people' when talking on a global scale, and 'black and ethnic minority people' when talking about individual countries that have white majority populations. I recognise that race is a social construct – there is no such thing, for example, as a 'white race'.

Throughout this book I tend to use 'women and girls' to identify the people most affected by the far-right attack on reproductive rights. This is for two reasons. The first is that they make up the majority of those who are impacted by any abortion bans. The second is that far-right attacks on abortion are rooted in a past and present of misogyny. That misogyny is rooted in centuries of oppression and reproductive exploitation. I fully recognise that people who don't identify as women or girls – such as transgender, genderqueer, and non-binary people – will also be impacted by any restrictions to abortion and where appropriate I make this clear by using the term 'women, girls and pregnant people'.

Preface

Towards the end of my second edit of this book, I heard the news that *Roe v. Wade* – the 1973 Supreme Court ruling that guaranteed abortion rights across the United States – had been overruled. I had just returned from a reporting trip in Kenya where I had spent an incredible ten days interviewing pro-abortion activists. To get this news the very day I arrived home, bleary-eyed from a night flight, was devastating.

But it was not surprising. For years, I had been predicting the end of *Roe*. I had felt like a sad Cassandra, warning of disaster to a disbelieving and unreceptive audience. The process of researching this book, and the investigative journalism I had done in the years running up to writing it, meant that an end to nationwide abortion rights in the US felt terrifyingly inevitable. The rise of the white Christian nationalism which accelerated under Trump was not going to quit until women's human rights were crushed. Now, as a pro-abortion movement, we cannot give up.

I'm a journalist by trade, but this book is not a news article – and so while I obviously updated the text during the final edit to acknowledge the end of *Roe*, I don't go into detail about its overruling or the horrors inflicted on women's and girls' bodies since the decision.

Instead, this book is intended to demonstrate the patterns of misogyny and white supremacy that underpin attacks on abortion rights in the Global North.

Similarly, most of this book was written when Boris Johnson was prime minister, and before Brothers of Italy (Fratelli d'Italia) started surging ahead in the Italian polls. I have tried where I can to be as up to date as possible given the restrictions of publishing lead times, but the detail of the news cycle is not the point: rather, I want to draw attention to the patterns behind the shift in women's rights.

When I started reporting on the far-right attacks on abortion rights, which then led to a long process of putting a book proposal together and finally writing this book, I would often be met by bemusement when I tried to explain that the anti-abortion movement is fuelled by misogyny and white supremacy. People did not necessarily see it as a far-right project linked to conspiracy theories about 'white genocide'.

That has shifted now, in part because the process of normalising far-right ideas about women's bodies that I track in this book has taken place. Radical, neo-fascist ideas about abortion, race, and sex that lurked in dark corners of the internet have travelled the pipeline into the political mainstream. My central claim – that the far right sees abortion bans as a way to reverse the so-called Great Replacement – is no longer confined to creepy natalist Telegram channels. It is spoken out loud by anti-abortion political leaders.

Just take this quote from the head of the Conservative Political Action Conference, Matt Schlapp, during a speech at the event in Hungary in May 2022:

> If you say there is a population problem in a country, but you're killing millions of your own people every year through legalized abortion every year, if that were to be reduced, some of that problem is solved. You have millions of people who can take many of these jobs. How come no one brings that up? If you're worried about this quote-unquote replacement, why don't we start there. Start with allowing our own people to live.'[1]

This isn't some fringe far-right leader, but a confidante of Donald Trump and the head of the biggest conservative gathering in the world.

What happened in the United States in June 2022 was one

painful and devastating result of the forces and ideologies I explore in this book. But there is hope, too. When *Roe* was overruled, I spoke to the Center for Reproductive Rights in Geneva to find out about the implications of the Supreme Court decision for the rest of the world. Senior Regional Director for Europe Leah Hoctor explained to me that since 1973, a total of fifty-five countries have improved access to abortion. Only four had rolled back abortion rights.[2]

Siân Norris
August 2022

Introduction

The coronavirus pandemic is raging across the UK. Families have been kept apart, friends forced to communicate via Zoom, and – for those of us homeworkers without gardens – the only fresh air we could enjoy was during our state-sanctioned twenty-minute walks, runs, or cycle rides. We have accepted the restrictions to stop the spread of a little-understood virus that is killing hundreds of people every day. But outside Britain's abortion clinics, those claiming to be 'pro-life' appear willing to risk spreading a deadly disease in order to prevent women from accessing reproductive care.

Not even pandemic restrictions on free movement could deter anti-abortionists from the streets during Lent, as they took part in '40 Days for Life', an annual campaign to harass abortion clinics; it is organised by a US anti-abortion group which now has branches all over the world. Holding their graphic posters emblazoned with foetal tissue and cruel messages, the protesters murmur their prayers. They say they are here 'to help young ladies' with information about abortion. They chastise, antagonise, and upset clients with literature urging women 'not to be a murderer'; they tell them to ask the abortion clinic staff 'to see a scan'; and they show distressing images of living and aborted foetuses. They taunt abortion clinic workers as killers, sometimes physically accosting the nurses and doctors. In the US, protesters have bombed clinics and killed doctors, making a mockery of any claim to being 'pro-life'.

These Lenten protests take place every year in Britain, where abortion is legal under certain circumstances. Compare this scenario of an embattled yet still legal right to abortion with the rest of the world today, where 90 million women of reproductive age live in countries where abortion is prohibited altogether.[1] This is a world where just under 50,000 women die following unsafe abortions each year.

In El Salvador, where abortion is banned in all circumstances, three-eighths of maternal deaths comprise those under the age of eighteen who take their own lives after discovering they are pregnant. In Poland, during just one year following a tightened abortion ban, three women died after being denied a life-saving termination. Across Europe, 20 million women live in countries where abortion is banned in almost all cases, including Poland and Malta. Even more women live in countries where the right to safe, legal abortion is being continually undermined – as conservative and far-right MPs vote to restrict access as in Slovakia, Portugal, and Spain; sign anti-abortion declarations as in Hungary and Belarus; or declare their regions to be 'pro-life cities', such as in Verona, Italy.

In almost every country in the world, women, girls, and pregnant people are under siege. They face multiple legal and social barriers simply to access a basic human right – bodily autonomy. Those barriers can take the shape of draconian bans on abortion, but they come in other forms too.

In Britain, the barriers involve getting two doctors to confirm that continuing the pregnancy will put the patient's mental and/or physical health at risk, and until recently, even a medical abortion (taking pills forty-eight hours apart) had to take place on the premises of a registered medical provider, such as a GP's office, a family planning clinic, or a hospital. Nine European countries – including Hungary, Armenia, and Belgium – demand that those needing an abortion have counselling and/or a 'cooling-off' period before being granted the procedure. Other barriers include bans on organisations 'advertising' abortion services, requirements for parental consent for minors, the failure to fund abortion care, individual doctors refusing abortions on moral grounds, and a basic lack of healthcare provision and expertise – particularly when it comes to abortion later on in a pregnancy.

In the US, a 2022 Supreme Court decision overturned the 1973 *Roe v. Wade* ruling that offered the nationwide right to safe, legal abortion, leading to multiple states banning the procedure. As a result, women, girls and pregnant people wanting to access reproductive healthcare now have to continue with an unwanted pregnancy, or travel to a state where the procedure is legal. Even before the law change, millions of women and girls lived in states where access was severely limited; they would have to travel long distances to reach a clinic, only to be made to look at an ultrasound scan and/or endure a 'cooling off' period. Such restrictions meant that getting an abortion was expensive and time-consuming. Individual states have enforced so-called TRAP laws (targeted restrictions on abortion providers), which put draconian health and safety restrictions on abortion providers, forcing them to close because they simply can't afford to make the modifications needed to stay open – and of course, that was the whole point of the TRAP law.

The Supreme Court's eventual decision to overrule *Roe v. Wade* stripped human rights away from women and pregnant people, a major victory in a decades-long war of organised misogyny. A total of twenty-six states were ready to ban abortion, either completely or after six weeks of pregnancy (before most women know they are pregnant), and 41 per cent of women of childbearing age saw their nearest abortion clinic close. Women in some states would have to travel up to 500 miles to access the nearest abortion clinic.[2]

I've been reporting on the threats to abortion since 2017, having been a feminist activist for more than a decade before that. My wake-up call that the hard-won right to safe, legal abortion was under threat came when I travelled to Romania for the British news agency openDemocracy 50.50. I was sent to report on what seemed – at the time – to be a separate issue: a constitutional referendum about LGBTIQ rights. The referendum was about equal marriage, but in many of the conversations I had, the threat to abortion kept coming up. What I learned on that trip, quite frankly, changed my life. Because it was during quiet conversations on Bucharest's freezing streets, eating cheese pastries, and drinking beer in jazz bars, where I discovered how a global conservative movement was using a far-right playbook to wage a global attack on women, right there in the heart of Romania. That playbook is a mixture of anti-abortion, 'family rights' rhetoric, racist conspiracy theory, organised misogyny, and fascistic notions of a so-called 'natural order', all contrived to reverse progress on reproductive and sexual rights.

The more I looked into it, the more I discovered that Romania was not an isolated case. Across Europe and beyond, women's rights were increasingly under siege by international forces working in concert with local 'family rights' and 'anti-gender' organisations determined to overturn abortion and LGBTIQ rights. In Slovakia, Slovenia, and Estonia, cross-border networks had supported local groups launching constitutional referendums throughout the decade to stymie progress on what they called 'gender ideology'.

When I looked back to the previous year in Poland, and the unsuccessful attempt in 2016 to ban abortion, the same rhetoric, the same organisations, the same networks, and the same funders kept surfacing. Fast forward to Ireland's 2018 referendum to legalise abortion, and there they were again, fighting for the 'no' vote in the referendum. The same rhetoric. The same organisations. The same networks and funders. On both reproductive and sexual rights, a network of far-right and religious-right operators spanning Europe and the US were sharing tactics, duplicating strategies, and deploying their people to roll back progress on abortion.

But something else was going on too. Like most people, I had always believed anti-abortion ideas were rooted in a religious objection to reproductive healthcare. I might disagree with that objection, but so long as our opposing belief systems didn't actively prevent women from accessing abortion, I thought this was a difference both sides had to learn to live with. I was wrong. As I reported on this movement for openDemocracy, *Byline Times*, the Tortoise and NewsMavens, the obvious truth could not be ignored. Underpinning these organised assaults on reproductive and sexual rights were far-right conspiracies, white supremacist ideas, and a fascistic belief in restoring a supposedly natural order to reassert white male supremacy and reverse progress.

This so-called natural order is one where women and black people are inferior to white men, and where LGBTIQ people simply should not exist. As such, these far-right conspiracies are driven by a misogynist worldview that pins women to reproductive labour and puts their bodies under male control.

This book, then, is an account of how the attacks on abortion rights in the Global North is part of a larger misogynist and white supremacist project of the far right. It's about how women's bodies are under siege from extremist, far-right anti-abortion forces determined to lay claim to women's wombs and mark out women's bodies as exploitable territory. And whenever there's a siege, things end badly for women.

In these pages, I argue that the ideology driving the far right is travelling from extremists on dark web forums, to respectable religious-right conferences and into mainstream authoritarian governments. This ideology is focused on a racist and misogynistic conspiracy theory that a white majority is being deliberately (and malignly) *replaced* by migration from the Global South and causing a 'white genocide'. The so-called genocide, its believers claim, is enabled by feminists supressing the birth rate with abortion. In its most extremist iterations, the replacement is understood as a Satanic plot to 'de-Christianise' society, aided by feminists, Muslim migrants, and Jewish elites.

In order to restore a so-called natural order of white, male supremacy, the far right demands the exploitation of women's reproductive labour, positioning women as the 'wombs of the nation', while waging a race war against black and global majority people to create racially pure ethno-states across the world – with the Global North being reserved for white people.

This is the heart of my argument. It's designed to be a wake-up call about how we think about today's far right, creeping authoritarianism, and its involvement with the anti-abortion movement. I argue that the far right believes reproductive control can and must be the solution to its white supremacist anxiety about so-called white genocide. And while this belief may have started as an extremist idea, it has now become mainstream politics, supported by a network of deep-pocketed funders on the radical right.

It took me time to see this, but as it emerged as a revelation, I began to find more and more proof that such an architecture of thought existed.

It was a chilly morning in October 2019, and the sky was bright autumnal blue as I walked across Blackfriars Bridge in Central London. It took me three attempts to follow the blue dot on my Google maps app to the correct location, an anonymous-looking conference centre, where a smiling woman with a North American accent welcomed me to the Clarkson Academy, a two-day training seminar run by the extreme anti-abortion Centre for Bio-Ethical Reform UK (CBR UK). I was posing as a wide-eyed, naïve and newly interested anti-abortion activist called Marie, so I could report on how these groups operated. In the doorway was a banner illustrated with a picture of a light bulb; on closer inspection, I realised the bulb's filament was shaped like a foetus.

This would not be the only foetus I'd see that morning. On display tables in the crammed and stuffy room were little plastic models of embryos at different stages of development. Models like these are taken to protests and waved at women entering reproductive health clinics. The training session, which aims to 'help passionate pro-life advocates become effective instruments for change', also involved watching a video of abortions at different stages of pregnancy. As I stared at the vagina of the woman on the screen, I wondered if she had given her consent for footage of her vulva to be shared with me and this room of anti-abortion extremists. I wondered if any of the people sitting around me cared.

CBR UK's modus operandi is to bring so-called 'education displays' (graphic images of abortions and aborted foetuses) to abortion clinics, universities, and public spaces. This included, in October 2019, a billboard outside pro-choice MP Stella Creasy's constituency office after the Labour politician successfully proposed a bill to decriminalise abortion in Northern Ireland. The group defends its tactics by claiming that women need to see the *truth* of abortion: during his introduction to the training academy, CBR UK founder Andrew Stephenson claimed the 'real misogynists' are pro-choice activists who deny women access to abortion's 'truth'.

As I looked around the small but tightly packed conference centre, where veterans of the anti-abortion movement mingled with younger activists, it was clear that CBR UK was a fringe group. Their membership is not huge and they don't have a lot of money. But small or not, what I found to be more troubling is what organisations like this represent: they are just one node in the global network of anti-abortion extremist groups, intent on overturning the right to safe, legal abortion in the UK and elsewhere.

This is an organisation which is linked to the US, where the original CBR was established; that US organisation has branches in Canada and Europe, and ambitions to reach Latin America and Asia. Within the UK itself, the group is connected to a network of other anti-abortion, anti-LGBTIQ groups such as Christian Concern and 40 Days for Life. The latter's director of international campaigns was on the board of CBR UK. He also received training from the Leadership Institute, a US radical-right initiative designed to train conservative activists, and which counts former vice president Mike Pence among its alumni. While CBR UK alone is not much to shout about, its participation in a network of anti-abortion actors – a network that you will learn more about in the coming chapters –is real cause for concern.

The day began with Stephenson giving an introductory talk. This was quickly followed by a lecture from Wilfred Wong, an anti-abortion activist who launched into a full-scale conspiracy theory, claiming that abortions are ritual sacrifices designed to boost Satan's power and de-Christianise the West.[3] Wong told his audience how the UK is in the grip of Satanism, in part because of the high number of abortions in the country; he explained that 'with 500 abortions every day there are plenty of blood sacrifices they can offer to the Devil'. As I had seen others claim in Romania, Poland, and Ireland, he went on to link abortion rights with the 'homosexual agenda', saying both are 'fronts in the Satanic revolution'. Wong also spun a story of how Satanic ritual abortions in clinics were accompanied by women rocking and chanting, 'Our bodies ourselves' – a reference to the classic feminist text and slogan.

In a video interview recorded the following year, in September 2020, Wong expanded on his Satanic theories, joined this time by Stephenson.[4] At the academy, the latter had simply offered an introduction to the organisation and abortion more widely. This time, he explained to viewers how 'Satanic ritual abuse and Satanism is that love of death', an ideology he argued was 'institutionalised' in legal abortion.

In the video, Wong went further than at the academy, stating that Islam and Satanism share a common goal – the 'destruction of Christianity' – while falsely claiming that demographics show Muslims are starting to outnumber Christians in Europe. He explained how part of the Satanist plan for preparing 'society for the rise of the anti-Christ' involves Satanists 'actively supporting Islamisation of the West'.

Wong claims a UK politician, whom he labelled as being involved in satanic ritual abuse, proposed policies that would allow a 'huge flood of Muslims into the EU' until Europeans are 'outnumbered' by Muslims in the region. There was no ignoring it: this was the far-right Great Replacement conspiracy theory mixing with the far-right QAnon conspiracy to push an anti-abortion agenda. Anti-abortionists around the globe are using the manufactured threat of *replacement* – and claiming such a replacement is 'Satanic' – as justification for stripping away human rights from women, LGBTIQ people and migrant people.

In this book, I will escort you along the pipeline through which these far-right conspiracies travel from small conference centres, handfuls of protesters outside abortion clinics, and fringe websites into government buildings across the Global North.

We begin with an overview of the fascist thought architecture that wants to restore a natural order of white male supremacy. That natural order, it argues, can only be achieved by rolling back centuries of progress on human rights to a pre-Enlightenment phase. This thought architecture is then expressed in extremist conspiracy theories within far-right and anti-abortion movements, such as the Great Replacement theory or the QAnon/Satanic abuse conspiracy. That's stage two. The third part of the process involves respectable far-right faces who transform the ideology into government strategy and policy, and introduce it on the world stage via international bodies such as the European Parliament and United Nations. These groups are funded by radical and religious-right billionaires who want to restore a natural order that they imagine entrenches their power. In the final phase, those strategies and policies are adopted by national governments and their leaders who also wish to maintain their grip on power.

In the first chapter, I'll explain the thought architecture of contemporary fascism and demonstrate how this creates the far right's anti-abortion stance. I'll guide you through how the far right wants to reverse history to recapture a pre-Enlightenment fantasy world, known as the 'fascist mythic past'; and to wage race war. The natural order vision represents the end of history and demands that we return to a feudalistic state where progress is reversed, where nature dictates human behaviour and where society as such no longer exists. Men's role is to fight war (since battle is understood as part of the natural order), while women are pinned to reproductive labour. In contrast to the Enlightenment belief that humans create and change society, and can, in turn, be changed by the society around them, the fascistic natural order debases humanity to an eternal cycle of violence and childbirth, oppression and moral poverty. This is the first stage of the pipeline.

To demonstrate how this fascist construct manifests in the world today, I'll introduce you in Chapter Two to its most extremist iterations: the far-right conspiracists who populate dark web message boards, discuss the nonsense concept of 'white genocide', and ready themselves for a race war which, they hope, will create pure ethno-states. This is the second stage of the pipeline. I'll explain the Great Replacement conspiracy theory and show you how this baseless ideology is fuelled not only by extreme racism but by the belief that feminism is aiding replacement through abortion and contraception. I'll introduce you to how another far-right conspiracy about Satanism allows the movement's followers to position abortion as unnatural, and explore how the QAnon movement has taken hold among mainstream US political groups which want to ban abortion. I will explain how, according to the followers of this hateful ideology, feminism must be defeated and women must lose their bodily autonomy: women's bodies must, they believe, be put to work serving the white nation-state that will be the outcome of a far-right victory. By undertaking my own investigations into the nefarious world of extremist message boards and forums, I will show you how – in the fascist mind – so-called white genocide can only be reversed through reproductive control.

Through a deep dive into two extremist misogynist movements, the Red Pill and the incels, I will demonstrate how hatred of women and a desire for reproductive control acts as a gateway drug to the acceptance of white supremacist ideas *tout court*.

Away from the Reddit forums and far-right Telegram channels, the next chapter focuses on the public face of anti-abortion extremism: the networks, conferences, and organisations which bring extremist ideology about women's bodies into the United Nations, the European Parliament, and national governments. These men wear smart suits, not swastika badges, and they speak in the halls of international government rather than on message boards. But they share a basic ideology with their less polished comrades: that abortion rights are disrupting a natural order that can only be restored by rolling back progress and returning women to reproductive labour.

This section will focus on four major case studies which form the third stage of the pipeline: Agenda Europe and CitizenGO in Europe; and Alliance Defending Freedom and the Council for National Policy in the US. I'll describe how these organisations meet with and support one another, and share with you the tactics they employ to normalise an anti-abortion, white supremacist ideology in Europe and the USA. In fact, bringing these ideas into the mainstream is the key goal of these organisations. You'll learn how these networks target global bodies such as the UN in order to influence policy-making away from a human rights model and back to the so-called 'natural order', meaning white male supremacy and female inferiority. These groups are global as well as organised; they take fringe ideologies voiced in extremist spaces and seek to insert them into European and US laws.

Doing so costs money. Luckily for those determined to undo human rights for more than half the world's population, there are plenty of wealthy people keen to pour their billions into funding white male supremacy – both in Europe and in the US. Chapter Five tracks the funding sources coming from Russia, Europe and the US that fuel the transnational far-right anti-abortion movement. Following the money is fundamental to understanding that what may seem to be a crazy fringe movement is in fact a well-funded, highly organised mainstream phenomenon. Chapter Five describes the financial ties that create what political philosopher Hannah Arendt calls the 'alliance of the elite and the mob'.

The penultimate chapter brings us to those mainstream governments where the fringe ideas expressed by the extremists in Chapter Two have been nurtured by the respectable faces of white male supremacy from Chapter Three and then fertilised by the money-men in Chapter Five, before blossoming into government policy. In this section, I will demonstrate exactly why we need to worry about the roots of extremist anti-abortion, Great Replacement ideology as expressed on the scary Telegram channels and incel forums. From Hungary to Poland, from the Netherlands to Italy and Spain, the belief that a white majority is being 'overrun' by migration from the Global South – and that this so-called replacement can be reversed by controlling women's bodies – is being written into European laws. This is clear in Poland's highly restrictive abortion laws, imposed by an anti-migrant, far-right leadership; the repeated neo-Nazi attempts to ban abortion completely in Slovakia (aided by Catholic conservatives); the lining up of Spain's right-wing leaders with its neo-fascist party to attack laws protecting women; as well as Hungary's Viktor Orbán, France's Éric Zemmour and the Netherlands' Baudet using Great Replacement rhetoric to win electoral support and sow division and fear.

The UK is not an exception, although the mainstreaming of far-right ideology has manifested slightly differently due, in part, to its parliamentary make-up, its old-fashioned abortion laws, and its increasingly isolated post-Brexit status within

Europe. In Chapter Six, I'll analyse how the culture war that was intensified by the EU membership referendum tries to pit white men against the values of equality and fairness; it has also whipped up hostility to migrant people and enhanced the influence of radical-right US interests on UK lawmakers.

If Chapters Two to Six focus on the *how*, the final section asks *why*, and more specifically *why now*? In Chapter Seven I'll discuss how the crisis facing capitalism since 2008 has created a breeding ground for far-right ideology to take hold. A perfect storm – fomented by an ageing population, low birth rates and the end of neoliberalism – has left capitalism with shrinking options for regeneration and stabilisation. One route to capitalism's survival involves the alignment of corporations and the wealthy with the far right on reproductive control, with the goal of pinning women to reproductive labour. It would not be the first time.

But just as capitalist elites are making choices, so are we. This book doesn't claim to have answers about how we revolt against this siege and break out towards freedom. Instead, my hope is that by *understanding* and *exposing* far-right ideas about reproduction and women's bodies, we can see how those ideas are being made respectable and turned into laws across the Global North. I demonstrate the path from the fringe white supremacist invention of a white genocide that could be fixed through reproductive control and violent anti-migrant measures, to its infection of mainstream governments and businesses interests who fear their power is waning in the face of women's bodily autonomy, and of movements such as Black Lives Matter, Open Borders and the fight for LGBTIQ rights. There is no longer any possibility of ignoring the link between anti-abortion, the far right, misogyny and racism, now that misogyny and racism are dictating mainstream politics.

If you don't want to submit to this siege on our bodies, and instead want to understand it so we can fight back, please keep reading.

1

The Ideology: The Place of Women in Fascist Thought

What is driving the far-right war on abortion? How has the abortion debate shifted from being one of religious morality to one where women's bodies have become a political battleground for the rise of the far right?

Before diving into an investigation into how the far right in Europe and the US is attacking abortion as the first step of a larger fascist programme, we need to take a step back and understand more about the aims of that programme and where they come from. In this chapter, I will explore the theoretical concepts of modern fascist ideology in the twentieth and twenty-first centuries. From there, I'll demonstrate how those concepts relate to reproductive rights in particular, in order to illustrate how women's freedom has become antithetical to fascism's aims. Understanding this can help to explain why the far right is determined to smash those same freedoms.

The theoretical underpinning of contemporary fascism can be divided into three broad concepts. The first is a belief that progress – including abortion rights, gender equality and sexual and reproductive freedoms – are subverting an imagined natural order that needs to be restored. That natural order is one of patriarchal authority over women, and white supremacy over black and global majority people. In order to achieve that natural order, progress needs to be reversed so that society returns to a pre-Enlightenment phase where nature rather than reason dictates human behaviour. This reversal of history creates what historians and philosophers such as Mark Neocleous and Jason Stanley characterise as the 'fascist mythic past' – the second concept. The third concept is that humans are inherently violent, so must inhabit a state of endless war. Gender roles within that war are biologically essentialist: a man should fight and a woman should reproduce.

These three concepts – the natural order, the reversal of history and endless war – are central to fascism, both in its historic and in its contemporary form. Those concepts underpin the rhetoric and beliefs of far-right communities found on extremist message boards, the suited men attending secretive conferences, and the authoritarian governments enacting far-right policy. The thought architecture for fascist ideology remains the same.

My research on the contemporary far right, whether manifested on extremist Telegram channels or in European parliaments, has repeatedly demonstrated a unifying message – one succinctly articulated by the anti-fascist writer, journalist and campaigner Paul Mason: that fascism 'is a fear of freedom, triggered by a glimpse of freedom'.[1] This is fundamental to understanding the far-right objection to abortion rights. Abortion rights are the glimpse of women's freedom, and the backlash comes from the fear of what women's reproductive freedom means for white male supremacy.

Without access to reproductive rights, women can never be free. Women's liberation depends on access to abortion and contraception, but that freedom is antithetical to the three concepts underpinning fascist ideology. In order for fascism to thrive, women must therefore be subject to reproductive control in order to fulfil their natural role, submit to a mythic past of patriarchal authority and reproduce the ideal subject to fight for the fantasy of a pure nation-state. This chapter will show that this is not a state of affairs invented by the contemporary far right: it is the way fascism has always operated in relation to women's bodies.

Exposing these three building blocks of fascist ideology is important because it demonstrates that the current attack on reproductive freedoms is neither a sideshow nor a fringe movement. Instead, attacking women's reproductive freedoms is central to fascist goals.

Understanding this thought architecture is central to the argument of this book: first, that white male supremacists believe their anxieties about replacement and 'white genocide' can be allayed via reproductive control; second, that their aims can be realised through reproductive control; and third, that what was once considered extremism has moved into the mainstream.

Let's dive in …

Concept One: A Natural Order

Fascism emerged as an ideology in 1920s Italy, when Benito Mussolini assumed his dictatorship of the country. It spread to 1930s Spain, where after his victory in the civil war against the left, General Francisco Franco ruled a fascist dictatorship until his death in 1975. The Nazi regime in 1930s and 1940s Germany is also recognised to be based within fascism.

For decades, fascism was deemed as something horrifying that had a specific lifespan in early twentieth-century Europe – an ugly relic from the ideologically driven past with no place in the modern, neoliberal world. Yes, there were neo-Nazi tribute acts storming London's streets in the 1960s and 1970s; and yes, there were always far-right political parties peddling new agendas – against the European Union, for example, or spreading vile Islamophobia disguised as concern about terrorism – in attempts to reach the mainstream, but none of these movements ever made it past the fringes. That began to change, however, as internet technology allowed a contemporary fascist movement to coalesce around a central ideology, propagate that ideology through social media networks, spread conspiracy theories (such as Holocaust denial) and form new fascistic communities. Crucially, the internet allowed fascism to grow through a networked society whose members never had to meet one another, march down the same street or be in the same room. Instead, with the creation of a shared thought architecture communicated via shared memes and vocabulary, a new fascist movement was born.

From its roots in Europe after the First World War, fascism has always fundamentally been an anti-humanist ideology. It believes humans have no power to change or improve society. Instead, followers of fascism argue that humans are bound by nature, red in tooth and claw.

Central to this supposedly natural order is white, heterosexual male supremacy and capitalism making the rules. The historian Ruth Ben-Ghiat, whose book *Strongmen* examines how authoritarian male leaders from Mussolini and Franco to Trump, Putin and Jair Bolsonaro exercise their power, explains how the success of fascist leaders throughout history depended on selling 'a fantasy of returning to an age when male authority was secure and women, people of colour and workers knew their place'.[2]

According to Mark Neocleous, professor of the critique of political economy at Brunel University, fascism is concerned with 'the sanctification of nature and thus that which it takes to be natural: war and the nation'.[3] It treats patriarchy, and therefore male supremacist control over women's bodies, as innate and primal. This misconception of nature is crucial to understanding women's position in the fascist mind.

Neocleous's analysis reveals something fundamental: central to fascist ideology is the belief that nation and nature cannot be separated. Reading Neocleous's analysis revealed something fundamental to me: he proposes that fascism considers the nation to be 'not an imagined community' but a natural entity, an idea expressed in the Nazi doctrine of 'blood and soil'. The slogan, still used by fascist movements today, is 'suggestive of an intimate connection between the blood of the people (nation) and the soil of the land (nature)'.[4]

Further, Adolf Hitler argued that nature obeyed 'stern and rigid laws', and that society's problems – in this case those of 1920s and 1930s Germany – were rooted in the pollution of nature by post-Enlightenment progress.

When it comes to obeying nature's stern and rigid laws, and rolling back progress, women's duty and social utility lie in reproductive labour designed to strengthen and purify the nation-state. By 'articulating nature as a standard by which the social order can be judged', writes Neocleous, 'the success of the nation becomes dependent on the natural laws of sexuality and gender ... This provides fascism with the grounds for distinguishing the normal from the abnormal, where the abnormal is read as a threat to the natural – and thus the national – order.'[5]

When I applied Neocleous's theory to the extremist white male supremacists I was studying online, the idea that women should conform to a natural order of reproductive control was clear to see. Take this post from the misogynistic Red Pill Reddit forum:

> Back in the day, women would likely hit puberty, have sex, and within a couple of years they were having kids. That is the natural order of things. Now it's just a fucking free for all with consequences that we will have to deal with.[6]

In this order, women must fulfil their natural role and obey nature's strict laws by devoting themselves to reproduction. Further, because the success of the nation relies on its people following natural law, women's so-called biological destiny under fascism becomes inextricably linked to that of the nation. In fascist ideology, the ideal nation is an expression of racial purity, linking race and nation. Thus, the future of a nation/ race lies in the womb. A woman who disobeys those laws by ending a pregnancy is therefore corrupting nature and betraying her race/nation.

It's for this reason that the religious-right network Agenda Europe, which during the 2010s helped to strategise and coordinate regional attacks on reproductive and sexual rights across Europe, supporting campaigns against abortion and equal marriage in countries as diverse as France, Poland, Romania, Sweden and even the UK, titled its manifesto *Restoring the Natural Order*. This document rails against all that the group considers unnatural – abortion, women holding any form of political power, LGBTIQ people and rainbow families – and it lays out a plan to restore the 'natural order' by offering an 'agenda for Europe' linking nation and nature.

The 144-page manifesto lays out the importance of natural law in its introduction:

> For a society to live in peace and justice, it is necessary that its legal order is in compliance with Natural Law. Moral principles and positive legislation that are not in conformity with Natural Law will ultimately destroy any society that embraces them … The moral decline of a society usually takes place in several steps that can easily be distinguished. The first step is that just and equitable laws, while they are still in place, are not complied with. The second is that they are not enforced. The third is that they are publicly derided. The fourth is that they are 'liberalized', so that compliance with the precepts of Natural Law is now an option, but no more an obligation. Later on, they are modified once again, so that acting in contradiction to Natural Law is turned into a 'duty', and complying with Natural Law into a 'crime'. As a last step, criticising the novel moral code is turned into a thought crime, and the critics are persecuted for merely expressing their opinion … the moral code of the past complied with Natural Law, whereas the moral code of today opposes it.[7]

In contrast, it is now clear why the right to abortion is so antithetical to fascists: it contravenes what they believe to be a natural order and allows women to decouple themselves from their presumed biological destiny. Feminism argues on the other hand that women's oppression is unnatural and that women's role should not be solely reproductive. It identifies gender oppression as an artificial social and economic structure created by men, and therefore men's self-claimed authority over women cannot be natural. Abortion rights give women a route to freedom.

In their designation of childbearing as an optional part of women's identity, feminism and women's sexual freedoms are therefore perceived as *abnormal* or *unnatural* by the far right. Worse, they are considered an existential threat to the nation itself because they threaten racial supremacy, which is synonymous in the fascist mind with the nation (in 1930s Germany, for example, the Nazis declared 'only those of German blood … may be members of the nation'[8]).

This is why the far right links abortion to an imagined conspiracy it calls *white genocide*. The conspiracy theory posits that abortion, combined with migration from the Global South, is working to eradicate racial purity and destabilise white-majority nations. To save the nation/race and to restore the fascistic natural order, women's rights (along with migrants' rights) must be cancelled; women must be returned to reproductive labour in order to regenerate the nation/race and maintain white supremacy.

There is a reason the far right describes women's and minority rights as *against nature*: they see all equal-rights movements as unnatural, and women's liberation is no exception. They want human societies to be closer to how they consider animal societies function, with clear social hierarchies based on sex and race, and women and minority groups trapped in inferiority, and white men secure in their authority.

Concept Two: A Constant State of War

Fascism's obsession with its false image of the *natural* is at the heart of its embrace of constant war. As Neocleous explains, it is in the 'conjunction of nation and nature that war is crucial … War sustains the dynamic of nature and contributes to the power of the nation.' Fascism needs to be in a constant state of war, as its followers believe this 'shapes man's spiritual character and is the *defining characteristic of nature*.'[9]

The belief that a constant state of war is humanity's natural state means that fascism must always wage a conflict against modernity, progress and humanity. The fascist fight is for the nation where nation is race – hence the need for its followers to wage a race war to create individual ethno-states.

Those individual ethno-states are the end goal of all fascist movements. The US far-right group Identity EVROPA advocated for pure white states. In order to create a veneer of respectability and non-violence, the way to achieve these monocultures was presented as giving black and ethnic-minority citizens, including Jewish people, the opportunity to leave their white-majority country – something the neo-Nazi leader Richard Spencer chillingly described as 'peaceful ethnic cleansing'.[10] Of course, no such thing exists. The only way to achieve the fascist dream of individual ethno-states is through violence.

Again, when I applied Neocleous's framing of fascism and war to the rhetoric and actions of contemporary fascism, it became clear how this same thought architecture underpins the actions and ideology of the far right. On the extremist message boards, the movement discusses a coming war – codenamed 'boogaloo' – that would be triggered on 'Day X'. When the Taliban took over Afghanistan in August 2021, with the US forced to withdraw troops, the far right celebrated, seeing it as a model for their own planned state of war: they framed the activities of the Taliban as a success because it showed how quickly a militia force could rage through a country and take over with little resistance. On the social media platform Gab – notorious for its far-right membership – groups discuss and plan 'for the civil war between the communistic Left that has hijacked America, vs the rest of us', and share 'news, information, after action reports, KIA, WIA, combat vids, intel, analysis, discussion on the civil war that is also looking to be a 2nd American Revolution'. They predict 'the great coming bloodshed' in the West, and claim they are 'seriously discuss[ing] the writing on the wall. The great coming FIGHT. Or the great coming abject capitulation. The survival of American culture. Or its EXTERMINATION under a tsunami of Democrat sponsored gimmigrants.' Neo-Nazi posters bemoan how they 'lost' the Second World War, despite being US citizens – they identify instead with Nazi Germany. This time, the far right believes it will win.

Where we saw this obsession with war play out in real time, live on our TV screens, was at the insurrection at the Capitol, Washington, DC, on 6 January 2021. For many of the participants (mostly white men), this was Day X, the start of boogaloo. No wonder so many wore combat gear, carried weaponry and equipment to take hostages, and called to hang the vice president. Ultimately, such groups need combat, both to reverse progress and to restore the natural order – understood as a permanent state of war.

The lack of women at the insurrection also tells us something interesting about women's distinct role in the far right and explains why a ban on abortion has always been a key weapon in the far right's armoury, both to create its individual ethno-states and to defeat the so-called replacement of what it considers to be the white race. Put bluntly, the far right cannot win its race war without women's reproductive labour. Any 'white' woman who therefore asserts her right to bodily integrity is seen as betraying her race/nation (this attitude is shared by states with nationalistic governments such as Iran). To ensure this treachery does not take place, she must be placed under patriarchal control.

Concept Three: The Mythic Past

The far right justifies its notion of the natural order through its dissemination of the fascistic mythic past, typified by patriarchal authority and achievable through warfare. This myth is a rejection of modernity, which falsely claims white male supremacy as a better, greater, past to return to – an imagined world based on a moment in history that never really existed. The obsession with an imaginary past is key to fascism: as Neocleous explains, it invokes a return 'to past values, to a social and political order prior to the current one of constant change'.[11]

Hitler's Nazis idealised medieval Europe and feudalism as their version of the mythic past, a time when society was organised according to man's relationship to the soil, and when workers and the propertyless had no rights. The party used runic symbols to connect the regime to its mythic past. In Mussolini's Italy, the mythic past was Ancient Rome and its empire, which he described as 'our guiding star; it is our symbol or if you prefer, our myth'.[12] Crucially, all (Western) fascist mythic pasts are pre-1789; they are based in a period before humanism, before the social revolutionary movements across Europe that decoupled humans from nature and argued that inequality was not natural and predetermined, and that a more equal society was possible. Fascism demands we reverse the progress made on human rights since 1789 and freeze historical time to a period that naturalises inequality. No wonder that Nazi Germany's chief propagandist Joseph Goebbels described the party's rise to power as the moment '1789 becomes expunged from the records of history'.[13]

This fascist mythic past is always gendered and, writes Yale philosophy professor Jason Stanley, 'invariably involves traditional, patriarchal gender roles'.[14]

In fascist Italy, this was demonstrated by Mussolini's strategy of baby-making to make the nation great again, where women were rewarded for pregnancies and men were valued for violence. Mussolini declared that 'war is to man what maternity is to a woman'.[15] Similarly, in Nazi Germany, the burgeoning women's movement in the wake of the First World War was swept away in favour of rewarded fecundity. Men and women were expected to fulfil clear gendered roles: even from a young age boys were encouraged to join the Hitler Youth and girls the BDM (Bund Deutscher Mädel, or Band of German Maidens); these groups, with their nostalgic gendered uniforms and activities, sent a message that girls were for *Kinder, Küche, Kirche* (children, kitchen, church), while boys were for fighting.

In my research, it became clear the fascist mythic past is still inspiring both the far right and more mainstream conservative movements today. Consider how often right-wing leaders evoke a mythic past in order to rile up their base and win support. In the UK, the right-wing Brexit project promoted 'Rule Britannia' nostalgia – an Empire 2.0 in which Britain would be restored to its former status, swashbuckling around the world extracting wealth from the Global South. Proponents of Brexit made much of posing with pints of dark brown ale while wearing tweed – again, evoking a nostalgic mythic Great British past that rejects modernity. Brexit-favouring political leaders often invoked the Commonwealth, the group of countries that once made up the British Empire: Theresa May said that Brexit would make Britain 'global' and strengthen trading ties with the Commonwealth; Nigel Farage claimed that Brexit would 'cultivate economic ties within the Commonwealth that would put its life in the EU to shame'; and Boris Johnson said the Commonwealth had a 'key role to play in the bright future for Britain'. This was taking place in a context where Commonwealth nations were increasingly leaving the community and rejecting the Queen as head of state. Needless to say, this focus on the Commonwealth demonstrates the attachment of the right to a past where Britain ruled supreme over its empire, as opposed to being an equal partner in the European Union.

In Hungary, as we will see in Chapter Six, the far-right prime minister Viktor Orbán inspires his followers by celebrating the medieval Magyar warriors and promising a return to Hungary's militarised past. In 2012, he unveiled a 10-foot statue of the mythical Turul bird, which, as legend has it, heralded the arrival of the Magyar warriors (a nationalist symbol that was banned under Communism). Orbán introduced the bird in a speech, claiming it as 'an archetype of the Hungarian people' that belongs to Hungarians' 'blood and motherland'. At the annual Great Kurultáj event, which recreates the Battle of Pozsony from 907, Speaker of Parliament László Kövér welcomed 'heirs and worshippers of Attila and Árpád's people', the latter name invoking the chieftain who formed Hungary's first royal dynasty.[16]

For Vladimir Putin in Russia, the mythic past harks back to an imperial tsarist version of history that existed prior to 1917 and all those pesky revolutionary attempts to achieve gender and workers' equality. He slams so-called western influence and promotes the image of Mother Russia and Russian imperialism. Most famously of all, Donald Trump in the United States promised to 'make America great *again*' – his allusion to a lost mythic past. It's been less than a century since racial segregation was banned in the US, and only fifty years since *Roe vs Wade* gave women the federal right to abortion which, in turn, helped to emancipate them from reproductive labour – so it's not hard to guess what kind of mythic past Trump was referring to.

The 1789 moment and the Enlightenment represented historical progress and the beginning of revolutionary class consciousness. In contrast, fascism valorises war, nation and nature. Little surprise then, that the need for the mythic past is fundamentally tied to the fascistic obsession with nature: the 'centrality of nation and nature to fascist theory is reiterated and consolidated, for the central myths invoked and the traditions invested either are *national* ones or concern some kind of repressed natural essence waiting to be reborn in the modern world'.[17]

'Mythic' is the key term here: the past evoked by far-right forces and authoritarian leaders never existed. Great Britain was never a 'white nation': black people have always lived in London; empire was a brutal, violent, cruel, genocidal operation; LGBTIQ people have always existed; and women have always had abortions. Even the Turul bird was mythical! There has never been a time of pure patriarchal dominance: women have always exercised their own economic independence, practised abortion and contraception, and fought back against male supremacy. But truth is beside the point when presenting a fascist mythic past that strains towards an imagined history where men were men, women and black people knew their place, and LGBTIQ people were forced into the shadows. Creating this past allows the far right to position liberation movements – such as feminism, Black Lives Matter and LGBTIQ rights – as malevolent, unnatural and destructive forces set on attacking the status quo and the natural order of un-freedom, which can only be restored via violence and conflict.

A Fear of Freedom

At root, as Mason argues, 'fascism is a fear of freedom, triggered by a glimpse of freedom'.[18] This is why the far right is so exercised about women's reproductive and sexual rights: they want to prevent all humans from enjoying liberated, self-determined lives. Freedom, fascists believe, is an ideological enemy and a threat to their project. Further, they consider freedom to be against nature: what's natural, innate and immutable is war, and the oppression of women and black and global majority people.

This makes even more sense when you realise how fascism's horror of freedom is linked to the far right's anti-Marxism.

Marx believed that humans had the freedom to change society, and to be changed by it. This symbiotic relationship allowed for progress, along with the development of what it could mean to be human. Marx's writing teaches us that the inequality that shaped his (and our) society is anything but natural, and that can be changed. Such changes can, in turn, alter the human condition. If humans have freedom, then they have the agency to shape and change society to become more equal. No wonder fascism still fears his ideas!

The liberation movements of the past fifty or sixty years have ultimately been movements for freedom – the clue is in the name! While the far-right assault on abortion rights is driven by the belief that feminism threatens both nature and the nation by allowing women to refuse reproductive labour, it is also driven by its anti-freedom creed. The Dutch far-right leader Thierry Baudet exposed the fascist antagonism towards freedom in an essay, purportedly about the French author Michel Houellebecq but really giving the opportunity for Baudet to lay out his own ideas. The article refers to 'modernity's joyless liberation', and argued that 'liberation has not made us happy. Instead, it has left our lives empty, without purpose.' Liberalism and socialism, he continued, base their vision for society on the

> principle that every individual enjoys certain 'inalienable rights', which by definition eclipse all other claims, and to which all other ties, loyalties, and connections must ultimately be subordinated. Over time, all such institutions that the individual requires to fully actualise a meaningful existence –such as a family and a connection to generations past and future, a nation, a tradition, perhaps a church – will weaken and eventually disappear.

Today we have the freest people in history, Baudet argued, who 'live the least meaningful lives'.[19]

This is a textbook example of the fascist repudiation of freedom. It claims that freedom has brought misery and suffering, that it is based on a false promise, and that true happiness can be found in going back to the mythic past and returning to the old certainties: nation, nature and war.

Abortion rights also come under fire in Baudet's essay, as he complains how 'today, even new life (in the womb) may be extinguished to avoid disturbing the individual's freedom'. The ultimate path to liberation from patriarchal authority is found in the right to abortion and reproductive healthcare. A woman's ability to control her own fertility – to exert her right to bodily autonomy and decide if and when she wants to have children – allows her to move towards some form of economic and social equality. Abortion and contraception help women to step out of the domestic and into the public sphere – freeing them from the imperative of reproductive labour. When we talk about the right to choose, this is what feminism is talking about.

What this means in practice is that access to abortion has the potential to free women from what fascism has prescribed as their biological destiny – thereby, according to the twisted logic of the far right, breaking apart the natural order and posing an existential threat to nation/race. Women's liberation and abortion rights fundamentally threaten and undermine the basic principles of patriarchal authority and female subordination upon which fascism is built. For this reason, the far right wants to reverse progress and take us back to the fascist mythic past where women knew their place in the natural order and could be an exploitable resource to fuel its endless race war.

2

The Extremists:
The Anti-Abortion Far Right

Now that we understand the theory, it's time to learn how it works in action. Throughout this book you will meet a variety of different far-right subcultures, organisations and politicians, all working to put the fascist objection to abortion into practice. The operations of these groups, individuals and networks demonstrate the extent to which white supremacists believe reproductive control is a way to resolve their anxieties around 'white genocide' and achieve their aims of restoring what they imagine is the natural order tied to a fascist mythic past, thereby entrenching white male supremacy. In this chapter, I'll show you how extremist racist and misogynistic ideas about migration, LGBTIQ people and women have moved from the extremist fringe and into mainstream governments, threatening the future of women, global majority people and minority groups.

I'll introduce two popular conspiracy theories rooted in the fascist thought architecture which are driving far-right opposition to abortion. It starts with the Great Replacement: a baseless conspiracy theory coalesces far-right anxieties about women's liberation and migration, to justify a race war in which reproductive control becomes crucial to 'restoring' the white race in the Global North.

This belief in replacement blossomed on far-right and neo-Nazi message boards, Telegram channels and in terrorist manifestos. But since then, it has moved out of the fringe and into mainstream politics. Hungarian Prime Minister Orbán talked about population replacement in a speech at a demographic conference, when he told his audience 'there are political forces which, for a variety of reasons, want to see population replacement'. Baudet has used Great Replacement rhetoric to attract support for his far-right Forum for Democracy party in the Netherlands, writing that women's liberation is causing 'demographic decline', and that nationalist movements offer 'an attempt to preserve traditional European culture or indeed to reestablish it: a world in which the family is once again at the centre, in which nations are restored'.[1] French provocateur and 2022 presidential hopeful Éric Zemmour promoted the theory in his book *French Suicide*, where he claimed 'the sovereignty of the nation has disappeared ... There are parts of France which feel like a different continent today.' This, he claims, means that France is in 'the phase of destruction'. In the UK, meanwhile, far-right activists are demanding that the government protect white people from being replaced, pressuring it to take a harder line against migration, resulting in the Conservative Party's adoption of a refugee policy that potentially violates international law. Although its replacement premise is baseless nonsense, the far right has successfully tapped into a more mainstream white male supremacist anxieties – about women's rights and migration – in order to turn conspiracy into policy.

The second conspiracy theory focuses on QAnon and the belief that abortion is a satanic plot to de-Christianise the West and aid the Great Replacement. This absurd conspiracy should be easily dismissed. However, fascism has set itself against the rationalism of the Enlightenment, and so we should not be surprised that this bizarre and violent belief system has taken hold in mainstream US politics, threatening women's rights and democracy itself.

In the coming pages, I'll use examples from extremist, anti-abortion actors to demonstrate how the Great Replacement and satanic conspiracy theories offer a framework for the far right and draw in its mainstream supporters, leading them to target abortion rights. The first of these conspiracy theories involves the demand that in order to prevent 'white genocide', white women's bodies must be pinned to reproductive labour so as to reproduce the lost or threatened population. To achieve this, the far right promotes natalism, with nationalist influencers challenging women in the movement to have three to six white babies. In contrast, abortion is designated a form of treason against the white race or the nation-state: to deliberately end a pregnancy when white people are supposedly facing a genocide is to aid those intent on destroying them. Alarmingly, this is not merely a fringe belief: governments in Europe are undermining or even cancelling abortion rights while actively incentivising women to have more children in order to reverse what right-wing politicians such as Italy's Matteo Salvini call a 'demographic winter'. To put this in context, I'll introduce historical examples where manufactured fears of replacement have been met with demands for reproductive control.

The satanic conspiracy theory works in partnership with this belief that abortion is genocidal, by positioning abortion as devilish and unnatural. Instead, the far right believes women should be fulfilling what it claims is their natural reproductive role.

From there, you will meet two white male supremacist subcultures on the far right, the incel and Red Pill movements, and discover how these conspiracies foment in extremist spaces and influence mainstream political culture. Both subcultures became established online, and both focus on removing women's sexual and reproductive freedoms in order to entrench white male supremacy. Both view women's liberation as an unnatural attack on patriarchal authority that must be overturned.

Our journey begins in some of the murkiest online spaces, where far-right extremists gather to share memes, swap hate speech and even find a marriageable woman ... welcome to a dark web of fascist forums and extremist channels.

On a Telegram channel focused on the Great Replacement conspiracy theory, a comic strip showing a woman in a niqab warns 'in 100 years Europe will be Africa'. On Gab, a social media network popular with the far right, members share pictures of football teams and classrooms with white and black players and pupils, captioned with phrases such as 'spot the invaders', before urging their followers to 'make white babies, a lot, now'. Back on Telegram, UK far-right activist and founder of Patriotic Alternative Mark Collett shared a cartoon of white women queuing at an abortion clinic and hijab-wearing women queuing in a maternity ward; it was captioned, 'this is white genocide'.

These hateful memes help us to understand the baseless Great Replacement conspiracy theory which drives the far-right attack on abortion, and which gained public notoriety and far-right popularity following the mass shooting at a mosque in Christchurch, New Zealand. The killer's manifesto, which can still be found on the dark web, was titled 'The Great Replacement', and stated, 'it's the birth rates, it's the birth rates'. His vicious document asserts that white women need to have 2.06 babies to 'replace' the population and blames 'individualism' for the fall in white birth rates that, combined with rising migration, is causing 'white genocide'.

If you haven't come across the lunatic Great Replacement conspiracy theory before, then as described above, it claims that white people in the Global North are being replaced by migration from the Global South. In turn, migration is being encouraged by so-called cultural Marxist elites – a manufactured enemy of the far right that doesn't exist in reality. Because there are very few actual Marxists for the far right to rail against, the term – which has its origins in antisemitism – has come to mean feminists, LGBTIQ activists, Black Lives Matter activists, human rights lawyers and neoliberal political structures such as the European Union and, in the US, the Democratic Party. The replacement, the theory goes, is aided by feminists suppressing the white birth rate through abortion and contraception. All of this is being coordinated by Jewish billionaire financiers, who are also accused of being Marxists.

Needless to say, the idea that there is a demographic threat to white people in the Global North has no basis in reality, not least because the idea of a 'white race' is a construct. In England and Wales, the 2021 census revealed 87.1 per cent of the population identifies as white, an increase of 2.1 per cent since the 2011 census.[2] In European Union member states, black and minority ethnic people make up only 10 per cent of the population.[3] The United States has a larger non-white community, and the white population has decreased from 80 per cent in 1980 to 60.1 per cent in 2019. But even with that shift, a 'replacement' is simply not happening, outside the deranged fantasies of white supremacists.

This fantasy fuels the fascist demand for reproductive control. At the same time, black and minority ethnic people must be – as we saw from Identity EVROPA – either incentivised to leave, violently removed with forced deportations, prevented from reproducing through forced sterilisation or, in the darkest fantasies of the far right, eradicated in a genocidal race war. The Christchurch killer's manifesto proclaimed, 'before we deal with the fertility rates, we must deal with both the invaders within our lands and the invaders that seek to enter our lands. We must crush immigration and deport those invaders already living on our soil.'[4] The Great Replacement is the perfect vehicle to drive forward the far right's violent ideology: it allows them to justify race war, terrorism and reproductive control, while positioning those who oppose its violent aims – including by ending an unwanted pregnancy, or by being gay or black – as traitors.

Bearing in mind the fascist thought architecture, it is clear that the manufactured threat of the Great Replacement plays a vital role in far-right politics. By claiming that the West is indigenously white, the far right links whiteness to Europe's *nature* and the nations within it. That natural order is being threatened, far-right activists claim, by 'cultural Marxism', as represented by immigration, abortion rights, Black Lives Matter and LGBTIQ rights. These movements represent freedom – freedom to move, freedom to decide what happens to our bodies, freedom to determine our own lives, freedom to love.

The Great Replacement builds on long antisemitic and racist traditions in Europe, but the term was coined by the French novelist Renaud Camus in 2012.[5] He argued that an onslaught of non-white, mostly Muslim immigration had endangered French culture and left it under siege. This line of thinking considers migration to be a form of reverse colonialism, with Muslim communities overwhelming their counterparts in Christian Europe, and is rooted in fascist ideology: the hatred of migration is born from the belief that crossing from one nation to another undermines the stability of the nation-state, and the idea that it is possible to change one's nationality poses a threat to the idea that there is something immutable and natural about a nation.

The attack on individualism as a driver of abortion reflects the way in which the far right seeks to subjugate women's reproductive rights and self-determination to the reproduction of the nation. They accuse white women who delay becoming mothers (or choose not to have children at all) of putting their individual needs before the needs of their racial collective.

The Great Replacement theory is also espoused by the far-right groups calling themselves Identitarians, the most famous of which is Generation Identity. The Dutch political scientist Cas Mudde explains in his book *The Far Right Today* that 'the central agenda of the Identitarian movement is to oppose the alleged "Islamization" of Europe and to renew the birth rate and identity of European nations'.[6] As key Identitarian activist Markus Willinger puts it, 'we don't want Mehmed or Mustafa to become Europeans'.[7] The neo-Nazi Telegram channel Full Haus is another apparently Identitarian group; it describes its membership as 'unapologetically pro-white and hostile to the forces that try to … make whites a minority in every country

36

on earth'. The group's desire to ban abortion is motivated by the perceived need for 'more healthy white children ... to secure the existence of our people and a future for white children'. This latter part of the sentence echoes the Fourteen Words slogan coined by neo-Nazi David Eden Lane, both to summarise the movement's aims and as a shorthand signalling political allegiance to other far-right activists.

The claims about white genocide and replacement can be found all over the far-right infosphere. For example, the UK far-right group Patriotic Alternative posts Great Replacement conspiracist content on its own Telegram channels: activist members drop banners emblazoned with the slogan 'we will not be replaced', while leader Mark Collett accuses migration of assisting 'demographic replacement' and fuelling 'the genocide of our people'.

Collett is a neo-Nazi who set up Patriotic Alternative after being suspended from the British National Party amidst allegations he was conspiring against the leadership.[8] The fringe group aims to combat the 'replacement and displacement' of white British people by migrants who 'have no right to these lands'.[9] Collett's grim career includes referring to people seeking asylum as 'cockroaches' and calling HIV AIDS a 'friendly disease' because 'blacks and drug users and gays have it'.[10] He bemoans the 'fall of the western man', and his annual conference platforms men who believe women should submit to male dominance.[11]

Collett's dissemination of the abortion clinic cartoon described above directly links reproductive rights and racism. This demonstrates how the Great Replacement conspiracy cements far-right fears about the threat to white male supremacy – and how those fears relate directly to some men's desire to control women's reproduction. The white women queuing for an abortion are not only positioned as traitors to their race by refusing to reproduce white babies, but also as free from male control: in an all-female space, they are exercising their right to bodily autonomy. The Muslim women are equally portrayed as a threat – they are having brown babies in an attempt to 'replace' the aborted white foetuses. Both dangers must, according to the movement's followers, be defeated through violence and reproductive control.

Where I first discovered the relationship between the anti-abortion and anti-immigration far right was not on Telegram, however, but in the UK Life League. This activist group was the brainchild of far-right activist and Calvinistic firebrand Jim Dowson, who cofounded the anti-Muslim Britain First group. An activist from Scotland, he melds extremist political views with fundamentalist Protestantism, and has been called the most influential far-right activist in Europe. He courted controversy by setting up a website that published the personal details of sexual health workers and learnt much of his anti-abortion trade from the US movement.

While researching the Life League, I realised just how much the far-right and anti-abortion movements were closely linked – and why. I pored over its *Rescue* magazine, scribbling in my notebook and wincing at the graphic abortion imagery, discovering article after article about Muslim people who 'speak of conquering Europe through the wombs of our women'.[12] Praise was reserved for far-right authoritarian leaders in Eastern Europe who, the authors claimed, cared about their native people, while in Britain 'the empty cradles, playgrounds, school chairs where our own children should be are occupied by aliens'.

Consider the similarity of this language to that of a speech given by Italian fascist leader Mussolini in 1927, whose regime promoted a precursor to the Great Replacement theory. He launched a 'battle for babies' and a National Agency for Maternity and Infancy, which, according to Ruth Ben-Ghiat, 'encouraged the right kinds of Italians to multiply'.[13] He banned abortion and contraception, taxed single men and rewarded prolific mothers. In one speech, Mussolini warned: 'Cradles are empty and cemeteries are expanding ... The entire white race, the Western race, could be submerged by other races of colour that multiply with a rhythm unknown to our own.'[14]

Dowson is now the pro-life figurehead of the Knights Templar International, where he presents its *Templar Report* – videos in which he rants and rages against women, migrants and LGBTIQ people, often in long monologues interspersed with Bible verses. The site blends photos of British cathedrals, far-right conspiracy and pro-Putin, pro-Trump content with bizarre ramblings about chivalry and virginity. One video compares two scenes showing the British seaside town of Blackpool. The first clip, dating from the 1970s, shows mostly white people enjoying the traditional British seafront, while a more recent clip features holidaymakers from a range of ethnic backgrounds. The accompanying text states that the increase in black and Asian people enjoying a stroll along the beach is 'the result of fifty years of contraception, propaganda and economic necessity making women work rather than have children, and *literally millions of abortions*'.[15]

Like the cartoon posted by Collett, this reveals much about how the far right views women in terms of the Great Replacement. First, there is the desire to return to the fascist mythic past, an imaginary time when Britain's population was all white and where women, free of economic necessity to work, were confined to the domestic sphere. The public sphere could therefore be a pure male space. Second, the text explicitly blames white women's access to abortion for the rising number of black and minority ethnic people in the UK – claiming that if white women had continued to have children at 'replacement rates', Britain's white population would be larger. The piece also rails against contraception, expressing a desire to do away with women's bodily autonomy altogether.

These extreme views have now become mainstream. In 2017, Iowa's then Congressman Steve King said, 'the US subtracts from its population a million of our babies in the form of abortion. We add to our population approximately 1.8 million of "somebody else's babies" who are raising in another culture before they get to us. We are replacing our American culture two to one every year.'[16] King's comments bring together a desire to ban abortion to restore a diminished white population while railing against migration that 'replaces our American culture' – by which he means whiteness. This far-right conspiracy was publicly shared by a man who served as a Republican Congressman for eighteen years. No wonder that his views were met with praise from Ku Klux Klan leader David Duke, who tweeted in response, 'God Bless Steve King.'[17]

Chapter Six will examine in greater detail how these fringe beliefs have become a real and present danger, as they are transported from the extremist corners of the internet into mainstream government policy across Europe and the US. Although often (but not always) couched in more polite language, parliaments across the region are enacting laws that track back to far-right demands for reproductive control and racist anti-migrant policies. Following on from there, in Chapter Seven, we will examine how anxieties about low birth rates and a crisis in capitalism is allowing far-right ideas about women to take hold in the mainstream, posing a threat to women's future freedoms.

There are historical precedents for manufactured panics about immigration and women's reproductive autonomy becoming mainstream political policy: this is not, after all, the first time that white male supremacists have laid siege to reproductive rights. In the 1860s US, women were starting to gain more freedoms, including control over their reproductive capability, and a louder political voice. Abortion drugs were widely available and, according to historian Leslie Reagan, 'the most common means of inducing abortion – by taking drugs – was commercialized'.[18] She writes: 'by the 1840s, the abortion business boomed. Despite the laws forbidding the sale of abortifacients [poison laws], they were advertised in the popular press and could be purchased from physicians or pharmacists through the mail. If drugs failed, women could go to a practitioner who specialised in performing instrumental abortions.' The clients for abortion were often 'married, white, native-born Protestant women of the upper and middle classes'.[19]

It's important to note here that while abortion was available for white women, it was criminalised for enslaved black women. If an enslaved woman ended her own pregnancy, or sought help to do so, this was treated as a property crime as the foetus belonged by law to the slave owner. As black philosopher and civil rights activist Angela Davis writes, 'the slaveholding class was forced to rely on natural reproduction as the surest method of replenishing and increasing the domestic slave population ... in the eyes of the slaveholders, slave women were not mothers at all; they were simply instruments guaranteeing the growth of the slave labour force'.[20] This cruelty emphasises the right's long history of viewing women's bodies as a reproductive resource, with enslaved black women treated as both productive and reproductive labour resource, exploited to enrich the white ruling class.

Two other political shifts were happening alongside white women's increased emancipation. The first was the economic threat posed to the ruling classes by the Civil War and the liberation of the enslaved people from whom they extracted their wealth. The second was rising immigration into the country from Ireland, Mexico, China and other non-WASP communities. The combined forces of migration, women's reproductive agency and abolition caused a growing anxiety that white male supremacy was under threat: 'Anti-abortion activists pointed out that immigrant families, many of them Catholic, were larger and would soon outpopulate native-born white Yankees and threaten their political power.'[21] Dr Harold Storer, an anti-abortion activist who led the charge against reproductive freedoms, asked whether the US would 'be filled by our own children or by those of aliens? This is a question our women must answer; upon their loins depends the destiny of the nation.'[22] Storer and his acolytes won the battle against abortion, and the procedure was criminalised in the USA until *Roe vs Wade* in 1973 established it as a federal right – before *Roe* was overturned in June 2022, that is. It's also worth noting that by 1924, quotas were put in place to limit the immigration of people from non-white countries as well as eastern and southern Europe. Chinese immigration was banned outright by the Chinese Exclusion Act of 1882. The far right won because they successfully played on white male fears about women's freedoms, along with those about migrant people replacing the WASP majority.

At the turn of the twentieth century, precursors to the Great Replacement once again appeared on the US political stage – this time from President Theodore Roosevelt. In 1905, he concluded his Lincoln Day Dinner Speech with the proclamation that 'race purity must be maintained'. A year later, he referred once again to the falling birth rate among native-born whites by asserting the impending threat of 'race suicide'. Angela Davis points out that in 'his State of the Union message that year Roosevelt admonished the well-born white women who engaged in "wilful sterility" – the one sin for which the penalty is national death, race suicide'.[23]

In 1930s and 1940s Nazi Germany, men won medals in recognition of killing while women won medals for childbirth, with gold medals given to the most fecund. The obvious reason for these awards was to encourage the reproduction of a white supremacist nation – to build the Aryan race for the Third Reich. But the reduction of women's role to reproductive labour in Nazi Germany was also a backlash against their growing sexual and reproductive freedoms during the preceding Weimar period.

According to a 1991 article by historian Charu Gupta, 'Nazis believed that the women's movement ... was part of an international Jewish conspiracy to subvert the German family and thus destroy the German race. The movement, it claimed, was encouraging women to assert their economic independence and to neglect their proper task of producing children ... encouraging contraception and abortion and so lowering the birthrate, it was attacking the very existence of the German people.'[24]

This backlash against reproductive and sexual rights is one of the horrifyingly long list of reasons the neo-Nazi Telegram channel Full Haus bemoans the defeat of Germany in the Second World War. One post sarcastically claims that 'the system is dedicated to destroying whites through immigration [and] abortion ... but hey, at least we're not speaking German'; while another poster muses under the heading 'what if Germany had won?' that there would be 'No Cultural Marxism or Liberalism and their devastating consequences: ... Abortion ... Open homosexuality; Radical feminist movement.'

The UK, US and Europe are a long way from Nazi Germany – a genocidal totalitarian state that murdered 6 million Jewish people, alongside 5 million LGBTIQ people, disabled people, people of colour and communist dissidents. But in the late 1920s and early 1930s, when the Nazis were launching their attack on women's liberation and claiming women's freedoms as a Jewish and Marxist plot, Germany was also a long way from what it was to become in the next decade. The point is that extremist views about replacement, race war and reproductive control can become increasingly normalised until they gather momentum among voters and, from there, impact government policy. This has been the case in Hungary and Poland when it comes to anti-migrant and family policy, in the UK when it comes to immigration and asylum policy, and in the rhetoric used by elected political parties and leaders in France, Spain, Italy, Slovakia and the Netherlands, as well as in the Republican Party reshaped by Trump.

Working in concert with the Great Replacement is a second far-right conspiracy: QAnon and its claims about satanic ritual abuse.

If you've been lucky enough to have escaped awareness of the QAnon conspiracy, your delightful state of ignorance must sadly end here. This movement claims that a left-leaning elite of cultural Marxists runs a large child abduction network in order to harvest the chemical compound adrenochrome from their victims for its supposed psychedelic and anti-aging effects; the theory states that this compound is more potent when harvested from a frightened child. This mythical cabal performs abortions as ritual satanic sacrifice, the theory goes, and its ultimate aim is to de-Christianise the West. The fantasy emerged on the messaging board 4Chan, a social media platform that airs views considered too extreme for Reddit: the story featured Q, someone claiming to work within government with high-level security clearance, and supposedly leaking deep state information in preparation for a 'coming storm'. Q's theories then moved onto Facebook, Instagram and Twitter, with hashtags such as #SaveTheChildren. Q-related accounts are now mostly banned from most mainstream platforms, but by the time the big tech moderators had caught up, the damage was already done.

The Q and Great Replacement conspiracy theories meet at the intersection of satanic tropes with the fear that the West is being de-Christianised. Its followers claim that migration into Europe from predominantly Muslim countries in the Global South is part of a satanic plot to eradicate Christianity: in order to save the West from this satanic takeover, both migration and abortion need to end.

It would be tempting to ignore this madness, but recent US history demands we give it some of our time. The QAnon conspiracy claims that progress on human rights issues such as abortion is unnatural (satanic) and must be reversed in order to restore the fascistic natural order and return to an idealised, fascist mythic past. These ideas have been mainstreamed by the far-right, conspiracist capture of the US Republican Party and its support for Donald Trump, with some estimates suggesting that as many as one in five Americans now believe in QAnon.[25]

Satanic ritual abuse conspiracy theories have a long and ignoble history, starting with the antisemitic blood libel myth in medieval Europe, through to Nazi propaganda in 1930s Germany and the McMartin case in 1980s USA, which attacked day-care centres. The latter was connected to women's growing freedoms, similar to the backlash in post-Weimar Germany, with women blamed for going to work and accused of putting their children at risk.

To understand how the satanic conspiracy theory first took hold among the far right, before becoming mainstream, we need to think back to the three concepts that underpin fascist theory: the natural order, the mythic past and a constant state of war. While it may seem illogical to link abortion, migration and satanism, such connections are valuable in the far-right project of rolling back progress on women's rights and trapping them in reproductive labour. This opposition to women's bodily autonomy stems from a belief system holding that abortion is a subversion of the natural order – as represented by the unnatural or corrupt figure of Satan.

To understand how such a bizarre and violent conspiracy took hold, it is worth considering that satanic panic emerged in the US after the passing of *Roe vs Wade*, as men claiming to be former satanists newly converted to Christianity warned that the world was being run by satanist cults. These men included the Christian evangelist Mike Warnke, whose book *Satan Seller* recounted his alleged experiences in a cult; unsurprisingly, he and others like him were affiliated with the growing Christian-right movement in the US, and committed to its anti-abortion agenda.

By the 1980s, satanic panic was hitting its peak with the McMartin case, which gripped the Global North, spread by Reaganite Conservatives and anti-rape activists alike. The case involved lurid testimonies about robed men killing rabbits among other things. No evidence for the claims was found, and no one was ever convicted.

The hysteria around the McMartin case sprang in part from a reaction to women's increasing social and economic equality, following increased access to reproductive healthcare and contraception which had brought more women into the workplace. According to Richard Beck, author of *We Believe the Children: Moral Panic in the 1980s*, 'in the '80s you had a strong, vicious anti-feminist backlash that helped conspiracies take hold'.[26]

Just as today's satanic ritual abuse conspiracy theories spread by QAnon and CBR UK, this panic was based in fear about women's control over their own fertility. In the 1980s, the women's liberation movement paved the way for middle-class women to move out of the domestic sphere and into the public realm – out of the home and into the workplace. While feminists celebrated this as progress, reactionaries accused working mothers of abandoning their duty to their children and – crucially – their duty to have children.

'You had this Reagan-driven conservative resurgence,' Beck told *Mother Jones*, 'and day care was seen as at least suspicious, if not an actively maligned force of feminism.' What was driving the panic, he argued, was the idea that 'families were being harmed' by women's increasing freedoms.

The figure of Satan represents the unnatural – the left hand as opposed to the right, the darkness to the light. By claiming that abortions are a sacrifice to Satan, the conspiracist far right can code women's rights as unnatural, corrupt and evil; to put it in old-fashioned terms, women's liberation is *devilish*. In contrast, a good woman is one who accepts her biological destiny of reproduction and submits to male dominance. To restore this natural order, thereby defeating satanic power, the far right claims it must roll back progress on human rights and revive the mythic past, reversing hard-won freedoms. Importantly, the satanic conspiracy theory also creates the state of constant war upon which fascism thrives. It requires its believers to engage

46

in an endless battle between good and evil, light and dark, until the satanic forces are defeated. During the 2020 US elections, Q followers believed that battle would be led by President Trump, who would launch an all-out assault against satanic abusers on Day X – the conspiracist term for the start of the far-right/Q revolution. Radford University's Chair and Professor of Religious Studies, Paul Thomas, explains how 'according to Anons, Trump is engaged in a battle of cosmic significance between the "children of light" and the "children of darkness" and is working to dismantle pedophile networks that are abducting children for Satanic rites'.[27] The key word in this analysis is *battle*: the conspiracy puts Q's followers on a belligerent footing where they are ready and willing to use violence in a global fight to end this supposed abuse (they carried 'save the children' signs on protests and used the hashtag #SaveTheChildren on social media).

Given that women's role in the fascist concept of constant war is reproduction, this adds another layer of meaning to the #SaveTheChildren hashtag: men must fight to save children from satanic conspiracies; women should stay at home and *have* children (avoiding abortion). The majority of QAnon believers vote Republican; in fact, of those who agree with the statement 'the government, media, and financial world in the US are controlled by a group of Satan-worshipping paedophiles who run a global sex-trafficking organisation' 23 per cent are Republican voters and only 8 per cent are Democrat voters.[28] This confirms that race is a factor in the QAnon conspiracy theory and how it has spread: Republican voters are more likely to be white, while white supremacists were wooed to the party by Trump and his electoral agenda.

The links between anti-abortion and the #SaveTheChildren QAnon conspiracy theory are not hard to find: at the time of the 2020 US Presidential election, a brief search for the Twitter hashtag generated numerous references to Democrat elites, satanic ritual abuse and abortion rights. As one tweet expressed it: 'Y'all literally voted for a pedophile a man who is gunna make abortions legal but wanna post about #SaveTheChildren. You just put children in danger as well as voted to kill thousands of children.'[29] Another tweeted, 'abortion is child sacrifice. If you vote democrat you are supporting child sacrifice. #SaveTheChildren.'[30] Twitter user 'TriALII was more explicit, tweeting on the day of the US election that 'abortion is not womens rights #SaveTheChildren from becoming #Sacrifice by this satanic cult.'[31]

Things came to a head when QAnon moved offline and into real life during the violent insurrection on 6 January 2021 at the US Capitol building in Washington, DC. The incident brought together the overlapping memberships of the QAnon movement, far-right militias, racists and anti-abortion activists in an attempt to overthrow the democratic process in the US and launch a race war that would echo the 1860s Civil War.

On that day, as Congress voted to confirm the electoral victory of incoming President Joe Biden, busloads of Trump supporters started to roll into the heart of US democratic power under heavy grey skies. Groups such as Turning Point USA had organised transport to the nation's capital in order to bring those determined to 'stop the steal' of the 2020 election. The far-right Proud Boys in their polo shirts mingled with Oathkeepers, wearing military costumes and face coverings to conceal their identities. The marchers carried flags emblazoned with the American Revolutionary War slogan 'Liberty or Death' and yelled slogans and battle cries into loud hailers. 'It looks like soldiers because we are soldiers,' said Proud Boy Eddie Block as he livestreamed the crowd marching through Washington, D.C. Men who looked little older than boys pulled faces into their iPhones, taking selfies for their far-right social media followers. Making a film as he marched was the blond, baby-faced Tayler Hansen, who had gained notoriety for painting the slogan 'Babies Lives Matter' outside of an abortion clinic. Veterans of the anti-abortion movement, such as John

Brockhoeft, who had conspired to bomb abortion clinics in the 1980s, joined the crowd.[32]

What could not be ignored in that febrile, feverish crowd was that this was a movement of *men* – of white men. There was the odd black person, a rare woman in the mob. But there were row upon row of white male faces – some in baseball caps, some in cowboy hats, and at least one in a horned headdress – marching on the Capitol that day. 'This is our goddamn city,' they called out. 'Be loud and motherfucking Proud Boy proud.'[33]

At least one group of people were not present: antifascists, or antifa. The resistance to Trump's increasingly far-right turn had deliberately stayed home, a decision credited with preventing the insurrection from spiralling into violent street conflict.

When Trump took to the stage on that freezing grey afternoon, he was greeted with whoops and cheers. The president praised the far-right groups and conspiracy theorists who had gathered to defend him, urging them to film the day's events. Shouts of agreement went up as he railed against big tech for supposedly rigging the election and praised the 'hundreds of thousands of American patriots who are committed to the honesty of our elections and the integrity of our glorious republic'. White faces nodded along to his castigation of the Democrats for being from the 'radical left'; they chanted 'hang Mike Pence' – Trump's vice president, a zealous Christian conservative who nevertheless refused to challenge the legal results of the election – as Trump railed against the Republicans who opposed him, calling them 'weak'. He said, 'Everyone here will soon be marching over to the Capitol building to peacefully and patriotically make your voices heard.'[34]

From a Q perspective, this was the start of the battle between the light and dark, between Satan's forces and their Trumpian superhero. For the far-right militias who are not aligned with Q but do believe in the Great Replacement, this was a moment to reclaim the US from the cultural Marxist, pro-women, pro–Black Lives Matter, pro-LGBTIQ elite represented by Biden's Democratic Party, in order to entrench white male supremacy through a race war. For both, this was Day X, the beginning of the 'storm' that would trigger the constant state of war inherent in fascist theory; and they were launching that war with the permission of the man who – at that time – was still the most powerful leader in the world.

The presence of anti-abortion forces across both conspiracist factions was key: in order to destroy Satan's power *and* to win the race war, this violent, genocidal movement required women to be placed under patriarchal control and devoted solely to reproductive exploitation.

The men did march – but neither peacefully nor patriotically. They smashed windows. They wrecked bookcases containing feminist literature. They shouted that they would come for Nancy Pelosi, as her staffers hid under desks in her office and texted their parents to say they loved them. When they finally broke into the chamber, they meandered around, looking confused and proud all at once. 'This is our house!' men shouted, whooping in the Rotunda. 'This is America!' they cried out – those white men who claimed the US was for them and only them. Race is nation in their world, after all. 'Derrick Evans is in the Capitol!' shouted the anti-abortion West Virginia state representative, a man whose presence linked the Republican elite with the rioting mob. 'We're taking this country back, whether you like it or not,' he continued, livestreaming his crimes with the arrogance of a man accustomed to harassing women outside abortion clinics.[35]

The day ended with Trump finally telling his supporters to go home. The last person to leave the Capitol steps, it seemed, was Eddie Block, a Proud Boy who uses a wheelchair and was assisted to safety by the police force. He left behind him others who lay dead: Police Officer Brian Sicknick; QAnon believers Ashli Babbitt and Rosanne Boyland; and Trump loyalists Kevin Greeson and Benjamin Phillips.

Because these twin movements, driven by conspiracy theories, met at the Capitol, we need to take them seriously (though it would be preferable to ignore lunatic stories about satanic forces). But the terrible truth is that, when the Senators returned to the Chamber to ratify the 2020 election and declare Biden the winner, the conspiracy theorists weren't just out there, smashing windows and screaming hateful slogans. They were in the room.

Representative Jim McGovern is the Democratic congressman for Massachusetts. 'I kind of assumed that after this terrible tragedy we would come back and maybe all come together and do the right thing,' he told BBC documentary *Four Hours at the Capitol*. 'I was here when 9/11 happened. Democrats and Republicans gathered on the steps of the Capitol and with one voice said "God Bless America." I assumed that would happen again. And it didn't.'[36]

As the Capitol cleared and the rebels retreated, more than a hundred Republicans lined up inside the Chamber of Congress to vote that the election had been invalid. Among them were those, such as Paul Gosar, Lauren Boebert and Marjorie Taylor Greene, who had shared anti-abortion beliefs and promoted the QAnon conspiracy theory; Taylor Greene had called Q a 'patriot' and said Trump's re-election would be a 'once in a lifetime opportunity to take this global cabal of Satan-worshipping pedophiles out'.[37] She later said she regretted these comments. In the 2022 midterms, at least forty-five candidates had actively supported or followed QAnon, or spread related conspiracy theories.

This illustrates the far-right capture of the Republican Party, and demonstrates why it is imperative we scrutinise the links between the political establishment, anti-abortion movements and the absurd conspiracy theories. In the months following the insurrection on 6 January 2021, the Republicans waged war on hard-won freedoms, including the right to safe, legal abortion. The attacks on abortion rights came from many Republicans who had either expressed their support for QAnon, or who had voted with the insurrectionists to overturn the election and return Trump to power. Fascistic ideas about abortion, fear of freedom and a genocidal desire for race war were blatantly expressed by the violent militias smashing the Capitol's windows – but these same attitudes are also gaining acceptance in formal politics by an increasingly fascistic Republican Party.

Extremist anti-abortion groups and far-right conspiracy theorists consider women's full access to human rights as an attack on the natural order they want to preserve. This order is built on the exploitation of women's reproductive labour and women's subordination to male authority. What 6 January and the subsequent 2022 Congressional candidate list proved was that such bizarre theories are no longer the preserve of an extremist fringe. The far-right capture of the American Republican Party – the world's oldest democratic party, one formed to oppose the spread of slavery and the power of the planter class – is an example of what philosopher Hannah Arendt has called 'the alliance of the elite and the mob'. The elite comprises the Republican Party's policy-makers, its billionaire backers and Supreme Court nominees. The mob are the street fascists, the militias and the anti-abortionists who attacked the Capitol. Together, they are pushing through far-right ideology about reproductive rights, bringing violence and conspiracy theories from the streets into the halls of Congress, where their beliefs shape judicial and political policy.

It comes as no surprise that Trump's presidency ended with a display of white male supremacist violence, and with anti-abortion voices joining the call to overthrow democracy. He was a president who was catapulted to power with the support of men who hate women – and men whose misogyny has been a gateway to white supremacy. This is the Red Pill community – a grouping of the so-called manosphere that started as a Reddit forum and soon became a hub for organised misogyny. It takes its name from the 1999 movie *The Matrix*, where swallowing a red pill allows the protagonist to see the reality of the world he is living in. Red Pill followers view women as sexual objects to conquer and exploit, and share the far-right belief that women's liberation is unnatural and leading to a societal decline.

Men in the Red Pill forums celebrated Trump as an 'alpha male' who could win a perceived 'war on men' waged by feminists and liberals and epitomised by the pro-choice candidate Hillary Rodham Clinton. Note that these are men who believe – in keeping with fascist thought architecture – that they are in a constant state of war, and that women's role in this war is to act as reproductive and sexual labourers.

In its earliest form, Red Pill culture was highly individualistic and built on a warped concept of male self-improvement: members were encouraged to develop their status from 'beta' to 'alpha male', by working out, building muscle and manipulating – or 'gaming' – women into having sex with them. The forum became increasingly politicised, however, in the run-up to the 2016 election, and votes for Trump were understood as votes for white male supremacy. Forum moderator redpillschool posted in October 2016 that it was important for men's rights activists and Red Pillers to vote for Trump and to secure the defeat of Hillary Rodham Clinton:

> This election season we're not going to be able to put up any walls between sexual strategy and politics, because the outcomes from these candidates are directly tied to the very cultural influences and trends we've been discussing here for the past few years. They're tied to sexual strategy ... Our presidential candidates are representing a system set up to increasingly damage the lives of men (and promote the choices, advantages, and positive outcomes for women) and those alienated by this system, respectively.[38]

Having won the Electoral College and therefore the presidency, Trump went on to meet the demands of his misogynistic base by weakening protections for women experiencing gender-based violence and launching an attack on women's reproductive rights. To understand how this happened, and how the electoral force of the Red Pill subculture helped shape Trump's misogynistic political programme, we first need to understand what draws men to this kind of extremism, what the members of the forums believe, and how they were convinced to support a mainstream presidential candidate. From there, we can analyse how Red Pill beliefs became policy under Trump's rule.

For the men in Red Pill and related subcultures, the sexual and reproductive freedoms that allow women to access the public sphere – to work *en masse* outside the home, enjoy political power and make their own decisions about sex and fertility disrupts, as we have discussed, the fascistic natural order. These are men who believe they are biologically superior to women and also that they have, as philosopher Amia Srinivasan has described it, a 'right to sex' – hence the focus on fitness and gaming women into sex. The fact that feminism denies these men unfettered sexual access to, and control over, women, means they feel, at best, hard done by – in other words, they believe that men are being oppressed or punished by feminism's gains. At worst, these men want to reassert that power and authority via violence and reproductive control. 'If you accept your own position as a man as biologically determined, as do so many foot-soldiers of the alt-right,' writes Paul Mason, 'then it's easy to see feminism as an attack on the biological order of things.'[39]

Further, as Mason explains,

> the importance of misogyny as a gateway drug to modern fascism lies in the broadness of the experience it draws on. Few racists have had their jobs taken by a migrant. But every heterosexual man can feel the difference between the ideology of "manliness" and the reality, where women are increasingly free to define their own norms of beauty and sexual behaviour.

And while only a minority of racists have physically attacked a person of colour, most violent misogynists have physically attacked a woman.[40]

In 2016, journalist Aja Romano explored how online misogyny led users towards white supremacy, writing in *Vox* that for communities of angry young men 'who ultimately feel threatened and rejected by women, the movement promotes a sense of male entitlement that is easily radicalised into white nationalism and white supremacy'.[41] Two years later, this was confirmed in a report by the Anti-Defamation League, 'When Women Are the Enemy: The Intersection of Misogyny and White Supremacy', which found that hatred of women was a 'gateway into the white supremacist world'.[42]

These online communities offer men a solution to their woman problem via organised misogyny. In 2016, organised misogyny got politically organised. Trump's election campaign gave these men focus and provided a vital tool for the far right to push their racially charged, anti-abortion agenda into the mainstream: it was an unprecedented opportunity for their views to influence both national and international policy. Like them, Trump appeared to believe that there was a war on men, and he was willing to deploy racism and misogyny to win that war.

With Trump's arrival on the scene, the men who populate these online subcultures started to recognise that, according to sociologists Pierce Dignam and Deana A. Rohlinger, 'if they identify and act collectively as men, they can effect political change … The election of a man who brags about sexually assaulting women illustrates the efficacy of this conviction'.[43] In 2019, Dignam and Rohlinger published a paper that revealed how the far right had radicalised the forum in order to rally support for Donald Trump. Influential Red Pillers started to promote Trump as the 'ultimate alpha'. The accusations of sexual harassment made against Trump further galvanised his

Red Pill supporters: they got behind a leader who, they believed, would restore women to their inferior natural position. Trump would reverse the decline brought on by women's liberation and entrench white male supremacy (think back to the fascist thought architecture that wants to undo progress and turn back the clock). When Trump talked to the Red Pillers about making America great again, they heard the promise of a mythic past based on patriarchal authority and women's subordination.

The Red Pill subculture had always fostered a collective identity among its members through a shared belief in their victimisation by women and minorities, and the community was strengthened by swapping fitness tips and pick-up lines. In the run-up to Trump's election, this identity was weaponised and politicised, moving away from self-improvement, working out and sleeping with or assaulting women, and towards a more political identity based on white male supremacy. Trump became a figurehead for men's political fortunes, and the fact that his rival was Clinton – a pro-abortion woman – gave the movement a sense of urgency. This was, they felt, their last chance.

Dignam and Rohlinger identified how influential posters in the Red Pill forums were able to shift their followers 'from understanding men's rights as a personal philosophy' to political awareness.[44] It 'quickly positioned Trump's candidacy as an opportunity to push back politically against feminism and destroy Hillary Clinton, whom they regarded as the epitome of everything wrong with feminists'.[45] In this way, the 2016 election became an almost existential battle for men's rights activists: vote Trump and win the war on men, or don't vote and let a pro-choice woman become the most powerful leader in the world.

The researchers found examples of Red Pillers becoming more supportive of Trump when it was revealed not only that he had been accused of sexual assault, but he had boasted of it. One Red Pill member set up a forum thread titled 'Sexual

Assault Is Why I'm Endorsing Donald Trump for President of the United States', before posting 'when somebody accuses a powerful or famous figure like Trump of "sexual assault," I don't look the other way. I don't denounce them or their behavior. Instead I run towards them, because there is no truer signal which side somebody is on, than when they're given a bogus accusation by the establishment. This is our beacon to find allies in the war.'[46]

The support Trump won from male supremacists after the allegations helped cement his position as the ultimate alpha who could restore men's sexual rights over women. Historian Ruth Ben-Ghiat argues that the revelations of alleged sexual violence 'merely strengthened the misogynistic brand of male glamour Trump had built over decades'.[47] Infowars, the infamous far-right conspiracy theory website, asked: 'During the Trump Era, will men finally start acting like men again?' The language is telling – the use of 'again' harking back to the fascistic mythic past and a desire to reassert the natural order of male supremacy.

At the same time, the Red Pill's hatred of Clinton exposed its members' own insecurity about their lack of sexual success. One poster on the forum feared that Hillary's victory would 'give the free card to all women in the nation to be complete deplorable corrupt whores'.[48] In this line of thinking, women's sexual and reproductive autonomy designates them 'whores', but a vote for Trump is a vote to make white American men great again.

Rohlinger and Dignam conclude that the politicisation of the Red Pill forum was short-lived but effective. Forum leaders such as redpillschool 'were able to quell dissent and link the Red Pill identity with voting for Trump. This clearly demonstrates that these extreme online enclaves can be dominated by a few powerful voices, which can help candidates holding distasteful views to get elected.'[49] Trump wasted no time in putting those views into action, delivering to his white male supremacist base the policy platform they had demanded. That meant a raft of anti-feminist initiatives, including the groundwork for ending the constitutional right to safe, legal abortion in the United States.

First there was the appointment of anti-abortion judges to the Supreme Court, which in June 2022 overturned *Roe vs Wade*. Trump appointed anti-abortion judge Neil Gorsuch, followed by Brett Kavanaugh – a man who was not only against abortion, but was publicly accused of sexual assault during his confirmation hearings. He denied all allegations. When he was nonetheless elevated to a lifetime appointment in the Supreme Court, it sent a bold message to Trump's following: women's bodily and sexual autonomy was out, and male dominance was in. Kavanaugh's appointment was met with glee on extremist forums, where the alleged abuser was praised as a 'supreme representative' of their community. This was a man, misogynists wrote online, who 'fought the feminists and won'. His appointment was followed by that of Amy Coney Barrett, an anti-abortion lawmaker and conservative whose approval was rushed through after the death of pro-choice Supreme Court judge Ruth Bader-Ginsburg in September 2020.

The four years of Trump rule were characterised by wave after wave of anti-abortion measures, led by the appointments of white male conservative judges and representatives. These lawmakers introduced so-called heartbeat bills which sought to ban abortion after six weeks; forced the closures of abortion clinics across the US; implemented a barrage of unnecessarily arduous health and safety regulations known as TRAP laws; and designed state laws requiring funerals for aborted foetuses, creating additional logistical, monetary and emotional hurdles for abortion providers and people seeking care. Outside the US, policies such as the reinstatement of the global gag rule withdrew funding for sexual and reproductive healthcare providers around the world. According to reproductive health charity MSI Reproductive Choices, the funding cut that denied federal funds to international NGOs offering abortions or abortion advice led to at least 1.8 million additional unsafe abortions and 20,000 maternal deaths.

Trump lost in 2020, but the damage had already been done. The rushing through of Coney Barrett's appointment, along with the judicial appointments across the nation, had created a conservative anti-abortion judiciary. This meant that in 2021, a conservative majority on the Supreme Court allowed Texas to ignore *Roe vs Wade* and ban abortion after six weeks, with a vigilante law put in place that criminalised anyone helping a woman to access abortion. As the decision by the Supreme Court not to intervene was published, one woman tweeted, 'Whatever you are doing now is what you were doing when Roe vs Wade ended.' Within a year, the Supreme Court had overturned the 1973 ruling and returned abortion laws to state level. The decision was made on a Friday and by Monday, nine states had already banned terminations. In one weekend 16 million US women and girls were stripped of their human rights.

The attack on abortion rights through mainstream government and judicial policy was fundamental to delivering Red Pill and far-right misogynistic aims. This is because, as we have seen, control over our own reproduction is absolutely fundamental to women's liberation: without bodily autonomy, women cannot be free.

Alongside the attacks on abortion rights, Trump's administration launched wide-ranging attacks on the rights of LGBTIQ people, and his regime oversaw the dismantling of protections for victims and survivors of domestic and sexual abuse. This included blocking the re-authorization of the 1994 Violence Against Women Act and a decision to legally redefine domestic violence so that only harms constituting a felony or misdemeanour crime could be considered abuse. The change meant that coercive and controlling behaviour, as well as financial abuse, were no longer defined as domestic violence.

The repeal of laws and definitions designed to protect women from gender-based violence is a key aim of fascist and far-right politics. From Vox in Spain to Putin in Russia to Red Pillers in the USA, the far right believes in patriarchal authority in the home that is protected by the state, or at least sheltered from state intervention. Trump's decision to dismantle women's protections against domestic abuse reflects the desires of his far-right base who believe that men should have ultimate authority over their family – wife, girlfriend, sister or daughter.

The Red Pill movement's greatest success, though, was the mainstreaming and normalisation of a hyper-misogynistic view of women. Their mobilisation took the subculture offline and turned the White House red. It was an example of how online extremist groups, so often ignored and derided, could successfully organise politically to affect mainstream politics and win what they desperately desired: a rollback of women's freedoms and a vindication of white male supremacy.

Although it was the Red Pill forum that arguably had the greatest influence on Trump's election and therefore helped to mainstream a fascistic attack on women's rights, it is not the only online subculture to bring together violent misogyny, conspiracy theories and far-right beliefs. Perhaps the most extreme example is the incel group – another forum that started on Reddit and now flourishes on other platforms such as incel.net and incel.is.

Incel stands for *involuntary celibates*: a group of men and boys who feel sexually rejected by women and who are very angry about it. Their grievance is associated with a sense of sexual entitlement: they believe they have a right to sexual access to women, which they can claim violently if necessary. These are men who feel cheated of what the writer Ta-Nehishi Coates describes as the one commodity all white men are supposed to have in common: the bodies of white women. They see women as a form of property, the object of sexual and reproductive exploitation.

The incel subculture is fringe and commands little influence, unlike the broader Red Pill and far-right movements. Its violent fantasies have spilled out into real-life terror, however, with extremists driving vans into cafes, shooting men and women in California, murdering Asian sex workers in massage parlours and stabbing people to death in Plymouth, UK. The group is worthy of our attention because it encapsulates how far-right, racist beliefs and conspiracy theories such as the Great Replacement combine with a violent desire to besiege women and girls, either to make them sex slaves, or to kill them.

When I visited incel forums using a fake identity, doing a keyword search for 'abortion', the results were revealing. What has often been missed in discussions of incel and Red Pill culture is its blatant white supremacism. Through my research I discovered that many incels believe in the Great Replacement, which, they claim, is being fuelled by women's reproductive rights. On the Purple Pill forum – which is less extreme than the Red Pill or incel movement – one poster wrote, 'abortion and women's rights lead to a sub-replacement birth rate. Either abortion or women's rights will end or those who implement them will die'. A second member of the forum shared similar views, writing that 'whites have lost the will to live as a collective. Birthrates in steep decline ... full-scale embrace of culturally self-annihilating movements like feminism, socialism, globalism and multiculturalism. White guilt, white inaction in the face of rising violence and hatred of us.' Further posts claim that 'extinction is imminent' and 'Western civilisation is in decline because of low birth rates and the slow dissolution of the nuclear family'. On the Red Pill, the general argument is summed up in a stark comment: 'decreasing the need for immigration is predicated on making women want to have more babies'.

In an incel thread titled 'What Pisses Me Off Most Is that Chad's Bastards Are Being Killed', GameDevCel, who has since been banned, rants that 'the same foid who claim to have abortions for population control are the same who see nothing wrong in mass migration and feeding n****rs, to the point they breed billions'.[50] (A *foid* or femoid is slang for woman; Chads are popular jock-style men who have lots of sex with women; Chad's bastards are aborted foetuses.)

These sentiments are echoed on a thread called 'Women Destroying Cultures and Countries'. Uncommon posted on 17 October 2020: 'The antifa and femoids support the invasion of africans and arabians in ALL Europe. In 50 years, thanks to the "diversity" … agenda, all Europe will turn into a third world shit hole full of wars and Sharia law everywhere.'[51] On another thread, titled 'Remember FOIDs are more than willing to genocide to see their "rights"' (genocide refers to abortion), the poster GameDevCel writes how 'foids' want the 'right' to 'fuck Chads', but 'they don't care if this will destroy their entire race'.[52] The fantastical accusation is that women who choose to have sex and then have an abortion are responsible for a white genocide.

You can see in this small selections of posts how the Great Replacement theory forms part of the far-right incel subculture – and yet, over and over again, the overlap between male supremacy and white supremacy in this closed-off movement has been ignored. This ignorance has to stop. The violent misogyny expressed in these spaces springs directly from the far-right agenda that proposes a demographic crisis in the Global North is caused by women's sexual and reproductive liberation. This means that, while incels' hatred of women is primarily driven by their horror at women's sexual and reproductive freedoms threatening *male* supremacy, it is exacerbated by the conviction that those same freedoms are threatening *white survival*. This is a far-right movement obsessed with white replacement and reproductive control.

The belief in fascist mythic past, an imaginary time when white men had unlimited access to women's bodies for sex and reproduction and no man was forced to be involuntarily celibate, further drives these ideas. Unsurprisingly, incels believe that the route back to this imaginary past is achievable by removing women's rights. On an incel thread about abortion, Cofffeee asserts, 'the woman shouldn't have rights over her body', and WelcomeToMyDNA adds, 'I am against anything that benefits femoids'.[53] GameDevCel would concur: 'there is no such thing as too many rights being taken away from foids'.[54] In response to a post pointing out that banning abortion leads to unsafe terminations that cause disease, GameDevCel says, 'so be infested with disease and illness'.[55]

A thread titled 'Strengthening Components in the Incel Brain' muses on the lost halcyon days of male supremacy. Tupolev, a forum staff member, believes that 'if we were born in an earlier timeline we would likely have wives and children … Divorce used to be shamed and frowned upon. Abortion used to be ILLEGAL, and women used to know their place in the world. They carried out their gender specific duties.'[56] On a thread called 'Confess to Me Boyos', Kaczor reveals that 'my fantasy is to live in a normal world without feminism, LGBT, abortion. Every man would be guaranteed a wife.'[57]

Linked to paranoia about the Great Replacement, incels think the rise of feminism and progressive movements is causing western society to degenerate. They share this view with far-right activists such as Jim Dowson. In a 2019 article, 'The War on Men', Dowson's colleagues in the Knights Templar claim threats posed by immigration and secularisation would not exist 'without female emancipation'.[58] Dowson has said that 'society is engulfed by silly women', and that women's presence in public space has caused 'the whole of society to degenerate'. He sees this degeneration in progress on women's, LGBTIQ and civil rights, as well as in more liberal approaches to migration.

Dowson and his incel comrades echo views expressed by Peter Thiel, co-founder of PayPal and Palantir, and the first outside investor in Facebook. Thiel said in 2009 that freedom and democracy were no longer compatible, in part because the franchise has been extended to women, who persistently vote in favour of social liberalism.[59] His stance is echoed in Kaczor's contribution to an incel thread, 'Women Destroying Cultures and Countries'. The poster claims that 'women, especially young women, also want to destroy their countries and societies by voting for left wing degeneracy', including support for LGBTIQ rights and abortion.[60] A comment from the Purple Pill forum on Reddit also shares in this belief that women's participation in democracy is harming society: 'the decline is not caused by female promiscuity but by female freedom and the right to work and choose'. Another proposes, 'what we have today is a decline which can be directly traced to the sexual revolution/feminist movement', and yet another asserts that 'the decline is because of the very high levels of female promiscuity' (that is, women's sexual emancipation).

The belief that women's liberation – from sexual and reproductive freedoms to the right to vote and occupy public space – is causing a decline in society is drawn from the anti-Marxist, fascist fear of freedom. Marx argued that humans have the power and the freedom to change society – and crucially, he argued that people could also be changed by society. This idea is intolerable to fascism because it undermines the belief that there is a fixed natural order. If a changed society has the power to change the people within it, populations can become still more progressive and more free. Women's freedom terrifies the far right because it means society can be changed, people can be changed in response to social progress, and white male supremacy is not a fixed, natural state. In other words, women's liberation takes a wrecking ball to the entire worldview of the far right – so women must be stopped.

Despite being rooted in a variety of different subcultures, there is clear crossover of extremist far-right groups on the subject of reproductive and sexual control. All the groups share an ideology rooted in the fascist thought architecture described at the start of this book. Even Thiel's intervention demonstrates a desire to return to a pre-1918 society where women had no democratic rights in the US or UK. It also tracks back to the definition of fascism as a fear of freedom. In this mindset, women's freedoms are so terrifying and dangerous, they are causing the destruction of Western society!

This is not about collusion: Dowson is not connected to Thiel, and neither have publicly identified as incels or Red Pillers. Rather, the far right shares an ideology of misogyny, and a shared ideology is relatively easy to push into the mainstream.

It's important to understand *how much* hatred against women exists in these spaces. Posters write about sending women to the slaughterhouse, keeping vaginas on leashes and shoving grenades up women's anuses. Women are described as 'rape fuel', as 'scum' who should 'rot in jail'. Men share videos of women being beaten, cheering on the violence, and they spread fantasies about child rape. When the Taliban recaptured Afghanistan in August 2021, the incels celebrated the 'Talichad' and approvingly shared images of women being flogged. One post on abortion reads, 'I care about abortion, women have to suffer and if they don't wanna suffer, we make them suffer.'

On Reddit's Purple Pill forum which, remember, is the *less* extreme space, a member has written: 'In theory I think all women should have access to abortion but to be honest I've learned to hate women, feminism and their sexual choices so much.' Another post says, 'I don't care if abortion becomes illegal and some women die during unsafe abortions.' There is no doubt that anti-abortion movements are rooted in misogyny.

While the far right urges white women to surrender as exploitable reproductive vessels, it decrees the opposite for black and brown women. Its belief in a race war means that its most extreme members instead call for a policy of forced abortion and sterilisation for black and minority ethnic women. One Telegram post reads, 'smol brain = pro choice; big brain = pro life; galaxy brain = what race is it?' This translates as 'stupid = pro-choice; clever = pro-life; really clever = ask the race of the foetus before deciding if abortion should be allowed'.

As feminist writer and founder of the Wages for Housework campaign Silvia Federici explains, 'The struggle in the feminist movement was always about the struggle *not* to have children, never about having the resources to *also have* children, which created a big division with Black women who were fighting against the question of denied maternity, from slavery on ... That's what they have had to fight against: sterilisation, not having money, always having to do housework, but in other people's homes.'[61]

Understanding the history of sterilisation of black and global majority women is important in revealing the genocidal obsessions of the far right; it also helps to expose the utilitarian attitude towards women's bodies – whether as white incubator or sterilisable labourer – in the fascist thought architecture.

A desire to destroy black and global majority women's reproductive capability is shared and amplified across far-right online spaces. I found posts on the 'The Great Replacement' Telegram channel, for example, which fantasised about reproductive control over white women and the forced sterilisation of black and global majority people. On the 'Opposing the Great Replacement' channel one post simply stated: 'abortion and birth control should be illegal for whites'.

This rhetoric is not confined to message boards – it's in mainstream politics too. Brazil's former leader Jair Bolsonaro may be anti-abortion, but he is also comfortable saying that the black *quilombola* communities 'are not fit to procreate'. Between 1909 and 1979, far-right ideas about race and sex meant that more than 20,000 men and women were forcibly sterilised in California alone.[62] Sterilisations were used in the USA as a means of controlling populations considered undesirable, including immigrants, people of colour, poor people, unmarried mothers, the disabled and the mentally ill, with federally funded sterilisation programmes taking place in thirty-two states throughout the twentieth century.[63] Angela Davis describes how in 'a National Fertility Study conducted in 1970 by Princeton University's Office of Population Control, twenty percent of all married Black women have been permanently sterilised. Approximately the same percentage of Chicana women had been rendered surgically infertile. Moreover, forty-three percent of women sterilised through federally subsidised programmes were Black.'[64]

California's sterilisation programme was an inspiration to Nazi eugenicists, with Hitler approvingly commenting that 'there is today one state in which at least weak beginnings toward a better conception [of citizenship] are noticeable. Of course, it is not our model German Republic, but the United States'.[65] In the 1970s, as feminist activists celebrated the end of illegal abortion in the USA with the success of *Roe vs Wade*, up to 50 per cent of Native American women were forcibly sterilised by the US government in an act of genocide.[66]

It would be tempting to think such policies are confined to the all-too-recent past. But in 2020, a whistleblower reported that women in immigration detention centres in Georgia, USA, were being coerced into having hysterectomies. Women held in prison-like conditions described how a gynaecologist completed the surgery with neither proper explanation nor adequate translation services. They described being yelled at by nurses when they resisted the procedure, and told human rights observers that the medical staff were 'experimenting with our bodies'. One woman submitted to a procedure for the removal of an ovarian cyst, but the doctor operated on the wrong ovary, leading to follow-up surgery which ended in a full, non-consensual hysterectomy.[67]

In East European countries such as Slovakia, the targets of forced sterilisation programmes have been women from the Roma community – a minority ethnic group that has been consistently persecuted across the region with racist and segregationist polices. A report published in 2003 collected 230 interviews from Roma women found that half had been forcibly or coercively sterilised. A woman called Agata told researchers how 'doctors came and brought me to the operating room [for a C-section] and there they gave me anaesthesia. When I was falling asleep, a nurse came and took my hand in hers and with it she signed something. I do not know what it was. I could not check because I cannot read, I only know how to sign my name. When I left the hospital, I was only told that I would not have any more children ... I was so healthy before, but now I have pain all the time. Lots of infections.'[68]

Agata's experience echoes that of indigenous women thousands of miles away in Peru, who were subjected to forced sterilisations throughout the 1990s. The programme led to the sterilisation of around 272,000 women and 21,000 men, most of them from rural indigenous communities. Women told activists and researchers how they would be in labour or having a routine gynaecological procedure, and were sterilised on the spot, without knowledge or consent. As with black women in the US and Roma women in Slovakia, Peru's indigenous women were specifically targeted in a toxic mix of racism and misogyny.

Testimonies collected by Bristol University's Quipu project told of the pain and suffering women endured. 'They took me,' says one woman. 'I went for a health check at the clinic. I was pregnant at the time so I went in for a check up. They told me "you are not pregnant so we will sterilise you." They put me in the ambulance by force and took me to the clinic in Izcuchaca by force.' Another woman described how 'we were forcibly sterilised. Because prior to that we did not know what sterilisation was. And that is how they did it to us, coming from Zurite, a campaign led by nurses from Zurite, because we had many children, like "guinea pigs."'[69]

Not all state-led sterilisation comes from right-wing or far-right governments, but they always come from a nationalist imperative and they are always bad for women. One of the most infamous sterilisation policies was generated by China's Communist Party. The imperative that families should only have one child within a patriarchal society where baby boys are valued more highly than girls led to femicide, with reports of mothers aborting female foetuses and newborn girls being left to die. The result is a skewed sex ratio, with 1.16 men for every woman in the country. During the 1990s, when the one-child policy was in full swing, twenty-six males per thousand live births died before the age of one, compared to thirty-three girls. The 2000s saw twenty-one boys per thousand live births dying and twenty-eight girls. In the 1980s, the number was equal, at thirty-six.

The past and present of forced sterilisation against communities deemed undesirable or alien by white supremacist societies offers a stark and devastating picture of the attack on reproductive rights. While white women's bodies are considered a resource to be exploited against the Great Replacement, black and global majority women's bodies are pegged for elimination. Forced sterilisation of black and global majority women deny women their reproductive choice in order to strengthen white supremacy and, at the most extreme, to build a pure ethno-state. A white male supremacist Global North is the goal, and women's wombs are the tool.

Alongside the genocidal threat of sterilisation, it is important to remember that abortion restrictions disproportionately impact black and global majority women. This is certainly the case in the US, where according to data from 1960s New York 'some eighty percent of the deaths caused by illegal abortions involved Black and Puerto Rican women'.[70] The Guttmacher Institute estimated in 2016 that black women had 28 per cent of US abortions, meaning any ban will disproportionately impact those women. This is, in part, because black women are more likely to be living in poverty than white women and therefore have less support to bring up children. Poverty removes women's reproductive choices just as does the denial of abortion rights. Without social security and support to raise happy, healthy children who can fulfil their potential, families can be denied the chance to have the children altogether, or socially punished for having children that the right dictates they 'can't afford'. The solution then is not to ban abortion but to promote social security and encourage reproductive choice.

Similarly in the UK, women from poorer backgrounds are three times more likely to have an abortion: those from the most deprived backgrounds accounted for 16.5 per cent of all abortions, and women from the wealthiest backgrounds only 6 per cent. As in the US, black and global majority women are more likely to live in poverty than white women. Almost two-thirds of women supported by the British Pregnancy Advisory Service cited financial factors as part of their decision to have a termination.[71]

This disparity demonstrates the need to talk about repro-ductive *justice* that recognises the right of women to have the children they want, and to end unwanted pregnancies. It demands that women have access to healthcare, housing, financial support and support at work. As Angela Davis wrote, the pro-abortion campaign 'often failed to provide a voice for women who wanted the *right* to legal abortions while deplor-ing the social conditions that prohibited them from having more children'.[72]

This history feeds into the black anti-abortion movement, which reflects the lived experiences of forced sterilisation, forced abortion and a legacy of medical experimentation. Anti-abortion activists capitalise on this horrific legacy, weaponising racism by claiming abortion is a form of black genocide in order to win support from (chiefly) black evangelical churches. Some have even gone so far as to co-opt the 'Black Lives Matter' slogan into anti-abortion materials and write that 'the most dangerous place for an African American woman is in the womb'. This appropriation of anti-racist movements to deny black and minority ethnic women access to reproductive health is not only cynical, it is dangerous.

The Southern Poverty Law Centre defines male supremacy as a belief system that 'reduces women to their reproductive and sexual function'; it is 'driven by a biological analysis of women as fundamentally inferior to men'. It is also 'driven by the belief that men are entitled to a superior place in society than women, which are biologically and intellectually inferior … and is driven by fear and anger at loss of white male status'.

Women's access to the public sphere was made possible (in part) by access to contraception and abortion, which decoupled a woman's value and purpose from her womb. This is why male supremacists, from the incels and men like Dowson to Trump and Bolsonaro, see women's advances into public space – advances enabled by having reproductive choice – as an attack. They are correct: women's liberation is indeed an attack on male authority, and feminism seeks to dismantle the gendered hierarchies that position men as superior and women as inferior, and which have caused so much harm and oppression to women for centuries.

As writer and lawyer Emily O'Reilly explains in her analysis of the historical success of anti-abortion laws, 'nothing threatened that [patriarchal] system more than when women are enabled to take control of every aspect of their lives, public and private.' There is nothing more critical to the exercise of that control than the ability to decide how to have children, if any, and when to have them.' She writes how in Ireland, the decision to put an explicit abortion ban in the nation's constitution came at a moment when 'patriarchal control was suddenly under threat and the fight back had begun'.[73]

This is exactly where we find ourselves now, with the success of feminist movements, the growing presence of women in public space, and increased access to abortion rights. It's what we saw with the rollback of abortion rights in 1860s USA,

1920s Italy and 1930s Germany. It is behind the urgent need from the far right to reassert male supremacy and female subordination.

What I learned from researching these extremist subcultures is this: the common strand connecting the far right's beliefs about women is that feminism is unnatural, harmful to the family and constitutes an attack on men. Because the far right envisions patriarchal authority as the basis of society, women's rights are considered harmful to society and an existential threat to the nation/race. Women's increasing success in the public sphere and the loosening of family structures, enabled by women's right to control their own fertility, are seen as an attack that can and must be defeated by reverting to the supposed natural order.

This is all rooted in a fear of freedom.

3

The Infiltration: The Networks That Bring Extremist Right Politics Into The Mainstream

In the previous two chapters, we established how fascist thought architecture relates to reproductive and sexual rights, and how its ideology is expressed through the twin conspiracy theories of the Great Replacement and satanic ritual abuse/QAnon. From there, we discovered how misogyny manifests in the incel and Red Pill subcultures, and how misogynistic far-right support propelled Trump to power in the US where he dutifully met the demands of his extremist supporters.

The Trump example shows that one way for fascistic beliefs about women to reach the mainstream is through the far-right capture of an existing political party. Another tactic is to create a conduit that filters extremist ideology through a respectable front: a middle man who can bring the fascist thought architecture into the corridors of power. Here, it can be transformed from conspiracy theories and violence into government policy.

Across Europe and the US, various organisations that hold extreme beliefs about women and abortion have created networks that act as this pipeline. They include (but are not limited to) Agenda Europe and its activist allies at CitizenGO, the Political Network for Values (generally considered Agenda Europe's successor on the world stage), Alliance Defending Freedom (ADF), the American Center for Law and Justice (ACLJ) and its European Arm (ECLJ), the Council for National Policy (CNP) and the World Congress of Families (WCF). They share strategic ideological goals as well as personnel and tactics. Those tactics include providing training to conservative activists; hosting networking events, meetings and conferences; launching petitions and lobbying campaigns in the European Union; legal interventions; and court cases – including in the US Supreme Court.

The pipeline from extremist fringe to mainstream works as follows: an organisation such as Agenda Europe or the Council for National Policy creates a network where anti-rights actors come together to devise a strategy rooted in far-right ideas about women's bodies, reproductive and sexual freedoms. That strategy is then enacted through campaigns or legal challenges by organisations such as CitizenGo and Alliance Defending Freedom. These campaigns go on to influence mainstream government policy. Crucially, while Agenda Europe and the CNP prefer to operate in the shadows, they use their affiliates to mainstream their ideology. Their members hold positions of power, including in international organisations such as the Parliamentary Assembly Council of Europe (PACE), the Trump administration, or as invited speakers at the United Nations – CitizenGO's Kenyan representative Ann Kioko has addressed the UN claiming that abortion and LGBTIQ rights are a form of cultural imperialism being imposed on East Africa, for example.[1]

'These groups are organising to get a political and legal system that is their ideal,' Neil Datta, founder of the European Parliamentary Forum for Sexual and Reproductive Rights, told me from Brussels. 'To do that, they have to destroy things to create their vision.'

In this chapter, I'll use the case studies of Agenda Europe, CitizenGO, the Council of National Policy and the Alliance Defending Freedom – as well as its European arm ADF International – to demonstrate how these organisations act as a conduit to transport extremist anti-abortion ideology from the fringes into the mainstream via a range of campaigning tactics, and by placing anti-abortion advocates into the heart of global decision-making. By doing so, they can bring extremist ideas about reproductive and sexual rights into the heart of national governments and international bodies where they become policy.

Agenda Europe is crucial to understanding how anti-gender ideology became mainstream across the region throughout the 2010s. First, because it took the fascistic concept of the 'natural order' and translated that ideology into a manifesto titled *Restoring the Natural Order*, which it used to inspire campaigning against reproductive and sexual rights across Europe. Second, because it brings together a myriad of leading anti-gender groups with political leaders and activists, taking the extreme to the mainstream. In the following pages, we will explore this manifesto in order to understand the planned attack on reproductive rights, as well as identify the power-players in this network and how they have taken Agenda Europe's blueprint into the world.

Picture the scene: Dublin in 2015, the year equal marriage is legalised by referendum and three years after Savita Halappanavar died after being refused a life-saving abortion when her seventeen-week-old foetus died inside her. As she begged for help, the nurse told her, 'This is a Catholic country.' Halappanavar died of heart failure triggered by sepsis, eight days after she arrived in hospital.

The referendum result shook the anti-gender movement in Europe, which thought it could always rely on Catholic Ireland to vote its way. No wonder, then, that Agenda Europe is hosting its 2015 summit in Ireland's capital city, at All Hallows College. The grey-brick Victorian establishment has educated generations of priests, leaders and professionals since 1842 in the values of justice, service and leadership, and their graduates go on to serve communities in all corners of the world. The delegates arrive through the neoclassical façade, taking Mass in the picturesque church. Conversations focus on how to campaign against abortion in cases of disability and foetal defect;

how to strategise for better 'sexual pedagogy'; and, crucially, what could be learned from the movement's defeat in the equal marriage referendum.

The first day is dedicated to optional discussions, sightseeing and lunch. Perhaps the delegates visited Trinity Library to see the *Book of Kells*, or wandered down O'Connell Street to examine the General Post Office's bulletholes from guns that blasted across the barricades during the Easter Rising for Irish Independence. Then, at 5 p.m., the Anglican theologian Phillip Blond took to the platform to open the summit officially. A strong influence on then Prime Minister David Cameron, he is there to talk about becoming a 'creative minority'. Afterwards, it's time for dinner and networking.

Agenda Europe brings together wealthy donors, politicians, religious leaders and activists at annual summits like the one in Dublin, where guests strategise and network to promote an anti-rights agenda. It courts Vatican surrogates: Datta explains how 'several prominent Catholic clergy representatives [have] graced Agenda Europe Summits with their presence. The first ever Agenda Europe summit was arranged by Austrian Gudrun Kugler and the American Terrence McKeegan, a pair of Catholic lawyers working with the Holy See. McKeegan had worked as a legal adviser for the Permanent Observer Mission of the Holy See to the United Nations.[2]

The group's membership includes politicians from across Europe, helping to reveal its mainstreaming strategy: Irish Senator Rónán Mullen, who heads up the anti-abortion political party Human Dignity Alliance; Italy's Luca Volontè, who ran a transnational anti-abortion group and was a member of the Parliamentary Assembly of the Council of Europe (PACE); the founder of the Croatian political party HRAST, Zejlka Markic; political adviser to the European Conservatives and Reformist Party (ECR) Paul Moynan; and Leo van Doesburg, director of European affairs for the European Christian Political Movement (ECPM). Ján Figel, former EU commissioner and the EU special envoy for freedom of religion or belief, spoke at its 2016 summit.

On the US side, Agenda Europe is connected via McKeegan to the US religious freedom giant Alliance Defending Freedom and the European Centre for Law and Justice (ECLJ), which employs Trump's former attorney Jay Sekulow. The ECLJ's Grégor Puppinck spoke in Dublin, as did individuals linked to the European arm of Alliance Defending Freedom (ADF International): Sophia Kuby, Robert Clarke, Roger Kiska and Paul Coleman. Brian Brown, founder of the anti-LGBTIQ, anti-abortion network World Congress of Families (WCF), frequented Agenda Europe summits; so did WCF's Russian representative Alexey Komov. This web of connections means that, far from being on the fringes, Agenda Europe can take its anti-abortion, anti-LGBTIQ aims into mainstream European, Russian and American politics.

Agenda Europe's plan for society is outlined in a manifesto titled *Restoring the Natural Order: An Agenda For Europe* – described by researcher Ellen Rivera as 'part theological tract, part anti-communist pamphlet, part far-right conspiracy theory, and part totalitarian roadmap'.[3] The document runs to over 140 pages and attacks feminism, Marxism, 'homosexualism' and 'gender theory' – which it claims 'go *against nature*' (my emphasis) – while designing a clear strategic plan to overturn laws on abortion, divorce, LGBTIQ relationships and families, IVF, and other areas relating to reproductive and sexual rights.

The manifesto's attack lines on abortion and contraception connect intimately with long-held ambitions of the church for women's role in society. Emily O'Reilly writes how 'the state's ban on contraception was central to the realisation in Ireland of the Catholic church's grand plan for the role of women in society.'[4] That role should be confined, for women at least, to the domestic sphere. They should be actively prevented from playing a role in the public affairs of the nation – something which of course links back to the far-right belief that women taking up space in the public sphere is causing a decline in western society.

Although Agenda Europe posed as the respectable face of the assault on progressive values, traditional far-right tropes sneak into its narrative. One of its 'possible strategies' to persuade people to back its anti-abortion aims is to 'use demographic decline as an argument'.[5] Such a plan taps right into the far-right anxiety about the Great Replacement and the fear that women's reproductive rights are enabling a white genocide. That Agenda Europe understands this as a possible tactic shows its importance in channelling ideas from the extreme to the mainstream.

Similarly, Agenda Europe signals its extremist beliefs through making references to the fascistic conception of nature – after all, its manifesto is cleverly titled *Restoring the Natural Order*. That order falls into three categories: the protection of life (an end to abortion); the protection of the family (defined as patriarchal authority within the home); and religious freedom. Its idea of a natural order is one where men complement women (that men should be masculine and the authority in the home, and women should 'complement' them through femininity and subordination – by its very nature, 'complementarianism' is heteronormative and excludes LGBTIQ families). It claims that the heterosexual, married family model 'is the only option that is morally acceptable'.[6]

The focus on patriarchal authority reflects the desire to rebuild the fascist mythic past emphasised by far-right extremists. Agenda Europe's purpose is therefore to give a respectable face to extremist ideologies based on the fascist thought architecture, before its members can promote them within international bodies such as the United Nations and European Parliament where its far-right attitudes can be realised as policy.

As such, Agenda Europe positions itself as a legitimate force for change, gaining respect and therefore influencing – even initiating – proposed laws and policy changes that have devastating consequences for reproductive and sexual rights. It explains that it will achieve this by bringing 'the right people into the right positions'. This means drawing up a 'list of key positions that will become vacant' in the UN, including treaty-monitoring bodies and special rapporteurs, the US Supreme Court, the European Court of Justice and European Court of Human Rights, the EU, the EU Commission for Justice and Fundamental Rights and within the high representative for human rights in the EEAS. Having identified vacancies, Agenda Europe could then 'proactively identify and promote suitable candidates' to these key positions, embedding its allies and agenda in high-level decision-making roles across the region.[7] It also sought to use academic institutions and likeminded journalists to spread its agenda by working with those who are 'capable of defending natural justice in the mass media'.[8]

Importantly, there is a two-way stream emanating from Agenda Europe. Through one channel, its strategies influence extremist groups, providing tactics for aggressive anti-abortion campaigning; and through the other, it carries the beliefs of extremist groups into mainstream media and the halls of government.

There is clear evidence that extremist anti-abortion groups are connected to these international networks. For example: a guest list for the 2013 London summit revealed that 40 Days for Life's international campaigns director, Robert Colquhoun, was present – and who is Colquhoun? A board member of CBR UK. Top of the summit's agenda was a discussion on pro-life strategies that could then flow out of the summit's dining halls to reach activists at the grass roots.

Another connection comes via a 2015 initiative known as Mum Dad & Kids, which has emerged from within Agenda Europe and campaigned against equal marriage and wider sexual rights. One of its founding members was Roger Kiska, who at that time worked at ADF International. Kiska later became legal counsel to Christian Concern, which shares administration and works closely with CBR UK. Through Kiska and Colquhoun, we have a direct link between Agenda Europe and the anti-abortion extremists on England's streets.

The Agenda Europe manifesto opens with the assertion that 'there can be no reasonable doubt that life begins at conception' and that all laws allowing abortion, even in cases of rape and incest or a threat to the mother's life, 'stand in clear contradiction to the natural law of morality'.[9] It then sets out two long-term targets to achieve its vision for a restoration of the natural order: a legal ban on abortion in all jurisdictions and an explicit legal ban on abortion in international law.

To get there, Agenda Europe plans for incremental changes that seek to erode women's reproductive rights. The measures it advocated include:

1. tightening restrictions on abortion by implementing bans on terminations in cases of foetal defect;
2. decreasing the upper time limit on abortions;
3. minors having to request parental consent before accessing abortion;
4. mandatory counselling and cooling-off periods;
5. the father's consent – this is particularly dangerous for women in violent relationships whose abuser may use forced pregnancy as a form of coercive control.

All five measures create a chilling impact that chips away at access to safe and legal abortion. Bans to prevent abortions for foetal anomaly create room to debate further restrictions, even in cases of threat to mother's life. Once the upper time limit is reduced from twelve weeks to ten, it becomes easier to say, 'Why not eight? Or six?' Once it's written into law that the father must give consent, women's bodies become the legal property of an external patriarchal authority: women's bodies are not their own, they can be controlled by an outside force. This is of course the ultimate aim of *all* anti-abortion movements: to put women's bodies at the service of white male supremacy.

Other mid-term goals outlined in *Restoring the Natural Order* include making it harder for abortion clinics to operate by introducing draconian hygiene regulations – something we will explore more as a tactic of the US anti-abortion lobby. Funding is also in the spotlight: Agenda Europe wanted to see an end to funding for abortions from the UN, the EU or national governments, and to exclude abortion from public health insurances. To put this into a UK context, Agenda Europe would ban abortions from being available on the NHS, meaning women and girls with an unwanted pregnancy would have to pay for reproductive healthcare (in the UK, abortion care is free to most women and girls via the NHS – although women with specific immigration statuses are expected to pay). Defunding would ultimately exclude the poorest women from being able to ask for a termination and create a tiered system where only the wealthiest women in society have full access to human rights.

A policy copying the US global gag rule – banning international aid funds to support abortion providers around the world – is also suggested. Again, to it put this in a UK context, in 2021 the Conservative government cut international aid on reproductive and sexual health by £130 million, unintentionally supporting the Agenda Europe plan.

Alongside legal and economic policy changes, Agenda Europe's 'possible strategies' are designed to influence public opinion against abortion, including by the publication of abortion statistics to help people 'understand the size of the problem'. So-called 'pro abortion propaganda' would be banned, while 'pro life counselling and poster campaigns' would be permitted.[10]

Ways to achieve these goals include 'making abortion visible' through films, posters and events, as well as 'erecting monuments to the unborn' and creating 'special places of remembrance for unborn children'. This reflects some US campaigning, such as Mike Pence's demand that women hold funerals for aborted and miscarried foetuses. Again, all of these techniques either diminish access or they erode public trust in a woman's right over her body. One of the defining posters during Ireland's abortion law referendum in 2018 was 'Trust women' – Agenda Europe says, 'Don't.'

If this simply existed in a frightening manifesto discussed in secretive networking events in European dining clubs, we could rest easy. But think back to my experience in Romania, where I saw country after country deploy the same campaign tactics to frustrate progress on women's and LGBTIQ people's rights. Watching multiple European movements and political parties try to undermine these rights showed me that the problem with Agenda Europe is precisely its mainstream success. Across the region, the anti-abortion goals laid out in *Restoring the Natural Order* have leapt off the page and into voting booths and legislation – often via organisations and individuals linked to Agenda Europe's network. This an instance of extremist anti-abortion ideology travelling along the pipeline from the fringes, via Agenda Europe's members, into government policy.

In Slovakia, where leading anti-abortion politician Anna Záborská is linked to Agenda Europe via the World Congress of Families, public funding for abortions for women over the age of forty has been scrapped. In Poland, draconian anti-abortion laws have been extended to include a ban on terminations for foetal anomaly. The organisation Ordo Iuris has been central in the campaign for more abortion bans in Poland and – surprise, surprise – is linked to Agenda Europe, hosting its Warsaw summit. In Spain up until a law change in June 2022, minors had to gain parental consent before accessing abortion – a campaign spearheaded by CitizenGO, which, as you will soon see, is effectively the public face of Agenda Europe.

The pattern is repeated across the region. In Germany, 'pro-abortion propaganda' was, until June 2022, banned – while there were no restrictions on disinformation campaigns from anti-abortion groups. Hungary leads the way in pro-life poster campaigns, where the government uses family rights rhetoric to create suspicion around abortion. Numerous countries demand mandatory counselling for women wanting an abortion, including Albania, Armenia, Belgium, Bosnia, Slovakia and Iceland. Portugal and Luxembourg have a cooling-off period, while Hungary demands both counselling and a cooling-off period. The World Health Organization has condemned the requirement for a cooling-off period, saying such measures 'demean women as competent decision-makers'.[11]

In the UK, a defeated bill tried to ban abortion providers from offering counselling to women with an unwanted pregnancy. Its author, former secretary of state for digital media, culture and sport Nadine Dorries, had worked with the organisation Christian Concern and attended World Congress of Families events. Christian Concern's legal adviser has connections to Agenda Europe, and another anti-abortion MP, Fiona Bruce, has repeatedly tabled bills designed to increase restrictions, including on sex-selective abortion and abortion in cases of foetal anomaly. All over Europe, organisations and individuals linked to this shadowy network are advocating to restrict abortion, and in many cases they are succeeding.

Its overarching plan for how to rid the world of abortion explained, *Restoring the Natural Order* gets specific about its campaign – what Neil Datta describes as a 'living action plan which Agenda Europe members have actively pursued at the EU and PACE and in various national settings'.[12]

Strategy one advises co-opting the language of *rights* when promoting far-right aims. Agenda Europe recommends that its members 'use the weapons of our opponents and turn them against them'. The pamphlet continues, we should not be afraid to draw upon the ideas and concepts that currently prevail in public debates and make them work for our purposes. For example, concepts like 'freedom of opinion' can be used or 'freedom of assembly' can be used not only by the organisers of 'Gay Pride' events, but also by their opponents ... Contemporary mainstream culture paradoxically gives rewards to groups who manage to posture in the role of 'victims of discrimination'. Even if we can find this posturing questionable, there is no doubt that we can use it very successfully as a strategy.[13]

Put into practice on the abortion debate, the document argues that Agenda Europe should lay claim to equality, and its activists should position themselves as victims of discrimination when talking about men and women, as well as promoting discussion about disabled people's rights as 'an argument against abortion'. It recommends members 'use freedom of conscience as an argument' and talk about the 'right to information' as an 'obligation for States to ensure that everybody is *correctly* informed what an abortion is. The right to information can be used for our purposes'.

Agenda Europe's advice encourages anti-abortion advocates to portray men as victims of inequality when it comes to abortion rights, as fathers do not have a legal right to prevent a woman from accessing a termination. This was epitomised by a 2022 headline in the *Daily Mail*: 'Anguish of the Men Whose Babies Were Aborted Against their Will'.[14] Using the 'right to information' argument also allows anti-abortion activists to display graphic anti-abortion imagery and films, with Andy Stephenson of CBR UK defending his tactics for showing the 'truth' of abortion.

This strategy is most commonly seen in connection with the term *family rights*, which, while sounding cuddly enough, is often code for attacking protections against gender-based violence in the home, or demanding that fathers have the right to prevent women from accessing abortion. *Restoring the Natural Order* even goes so far as to provide a glossary of terms, claiming, 'to a large extent, such cultural wars are about who can impose his use of terminology'.[15] Its glossary outlines what 'our opponents mean' when they use certain words, translated into 'what it really means' for Agenda Europe. Marriage, for example, is not 'a union of two persons [providing] them with a formal legal recognition and with social and fiscal benefits', but 'the life-long union between a man and a woman which has the purpose of founding a family'. 'Rainbow families' should instead be called 'broken-up families'; 'equal treatment for homosexuals' is defined as 'privileges for homosexuals' and 'reproductive rights' means 'free abortion'. It defines 'homosexual love' as 'sodomy', and 'freedom of choice' as 'freedom to kill.'

The anti-abortion movement in the USA has long understood the need for co-opting the left's language when trying to persuade people of its cause. The authors of the 1990s publication *Abortion: Questions and Answers* urges readers to borrow the 'feminist credo' around a woman's 'right to her own body' and apply it to the foetus.[16] Joseph Scheidler's *Closed: 99 Ways to Stop Abortion* advises its readers they should 'rarely use the word "foetus". Use "baby" or "unborn child"'. He continues, 'you don't have to surrender to [the opposition's] vocabulary', as 'they will start using your terms if you use them'.[17]

A key example of how language is used to infiltrate the mainstream with anti-abortion messaging is the US debate around the medically inaccurate term *partial birth abortion*, referring to a late-term, lifesaving procedure that ends an unviable pregnancy. The introduction of the phrase into political discourse and eventually the law is a deliberate tactic of the far and religious right to undermine trust in reproductive healthcare. In 2017, Robert Arnakis, senior director of domestic and international programmes at the radical-right Leadership Institute, told his friends at the anti-abortion, anti-LGBTIQ Family Research Council that the institute had started using the term in 1995 to spread unease about the procedure. The Leadership Institute was set up to train conservative activists; its alumni include former vice president and anti-abortion ideologue Mike Pence.

'We were discussing the abortion bill, and what we had was "late-term abortions"', Arnakis explained, referring to an attempt to ban abortions taking place late in pregnancy (the first attempt was vetoed by President Clinton in the mid-1990s).

> It went from 'late-term abortions' to a 'partial birth abortion ban'. We started talking about 'partial birth abortions' ... we kept hammering on this idea of 'partial birth, partial birth' ... And how we were winning that argument ended up being because the terminology we were using, the media started using. And eventually our opposition started using the terminology. And I would ask you today, when you heard the word 'partial birth', what image do you think of? You see, I think of a child, I think of a young child. And that's a powerful, powerful image. When we can use images to tell stories, when we can use images to convey emotions, we begin winning the debate in public policy.[18]

The tactic represents the deliberate introduction of a term designed to distort people's perceptions about abortions taking place late in pregnancy – what they are and why they happen. Rather than seeing this procedure as a lifesaving last resort or an act of care towards parents who know their baby will die at birth, late-term interventions in cases of fatal foetal abnormality or threat to the mother's life were portrayed as an act of cruelty. This offers a chilling example of how the far and religious right have controlled the debate on access to abortion in the USA: the phrase didn't exist before the mid-1990s when they invented it – now it's written into US law, thanks to the 2003 Partial-Birth Abortion Ban Act. This happened in the US. But Agenda Europe, for example, has relationships with

US organisations such as the World Congress of Families and the Alliance Defending Freedom. These relationships allow for successful strategies to be shared and adopted globally.

A second strategy involves portraying human rights advocates as all-powerful lobbies that use coercive tactics to get their way on issues such as reproductive freedoms and LGBTIQ equality. In this, Agenda Europe sets itself up as the David to a progressive Goliath – the little man with puny weapons against a behemoth of pro-abortion ideologues intent on crushing dissent. It positions what are often small and underfunded NGOs or individuals campaigning for reproductive freedoms as mass industrial complexes set on silencing an oppressed majority who lack that same power and influence to advocate for their rights. The *abortion industry* or even the phrase *big abortion* have entered common parlance among these groups. This framing deliberately ignores the fact that most anti-rights movement organisations are in receipt of vast amounts of cash from US funders and Russian oligarchs – let alone that Agenda Europe is connected to the Catholic Church, one of the most powerful and wealthy institutions in the world. It also ignores how those promoting reproductive and sexual rights aren't interested in removing rights from conservatives or Christians – our interest is in expanding human rights and freedoms to those who *are* oppressed.

Another way in which Agenda Europe brings far-right ideology into the mainstream is via its anti-Marxism and its anti-feminism. It calls feminism 'Marxism in a new clothing', and claims that it 'aims at masculinity for everyone': 'despite its name [feminism] … deprecates and holds in contempt all of that is considered typically feminine, especially the role model of a married wife and mother caring for her husband and children'. Agenda Europe's manifesto warns, 'according to the feminist agenda, wives should be economically independent of their husbands – an idea that in a certain sense contradicts the fundamental idea of a marriage'; and 'feminism is a highly destructive ideology that will undermine and destroy any society that commits the error of embracing it'.[19]

In *Restoring the Natural Order*, special hatred is reserved for women working in public policy – women who, the authors decide, are likely to be lesbians and unlikely to have children. Criticising the European Women's Lobby, a group within Europe dedicated to working on women's issues, Agenda Europe writes that it is 'independent from the millions on [*sic*] women with *real* lives – in particular those who actually have families and raise children'. The implication is clear: women with children and families are real and natural, because the domestic sphere is their natural place; women who occupy public space are therefore not real, or unnatural. The manifesto goes on to say:

> The fundamental problem is that women with a family and a job in the real economy usually are too busy to engage in politics. As a matter of consequence they are under-represented in politics, whereas childless and/or lesbian women are over-represented. The result is that policy on 'women's rights' often is openly hostile to marriage and the family, as these are not choice that those female politicians have made for themselves.[20]

Once again, a clear link emerges between the far-right extremists who rail against women in public spaces and the respectable face of the movement: these sentences reflect the far-right view that women's presence in decision-making roles, or even women's access to democracy, has corrupted the West and caused society to degenerate. The argument that feminism seeks to destroy women's natural roles corresponds to far-right ideas about men and women. Only by reversing those trends – rolling back our reproductive freedoms, and creating a false enemy of radical feminists and childless or lesbian women – can male supremacy and women's subordinate status be maintained and the so-called natural order restored.

As well as seeking to end abortion rights, Agenda Europe

had long-term goals for 'marriage and the family'. Its primary aim here – to 'prevent states from introducing same-sex partnerships' – has also been its most successful. It suggests forcing states to adopt a 'clear definition of marriage as between a man and a woman in an international agreement, explicitly excluding same-sex marriages', and it recommends the 'repeal of all existing laws on same-sex partnerships' and 'constitutional amendments to define marriage as between a man and a woman in all constitutions'. It also has a long-term goal of repealing laws allowing divorce and the 'adoption of anti-sodomy laws'.[21]

The 'possible strategies' section of its manifesto explains how Agenda Europe's members can prevent the adoption of equal marriage by ensuring that 'when marriage is already correctly defined at the level of ordinary law, such protection should be re-enforced through constitutional amendments'. Agenda Europe members have succeeded in lobbying against LGBTIQ equality in countries across Europe. In Croatia, for example, Agenda Europe affiliate U Ime Obitelji (In the Name of the Family) campaigned for a referendum that led to the nation's constitution being amended to state that marriage is a union between a man and a woman, thereby delaying progress on equal marriage. Similarly in Slovenia, Agenda Europe affiliate Children Are at Stake helped to prevent the adoption of equal marriage laws – a trend finally reversed in July 2022 when equal marriage was legalised.

Even unsuccessful attempts to bring extremist anti-LGBTIQ ideas into mainstream policy have frequently been spearheaded by Agenda Europe operatives. Slovakia's Alliance for the Family called for a referendum on three questions about marriage rights, gay adoption and sex education. The vote was declared invalid due to low turnout, but gay couples in Slovakia still do not have legal recognition. You'll remember that it was reporting on the tactics of Coalition for the Family (another Agenda Europe affiliate) in Romania that woke me up to the far-right threat across the region. The coalition led a referendum to write marriage as between a man and a woman into the constitution, but again the vote had such a low turnout that the result was void. On one measure, however, Agenda Europe's approach in Romania did succeed: the architects of the referendum were elected as far-right Alliance for Romanians' Unity (AUR) MPs in the 2020 election. The extreme is now the mainstream.

In recent years, Agenda Europe has shifted its strategy away from focusing on international bodies, with affiliates instead targeting national governments. Since 2018, Datta told me, 'we have seen Agenda Europe retreat from European space such as the EU and Council of Europe, but mainly from the EU. Instead, they've entrenched themselves at national level in a certain number of countries. So during the same time that we see a retreat from them from Brussels, we see an increased presence of the Alliance Defending Freedom in the UK, or Ordo Iuris in Poland, where they've exploded to being a very dominant actor. And from there, they've expanded to other countries. We see them trying to entrench themselves in a few other countries. They tried in Croatia, now in Slovakia, in Spain.'

In its place, we have seen the rise of the Political Network for Values – an organisation that features many of the same members, tactics and strategies as Agenda Europe, including annual gatherings for anti-abortion actors. The network brings together activists with politicians and funders – even disgraced actor Mel Gibson turned up to speak at its Budapest meeting in May 2022. On the Political Network for Values board are two influential actors that were close to Agenda Europe: Brian Brown from the World Congress of Families; and Ignacio Arsuaga, the founder of CitizenGO.

CitizenGO adopted the strategies and ideologies of Agenda Europe's manifesto and put them into practice, in order to normalise and popularise anti-abortion feeling. It is the public, colourful and controversial face of the anti-gender movement in Europe, and increasingly in the Global South – pulling stunts including driving a 'feminazi' bus around Madrid, and an 'anti gender ideology' bus in South America. It's well connected and global – and it transforms anti-gender ideology into campaigns which then influence mainstream governments.

Self-described as 'community of active citizens working together to defend and promote life, family and liberty', CitizenGO was founded in Spain by arch-conservative activist Ignacio Arsuaga. He had previously set-up the Spanish anti-gender organisation Hazte Oir. It has links to far-right parties in Germany, Italy and Hungary; oligarchs in Russia; family rights advocates in the US; the Kenyan government; and shady networks in Mexico. It is famous for its online petitions which promote a conservative Christian agenda and cover a bafflingly wide range of subjects, from protesting against Disney characters and Netflix programmes, to demanding that the UK government reverse a policy offering telemedicine for early-term abortions during the coronavirus pandemic.

CitizenGO claims 15 million active members – although how it defines 'active' isn't clear – across three continents, and it uses its network to influence political outcomes on sexual and reproductive rights in fifty countries.[22] It is extremely well connected to the global anti-rights scene, not least through its board member Brian Brown, president of the World Congress of Families (WCF) who also founded the National Organization for Marriage. The WCF, designated as a 'hate group' by Southern Poverty Law Center, is a conference where anti-abortion, anti-LGBTIQ actors come together to discuss strategies and tactics to achieve their reactionary aims. Although playing host to anti-abortion extremists, WCF also welcomes mainstream politicians to its stage, including Hungarian Prime Minister Orbán and far-right Italian politician Matteo Salvini.

The World Congress of Families was further linked to CitizenGO's board by its Russian representative, Alexey Komov of the St Basil the Great Foundation. Handsome, with designer stubble and grey eyes under his trendy glasses, Komov is connected to almost all the leading anti-gender movements through his relationships with CitizenGO, the World Congress of Families and the Russian oligarch Konstantin Malofeyev. He shot to prominence after spreading disinformation in Ukraine, including that claimed legalising equal marriage was a precondition to joining the European Union (it's not). Komov was removed from the list of CitizenGO's board members following Russia's invasion of Ukraine. Other board members include Luca Volontè, Walter Hintz, Blanca Escobar, Gualberto García, Alejandro Bermúdez and John-Henry Westen.

It's through CitizenGO that Agenda Europe can put its aims into action: it transports extremist ideas about women's bodies into the mainstream, by putting Agenda Europe's strategic platform into campaigning practice. At the start of the pipeline is the fascist thought architecture as it relates reproductive rights. This is voiced on the streets and online by extremist groups before being adopted into a strategic framework by Agenda Europe to rollback progress on abortion. CitizenGO turns that strategy into action through public-facing petitions, lobbying actions and campaigns directed at the mainstream. That lobbying reaches international and national decision-making bodies such as the European Parliament, as well as national governments and political parties, where it feeds into policy and law.

This is demonstrated by one of CitizenGO's formative successes: its campaign to prevent the adoption of the Estrela Report, a European Union initiative to ensure member states provide comprehensive sex education in schools and access to safe abortion. The report aimed to put sexual and reproductive rights on a par with wider human rights. Portuguese Social Democrat politician Edite Estrela summarised her goal as giving everybody the right to make 'their own informed and responsible choices on their sexual and reproductive life'. The report was non-binding, meaning no EU member state would be coerced into implementing its recommendations, but that did not stop CitizenGO doing everything in its power to destroy it. The action set the tone for future campaigns designed to prevent the European Union guaranteeing women's and minority groups' human rights. CitizenGO did what it does best: it launched a petition, which claimed that 'the Estrela-resolution contributes to make abortion and population control the political priority of the international development' and that the report 'promotes the pro-abortion-lobby getting more money from EU tax payers'.

This description is a clear example of Agenda Europe's strategy in action. First comes the claim that access to safe, legal abortion is some kind of nefarious plan for population control. As you will recognise from the previous chapters, this plays direct into the far-right conspiracy theory of the Great Replacement. The idea that the EU is advocating for abortion in order to keep white birth rates down, while allowing migration from the Global South to maintain population numbers, is a key component of the white genocide panic. Immediately, we can see how CitizenGO is mainstreaming a far-right trope to rally support for anti-abortion measures.

Second comes the mention of the 'abortion lobby' – Agenda Europe's clear tactic of positioning sexual and reproductive rights as a well-funded, all-powerful campaign overriding the concerns and beliefs of a victimised and silenced Christian majority. Not only does this ignore the reality of the pro-abortion movement's status, it also obscures the wealth and influence of anti-rights organisations.

Linked to this concept of an abortion lobby is the whipped-up paranoia that EU taxpayers are being forced to fund abortions. This technique is allied to Agenda Europe's arguments about conscientious objection and religious freedom – as well as its strategy of using the opposition's weapons against them. The debate becomes an individual rights issue: the right to oppose abortion is being undermined – and *my taxes* are being used to pay for something *I disagree with*.

The petition text goes on to address sex education, claiming 'the Estrela report calls for minors to act as sex education propagandists in the EU and in candidate countries'. This represents far-right fears around the corruption of children, and, perhaps even more importantly, an anxiety that the EU wants to estrange children from their parents – the text goes on to say the Estrela Report will mean fathers and mothers are 'disqualified' and 'are no longer recognized as first responsible of their own children'. CitizenGO's framing deliberately positions sex education as an attack on the family and, crucially, on patriarchal authority within the family. In the far-right mind, the family must be an autonomous entity: sex education is therefore treated as an encroachment on patriarchal authority in the home, while the threat of turning children into propagandists suggests that the curriculum seeks to position child and parent at odds with one another.

Finally, the petition uses the Agenda Europe tactic of co-opting rights language. It's presented as 'a perfect platform for the European Parliament to show its respect for the human right of all women, mothers and the unborn, and to show that the EU is indeed respecting the international human right.' This designates the pro-abortion, pro-LGBTIQ organisations as in conflict with human rights, and mirrors the method pioneered by the anti-abortion Wilkses in the 1990s to adopt the language of the feminist movement and apply it to the foetus.

The strategy is a masterpiece of manipulation, co-option and misinformation – playing on far-right fears about replacement and usurped patriarchal authority while also providing its supporters with a victim narrative that makes them feel like a brave David facing a women's rights Goliath. The petition's language persuaded more than a million Europeans to sign it. Delivered alongside a barrage of mail to politicians within the European Parliament, it led to the watering-down of the Estrela Report, which became a much more conservative document. Needless to say, comprehensive sex education and guaranteed safe abortion access is not the universal reality in the European Union at time of writing.

The backlash against the Estrela Report illustrates how successful Agenda Europe and CitizenGO have been in injecting extremist ideas about reproductive and sexual rights into mainstream European politics. Opposition to abortion and contraception moved from the extremist fringes, and was disguised, through petitions and lobbying, as respectable objection based on parental and taxpayers' rights: the result was a far-right message reaching the centre of European democracy, where it was heard and, most importantly, *respected*.

In 2021, a second report was authored focusing on reproductive and sexual rights in the European Union – the Matić report. The European Parliament adopted the non-binding report, despite opposition from CitizenGO and far-right and populist-right politicians. The success of this campaign shows the potential for the pro-abortion, women's rights movement to secure wins even during a period of backlash.

Following its success in opposing the Estrela Report, CitizenGO supported the One of Us citizens' initiative. The initiative's members included like-minded organisations from almost every European country including the UK's Right to Life, and sought to 'greatly advance the protection of human life from conception in Europe' by ending 'the financing of activities which presuppose the destruction of human embryos, in particular in the areas of research, development aid and public health'. The campaign gained 1.7 million signatures and, while it failed because the EU's budgets had already been decided that year, it provided another opportunity to test tactics and the campaigning model across the international stage. The One of Us campaign shows that legislative success is not always the point – it was a galvanising strategy as much as anything else, bringing together anti-rights groups and building a narrative that a grassroots silenced majority was being victimised, ignored and undermined by European Union political elites.

This is probably the point on which I am in agreement with Agenda Europe. It cites the One of Us initiative as a successful example of how to turn anti-abortion, anti-LGBTIQ ideas into a campaign that can influence mainstream policy, and *Restoring the Natural Order* praises it as a 'possible strategy' to achieve the long-term goal of banning abortion. The text advises, 'follow-up on ONE OF US: reiterate the demands of the successful petition at every occasion, until the EU takes action'; 'use ONE OF US as a model for similar petitions at a national level.' It explains that 'in the aftermath of the European Citizens' Initiative ONE OF US, there is now a momentum towards a European federational of pro-life organisations'.[23]

Where all of this becomes more concerning is the relationship between pressure groups, such as Agenda Europe and CitizenGO, and elected politicians in the region, including members of Spain's far-right Vox party. Such relationships show that these are no longer issues and agitators confined to the fringes – they are having direct influence on national government policy. This was evidenced in the campaign around the 'parental pin', which sought to which would give parents in the Murcia region of Spain, where Vox is popular, the right to withdraw their children from sex education lessons.

The parental pin campaign is a frightening demonstration of the pipeline in action. Stage one is a far-right objection to sex education, which is presented as usurping parental authority over children and promoting a homosexual and pro-abortion agenda. In stage two, Agenda Europe translated that objection into a strategic aim to end sex education. During stage three, CitizenGO turned this issue into a public-facing campaign – and at stage four, an elected political party proposed restrictions on sex education in a national parliament.

We will explore more in Chapter Six how mainstream governments have co-opted far-right ideas on reproductive rights to push a reactionary agenda. In the meantime, the example is an important signifier of how extremist religious-right networks are sharing tactics, strategies and campaigns to increase their influence in European parliaments and to attack reproductive and sexual rights. Indeed, CitizenGO's close relationship with Vox led to the former being accused of working as a super PAC (political action committee – controversial groups that can spend unlimited sums influencing elections in America and are renowned for their aggressive, negative campaigning) for the far-right party in 2019's Spanish and European Parliament elections; and a senior member of Vox even likened the organisation to a super PAC. The comparison is apt: CitizenGO supported Vox in its electoral ambitions and helped to make it the first far-right party to win seats in the Spanish parliament since Franco. The campaign included running attack adverts against Vox's political rivals: as CitizenGO director Ignacio Arsuaga explained, 'we are going to show bad things that have been said' by the leaders of other parties. Those 'bad things' were statements 'in favour of abortion or in favour of LGBT laws'. Arsuaga was reported to have said that CitizenGO was 'never going to ask people to vote for Vox ... But the campaign is going to help Vox indirectly'.[24]

CitizenGO is now exporting its model of anti-rights tactics, strategies and aims from the Global North to the Global South, where reproductive and healthcare infrastructures are often more fragile. Its influence in rolling back women's rights and risking women's lives has been particularly felt in Kenya, where I travelled in June 2022 to report on its activities for the *Byline Times*.

In Kenya, CitizenGO has spread misinformation that 'gender ideology' is being imposed on a vulnerable, victimised and 'traditional' population. Its local representative Ann Kioko presents reproductive and sexual rights as a form of cultural imperialism, while pro-abortion MPs are accused of being 'used' by 'abortionists in the West'. This argument of course ignores Spain's own history of violent imperialism, and how the tradition being defended is a western, Christian and colonialist imposition on an existing culture. It also ignores the fact that CitizenGO is a European initiative, exporting its hateful ideology to countries in the Global South.

While I was in Kenya, I spoke to Ayason Mukulia Kennedy, a member of the East Africa Legislative Assembly who had sponsored a bill promoting sexual and reproductive health in the East Africa Community's seven member states. His actions had led to CitizenGO launching a petition calling him an 'abortionist' that demanded his recall from the EALA. He told me how he received threatening emails from anti-abortion activists ('we are watching you'), and that whenever there was an uptick in news about the bill he would receive hundreds of tweets attacking him. During the public hearings on his bill, Kioko accused the policy of 'sneaking in' the 'murder of our children', while a petition against the bill falsely claimed it would introduce abortion on demand.

Other pro-abortion activists I spoke to reported similar attacks and explained how anti-abortion actors had effectively captured Kenya's Ministry of Health, leading to weakened public health policies. This had a particularly powerful impact on a reproductive health policy launched in July 2022, which many pro-abortion organisations had to disown for its lack of focus on the impact of unsafe abortion on maternal health. CitizenGO had been active in the public hearings on the policy and, activists told me, had influenced the ministry with its anti-abortion ideology. I was disturbed by the extent to which an apparently respectable organisation could bring extreme ideology into the heart of political decision-making. More than 2,500 women die of unsafe abortion in Kenya every year, and one brave young activist told me that she knew girls who drank disinfectant to terminate an unwanted pregnancy.

The model has also seen some success in Latin America, where CitizenGO campaigned on the streets in Colombia and worked with local anti-abortion actors in Argentina to frustrate moves to legalise terminations in the country. It didn't prevent legislative change – Argentina voted in favour of safe and legal abortion in December 2020 – but once again, its campaign enlarged its sphere of influence.

Then there are the connections with the US. A host of European anti-gender networks collaborate with anti-abortion colleagues across the Atlantic – sharing tactics, speaking at each others' events (including the WCF), and offering practical support to local European organisations on the ground. For example, US religious freedom giants Alliance Defending Freedom and the Liberty Counsel played a pivotal role in spreading anti-LGBTIQ propaganda in the run-up to Romania's equal marriage referendum, working in partnership with the Coalition for the Family.

But what does this look like in the US itself? Just as in Europe, groups in the US work as a pipeline to transport fascist thought architecture and far-right ideology into mainstream politics. The most obvious example is the Council for National Policy (CNP), an analogue to Agenda Europe. Both are shadowy networks that devise strategy, bring together activists, lobbyists, funders and politicians, and exercise influence while remaining largely unseen. Both provide support to organisations that act out an anti-gender, anti-rights strategy through campaigns and legal challenges. Finally, both place their members in positions of national and international importance, from where their hateful agenda can reach the mainstream.

The Council of National Policy is a highly secretive organisation set up in the 1980s for conservative activists and thinkers to strategise and network. Its members are interested in radical-right economic policy, disaster capitalism and deregulation. They are also engaged in anti-gender campaigning. This is a group that came to life during the anti-feminist backlash that followed *Roe vs Wade* and blossomed in the Reagan era – as conservative political actors campaigned for a traditional vision of America that was rooted in white male supremacy and free-market neoliberalism. This section will demonstrate how members of the CNP belong to a range of anti-gender, religious-right organisations which, more often than not, are linked in turn to mainstream Republican politicians and, of course, Donald Trump.

You may never have heard of the CNP, and little wonder – this is an organisation that likes to exist in the shadows. But in 2014, we got a glimpse into its world when the Southern Poverty Law Center published a list of its members.[25] The network was a who's who of anti-abortion, anti-LGBTIQ, radical-right ideologues and funders: Mathew Staver from Liberty Counsel; Tony Perkins and Ken Blackwell from the Family Research Council; Alan Sears from Alliance Defending Freedom; Heritage Foundation's Edwin John Feulner, Jr; and the anti-feminist activist Phyllis Schlafly (now deceased). Benjamin Bull, formerly of the Alliance Defending Freedom and later a board member of the Political Network for Values, was also on the list. James Dobson, founder of the anti-abortion, anti-LGBTIQ group Focus on the Family, is a former member of the CNP, while its vice president Timothy Goeglein was recorded as a member in the September 2020 directory, published online.

These groups and individuals inhabit stage three of the pipeline: the activists and campaigners who publish disinformation about abortion and LGBTIQ rights, lobby to roll back human rights protections and launch legal challenges to overturn abortion laws. They then share this strategy with their colleagues in the CNP who carry out stage four: the mainstream politicians and political actors bringing far-right ideology on abortion into Congress, the Senate and the White House.

To manage this stage in the process, the CNP counts among its members individuals linked to the Republican Party such as Paul S. Teller, chief of staff to former presidential candidate Ted Cruz. Others are acolytes of Trump, with former chief strategist Steve Bannon and former adviser Kellyanne Conway both listed as members. Jay Sekulow, Trump's attorney and chief counsel for the European Centre for Law and Justice (ECLJ), was both attorney for, and member of, the CNP. Richard DeVos, a former president of the CNP, is the husband of Trump's former education secretary Betsy DeVos. She and her brother Erik Prince were members, while their mother Elsa Prince Broekhuizen is a gold member of the CNP (its highest and most costly level of membership).

The CNP creates the network where anti-abortionists can translate far-right ideas about reproductive rights into actions, and then take those actions to political decision-makers; in other words, it is the US equivalent of Agenda Europe, with many of its members overlapping. That overlap is crucial to understanding the global reach of the far right's assault on reproductive rights, with US organisations exporting their successful tactics into Europe. This has certainly been the case with Alliance Defending Freedom and the American Centre for Law and Justice: both groups set up branches across the Atlantic, enabling them to share their anti-abortion and anti-LGBTIQ tactics and work in collaboration with local actors to overturn progressive laws in European courts.

Let's start with one of the largest religious-rights organisations with connections both to CNP and Agenda Europe – and the second biggest US religious-right spender in Europe – Alliance Defending Freedom (ADF). In the following pages, I will share with you how ADF in the US has used strategic litigation to push forward an anti-abortion agenda, taking cases to the Supreme Court in an effort to undermine women's rights. From there, we will look at how ADF International – its European arm – is hoping to replicate its US successes in the UK and the rest of Europe.

Alliance Defending Freedom was founded in Arizona in 1994 by thirty-five Christian leaders determined to 'defend religious freedom, free speech, marriage and family, parental rights, and the sanctity of life'. The founders believed it would 'take an alliance' to keep the 'doors open for the Gospel in the United

States' – an alliance of pastors, business leaders and, crucially, lawyers.[26] It argued that a legal system originally built on a moral Christian foundation had turned against principles of religious liberty, sanctity of human life, freedom of speech, and marriage and family. It planned to reverse that by challenging pro-abortion, pro-LGBTIQ laws all the way to the Supreme Court. Such legal cases are the cornerstone of ADF's strategy, designed both to change existing laws but, more insidiously, to change the culture. This shift in the conversation is a tactic for lasting victory on issues around abortion, marriage, family and religious freedom.

ADF boasts of winning 80 per cent of all cases, including fourteen victories at the United States Supreme Court. These include defending the city of Littleton so communities can protect themselves against the spread of sexually oriented businesses and the resulting social consequences; a federal ban on so-called partial-birth abortions; and dismantling buffer zones around abortion clinics that prevent anti-abortion protesters from blocking clinic doors – an approach later, albeit unsuccessfully, imitated by ADF International in the UK. ADF defended the Hobby Lobby lawsuit, successfully arguing that the owner's Christian faith meant the arts and crafts retail chain should not be required to pay for birth control included in private insurance plans. The case was a key gain in ADF's culture change aim: it helped normalise the attitude that contraception such as the Pill – legal for all women in the USA since 1972 – is in direct conflict to holding and expressing religious beliefs. That supposed conflict of rights builds an atmosphere of both medical and moral suspicion around contraception – a technique designed to inhibit a woman's access and right to reproductive healthcare, with the result that access to healthcare becomes a moral question, not a medical one.

As with CitizenGO, organisations such as Alliance Defending Freedom put into practice the anti-abortion strategic goals of the far and religious right. Ideas are rehearsed within the networks, before being played out in campaigns and court rooms. As we saw above, one example is the long legal battle over so-called partial-birth abortions in which the right portrayed late-term abortions as the murder of living babies, rather than an extremely rare procedure when either foetus or mother is unlikely to survive the birth.

During the Clinton administration, the anti-abortion right, backed by Republican lawmakers, had attempted to ban late-term abortions. Clinton vetoed the move after hearing evidence from women who were told late in pregnancy that their child would not survive birth. When pro-life President George W Bush was elected, however, he passed the 2003 Partial-Birth Abortion Act which led to a federal ban.

The strategy employed by the anti-abortion movement involved the use of emotive language to mislead the public about the necessity of this intervention and how it works medically. The anti-abortion movement used graphic descriptions and distressing imagery to make people believe that doctors were killing newborn babies because individualistic women had changed their mind about wanting a child. The pain of mothers who learn that their foetus has a fatal abnormality, or whose own lives are at risk, was totally erased by a narrative of murderous doctors and selfish women. So too was the crucial fact that only 1.3 per cent of abortions in the US take place after twenty-one weeks of pregnancy, with 91 per cent being carried out in the first trimester; of that 1.3 per cent, the majority are performed within the second trimester. Abortions late in pregnancy are vanishingly rare.

'The religious right has cynically weaponised and distorted the abortion issue, to the great peril of American women and girls,' the writer and journalist Anne Nelson told me. Her book *Shadow Network* investigates the CNP, and she has led the way in identifying the far-right creep in today's Republican Party. She went on: 'As of the 1970s, when the Supreme Court ruled on *Roe vs Wade*, conservative Protestants were in step with most Americans in condoning abortion under certain circumstances. Since then, political operatives tied to the religious right have employed polling and focus groups to promote (and in some cases invest in) misleading terminology to influence voters. For example, "partial birth abortion" is not a term recognised by medical science; it was designed to trigger a visceral, emotional reaction through visualisation. Other terms are equally spurious, including "abortion on demand" and "birth day abortion", suggesting that a woman about to give birth could simply change her mind at the last minute and undergo a procedure without an urgent medical crisis. These concepts are not practised, nor are they promoted by Planned Parenthood or Democratic policy-makers.'

So powerful was the anti-abortion argument against medical interventions late in pregnancy that the Family Research Council's Tony Perkins credits Trump's 2016 election win to the moment he referred to 'partial-birth abortion' during the Las Vegas debate against Hillary Rodham Clinton. That was the moment when, Perkins argued, Trump won the pro-life vote that helped catapult him to power.[27]

In 2007, the *Gonzales vs Carhart* case was heard at the Supreme Court; it sought to overturn the Partial-Birth Abortion Ban Act, with Planned Parenthood arguing that the procedure was sometimes necessary to protect the mother's life. The anti-abortion movement seized this as an opportunity to bring its history of manipulating the narrative about late-term abortions into the nation's courts – with ADF as the legal vehicle to deliver the strategy and tactics. ADF had provided funding for comprehensive efforts to coordinate an amicus curiae briefing defending the 2003 Act, as well as filing a brief with its allies at the Christian Legal Society informing the Supreme Court how and why the existing ban was constitutional. Their arguments were successful. The ban was once again challenged in 2017, but upheld, with ADF and CLS filing a further brief.

During the late stages of editing this book, the US Supreme

Court ruled on the *Dobbs vs Mississippi* case and overturned *Roe vs Wade*, the legal basis for abortion in the US. The impact was immediate: the ruling happened on the Friday, and by Monday nine states had banned abortion. Within a week, a pregnant ten-year-old girl who had been raped was denied an abortion in Ohio, being told she should consider the pregnancy an 'opportunity'. She was flown to Indiana where she received the medical care she needed. Twitter filled with stories of women being denied prescriptions that contained the same drugs as abortion pills, of reproductive health clinics closing their doors, and of women being forced to wait until they developed sepsis before a doctor would intervene on an incomplete miscarriage. It will come as no surprise that Alliance Defending Freedom had campaigned for and celebrated the end of *Roe vs Wade*.

In 2019, a firm whose attorney, Jonathan Mitchell, was the legal architect of the 2021 Texas abortion ban, received a $36,517 payment from Alliance Defending Freedom.[28] It was this ban that the Supreme Court allowed to stand in September 2021, signalling that *Roe vs Wade* was on its way out. Subsequently, Mitchell put his theory into an amicus curiae briefing to the Supreme Court as it judged the *Dobbs* case – this resulted in a ban on abortion after fifteen weeks, overturning the constitutional right to abortion in the US. In that brief, Mitchell argued that ending abortion in the US could cause women to practice abstinence from sexual intercourse as a way to 'control their reproductive lives'.[29] Men's role in heterosexual sex and pregnancy was not mentioned.

In the UK, where I live, the European branch of Alliance Defending Freedom – ADF International – has been busy replicating its successes in the US and importing its tactics and strategies to Britain's streets. In the Ashers Bakery case, for example, a Belfast bakery run by evangelical Christians refused a request from LGBTIQ activist Gareth Lee to decorate a cake with the slogan 'Support gay marriage'. The battle made it all the way to the European Court of Human Rights, which deemed Lee's case inadmissible in January 2021. Alliance Defending Freedom had successfully argued a similar case in the US Supreme Court. ADF International knew what had worked in the States when it came to gay cakes, and targeted the Belfast case with similar arguments to achieve a similar outcome.

The latest fight where ADF International is laying siege to reproductive freedoms in the UK is on the issue of buffer zones – designated areas around abortion and family planning clinics where protests and so-called prayer vigils are banned in order to prevent anti-abortion activists from harassing and intimidating women attending appointments. The campaign has two aims: first, to ensure that buffer zones are kept out of UK law; and second, to dismantle any buffer zones that currently exist. It seeks to do so by aping a successful intervention in the US, the 2014 *McCullen vs Coakley* case, in which the Supreme Court ruled to overturn a Massachusetts law that allowed for 35-foot buffer zones around abortion clinics. ADF had argued that buffer zones were unconstitutional because they 'intended to ban virtually all citizens from engaging in fundamental rights and liberties' by denying 'pro-life advocates' the chance 'to peacefully provide information on abortion alternatives'. The plaintiffs, it went on, 'engage in other peaceful expressive activities on the public ways adjacent to reproductive health care facilities including oral advocacy, counselling and prayer'. Allowing such zones, ADF continued, 'severely burdens Plaintiffs' and third parties' ability to win the attention of both willing and *unwilling listeners* and, consequently, from reaching the minds of their intended audience. Some people may have difficulty reading signs or hearing clearly from 35 feet away or less' (my emphasis). The zones also prevented the plaintiff 'from speaking to clients in a normal conversational tone'.

When ADF refers to *signs*, it means the kind of graphic imagery displayed by the US branch of the Center for Bio-Ethical

Reform (CBR) and similar groups, which cause distress and upset to pregnant women. *Speaking to clients in a normal conversational tone* involves individuals with no medical training using disinformation and manipulative techniques to persuade women not to access abortions. The mention of *prayer* refers to vigils advocated by Wilfred Wong, former board member of CBR UK, and others as a way to disrupt Satan's power and prevent an abortion from working. The Supreme Court unanimously held that the law violated the First Amendment to the United States Constitution.

In its fight against buffer zones in the UK, ADF International has invented the term 'censorship zones'. This focus on censorship has been key to my understanding of how this American anti-abortion movement is seeking to gain a foothold in the overwhelmingly pro-abortion UK. The anti-abortion movement seeks to undermine the right to safe, legal abortion around the world by presenting the pro-abortion movement as undermining human rights. Just as the Hobby Lobby case sought to create a conflict of rights between freedom of religion and the right to healthcare, the row over buffer zones tries to create a conflict between the right to free speech and the right to healthcare. This is the tactic devised by Agenda Europe, which, as you'll recall, advises its network to position the pro-abortion movement as being anti-rights. The right to bodily integrity is framed in opposition with the right to freedom of speech, creating a false debate to undermine the necessity of safe, legal access to abortion.

This approach has been voiced both by MPs in the UK parliament and by anti-censorship activists, some of whom might be expected to align themselves with the pro-abortion cause. The anti-abortion Conservative MP Fiona Bruce has led the charge against buffer zones by framing her opposition in rights terms, stating in a 2020 speech that she opposes them for a 'potentially damaging impact on free speech'.[30] A year earlier, Bruce had travelled to Vienna to speak to young people attending ADF

International's youth conference; the organisation covered the costs of Bruce's trip, with a modest donation of £927.

Bruce, who has a history of proposing anti-abortion bills to parliament, argued against the use of buffer zones by incorrectly claiming that aggressive tactics outside abortion clinics are rare and that introducing the zones would be a 'drastic overreaction' that could do 'damage ... to the more widely held freedom of speech in this country'. She went on, 'There is a long-standing tradition in this country for people gathering together to demonstrate their views and this is something to be rightly proud of ... freedom of assembly, freedom of expression, freedom of religion and the right to peaceably protest and the right to receive information – [are] fundamental liberties underpinning our democracy and many hard won.'[31]

The content of her speech shows how the global anti-abortion movement brings extremism into the mainstream via respectable organisations such as ADF International and networks such as Agenda Europe. A lack of buffer zones benefits extremist groups, including CBR UK, that promote far-right satanic conspiracy theories about abortion. Agenda Europe develops a strategy that defends intimidation and harassment as a freedom-of-information and freedom-of-speech issue. ADF International turns those strategies into legal arguments, ready to present at court if necessary. MPs linked to organisations such as ADF International bring the arguments to parliament where they become law (or, in the case of buffer zones, where a change to the law is stymied).

Interestingly, and arguably hypocritically, in 2021 Bruce voted in favour of the Conservative government's Police, Crime, Sentencing and Courts Bill that brought in draconian restrictions on the right to protest and gives the police unprecedented powers to shut down protests if they are 'noisy' and 'disruptive', although she claimed she had concerns about the Bill's reach. So did Sajid Javid, who when Home Secretary had ruled against buffer zones, saying they were a 'disproportionate response'. Protests outside abortion clinics have grown since then.

Of course, the right to protest and the right to freedom of speech must be protected. But so must the right to healthcare and access to medical treatment. Women in need of abortions have rights too: the right to ask for an abortion; the right to attend a clinic without being intimidated, harassed or fed disinformation; the right to safe and legal healthcare. Buffer zones do not prevent people from holding anti-abortion views – they don't even prevent anti-abortion protests. The groups who want to stop abortion have plenty of channels, means and places to peddle their message. A lack of protection around clinics can, however, prevent a woman from accessing healthcare that could save her life.

Exposing the specific activities of these groups in the UK demonstrates how the US is exporting its tactics to Europe, and how the extreme right has managed to enter mainstream discourse, with anti-abortion messaging travelling from rumours of satanic ritual abuse to being defended as free speech in parliament. The example also raises concerns about the UK's vulnerability to extremist ideology. We'll explore this more in Chapter Six, but suffice to say ADF International specifically set up in London because it sees the city as a place where it could 'better engage with crucial developments of law, policy, and media in one of the most influential cities in the world'. The organisation now spends more in the UK than across the rest of the European Union put together, around half a million pounds a year. Its focus on London echoes the ambition of Gregg Cunningham, US founder of the Center for Bio-Ethical Research, who in 2012 explained that 'the UK is a high priority for us because it is arguably the most influential country in Europe. Trends on the Continent often find their origins in the British Isles.'

Of course, since Brexit Britain's influence within Europe is diminished. But it's precisely because of Brexit that the UK now feels more vulnerable to extremist anti-abortion views moving into the mainstream. Brexit triggered a culture war in the UK between social conservatism and progressive values that can easily be exploited by groups like ADF International, particularly when it comes to freedom of speech. If you live in the UK, or are just observing far-right trends, you'll know that Britain's culture war these past few years has argued that white, conservative males are being silenced or having their history erased by a woke mob. This belief that conservative views are under attack or being silenced has led to far-right marches through London, ostensibly to protect statues of British war heroes; a rise in right-wing politicians using the term *cultural Marxism* to attack their opponents; a worrying number of white British people declaring the Black Lives Matter movement to be Marxist, divisive and harmful; and a growing population of young men raging against a feminim that they argue has gone too far.

At the same time, despite the claims that white male supremacist voices have been suppressed, rates of racially motivated and homophobic hate crime increased following the Brexit referendum. People with hateful or regressive views have been emboldened by Brexit and the arguments surrounding it, and the lack of clarity on the reasons for Brexit has allowed groups determined to exploit division and hate to intensify a culture war focused on race, sexuality, misogyny and a warped understanding of freedom of speech. This is intensified by the confused sense that Brexit is, in itself, about freedom, and that freedom is threatened by progressives.

The row provides fertile territory for groups such as ADF International, which understand women's access to contraception and abortion as an infringement on (white men's) fundamental freedoms – freedoms they are determined to defend by laying siege to reproductive rights.

The final mainstreaming tactic of the anti-abortion right focuses on crisis pregnancy centres – organisations that work to dissuade women from having an abortion and to continue with an unwanted pregnancy. While crisis pregnancy services exist all over the world, many of the global centres are affiliated with US-based organisations and use disinformation and manipulative tactics learnt from their US affiliates to prevent abortions. Critically, these centres take the anti-abortion message direct to women, girls and people who are already pregnant and seeking support to access a termination, often disguising themselves as medical centres or setting themselves up within hospitals. They present themselves as women-focused – as benign services for women in trouble – while painting the so-called abortion industry as fundamentally hostile to women, unsafe and motivated by profit.

In doing so, the crisis pregnancy movement uses tactics borrowed from the Agenda Europe playbook – namely, it portrays the opposition as an all-powerful lobby with a self-interested agenda that it seeks to impose on others. Further, crisis pregnancy centres adopt the strategy of 'using the language of our opponents against them'. They do this by presenting themselves as loving, concerned about women's health, and offering hope and care – even as they disinform, weaponise women's health conditions and seek to undermine women's fundamental human rights.

One of the largest crisis pregnancy networks is Heartbeat International – originally known as Alternatives to Abortion. It was set up in 1971 by a nun, counsellor and doctor who aimed to turn 'their passion for life and their compassion for women into the first USA-based pregnancy help center association'.[32] Although not affiliated to one specific church, Christian beliefs were placed at the heart of the group's mission. Heartbeat characterised itself as 'a community of God's people doing faithfully what God calls His people to do every day'. Its founders believed the legalisation of abortion in the USA following the 1973 *Roe vs Wade* ruling would lead to women feeling pressured into abortion: 'they would succumb or resort to abortion far more often than choose it. These visionaries determined to create a safety net of support and to reach these vulnerable women with "alternatives-to-abortion" services.'[33] They lacked evidence that women would be coerced into abortion, of course, but disinformation is the bread and butter of crisis pregnancy services. Ultimately, Heartbeat's vision remains to 'make abortion unwanted today and unthinkable for future generations'.

Heartbeat International has a network of national and international affiliates including 971 outside of the US; it has partners on every inhabited continent, and a global directory of crisis pregnancy centres. Affiliates receive a wide range of support from Heartbeat, such as discounts on training and resources, a listing on its Options Line helpline, support with web design and marketing, a retirement plan, and vaguely termed 'services' tailored to each individual organisation. The extremist anti-abortion group CBR UK directs women with an unplanned pregnancy to the Heartbeat Options Line. At the time of writing, Heartbeat had three affiliates in the UK: Tyneside Pregnancy Advice in Newcastle (along with Pregnancy Advice Sunderland); Stanton Healthcare in Belfast; and Pregnancy Crisis Helpline in London. As well as practical support, Heartbeat sends thousands of dollars to its partners and affiliates outside of the US each year: in 2015 it spent $149,194 across ten organisations; $63,601 of that in Europe. Countries in receipt of funds included Serbia, Italy, Ukraine, Macedonia and Spain.[34]

That money, along with networked support, is used to spread disinformation specifically designed to persuade women not to go ahead with a safe and legal abortion. Heartbeat also uses the same disinformation to try and undermine the legal basis for abortion. This is key, because in Europe it operates in countries where abortion is legally available and where women have the right to choose to end a pregnancy. The only exception is Malta, and, up until 2020, Northern Ireland.

In December 2020, I downloaded a training webinar called

'Answering Tough Calls', having the year before completed two other Heartbeat training webinars as part of an eighteen-country-wide undercover investigation with *openDemocracy 50:50*. In all three webinars I was told how to use disinformation and manipulation to prevent women from having abortions; I was taught to share inaccurate information about women's health and try 'slowing the caller down'– a key tactic that prevents women from accessing reproductive healthcare, including emergency contraception, in a timely fashion.

'Answering Tough Calls' is designed to 'cover how to handle a caller who is abortion bound or abortion determined. When a client calls, remember that no matter the purpose of her call you have three things you can offer. Faith. Hope. Love.' I accessed it by posing as a counselling student keen to volunteer at a pro-life organisation and wanting to get ahead of the game by picking up some new skills. Before receiving the webinar I had to tick a box affirming 'that this is an educational resource and is considered off the record'. However, it is in the public interest to share the contents of Heartbeat's training offering which impacts on the lives and well-being of vulnerable women across the world.

Throughout the training, which is designed to equip me for talking to the 'abortion bound', I'm reminded to be 'clear and factual' with the caller and let them know my service doesn't offer abortions. This demonstrates that Heartbeat is aware of its responsibility not to trick women into thinking they are talking to an abortion provider. But crucially, rather than acknowledging that the woman is 'abortion bound' and ending the call, the trainer encouraged me to 'quickly try to learn more about her situation'. The intention here is to slow the caller down and dissuade her from going on to access an abortion. The trainer narrated: '*It is important to slow her down and try to assess if she has in fact made an abortion decision.*'

'Slow her down' is a key tactic for crisis pregnancy services. In two of the webinars I took, I was told to offer women pregnancy tests, ultrasounds and urge them to take their time over the decision. While of course women should have space and time to think through their reproductive options, when it comes to abortion there are time limits – especially if you want a medical abortion, which is less invasive but can only take place in the first trimester. Slowing women down not only means they may be more likely to have to go through a surgical abortion, but diminishes the options for pursuing abortion, due to a lack of later-term abortion facilities and doctors, and the restrictions on abortions after twelve weeks in most European countries. This, of course, is the aim of these centres.

'As soon as someone decides to have an abortion, they're up against the clock,' Mara Clarke from Abortion Support Network explained to me.[35] Mara is a force of nature, setting up the Abortion Support Network which works in countries where abortion isn't available to provide women with financial, practical and emotional assistance to travel and receive reproductive healthcare. 'A lot of places have time limits in terms of how far into pregnancy an abortion can be performed,' Clarke continued. 'In places where abortion isn't covered by the health service, the further in pregnancy you get, the more expensive an abortion is. And while abortion is a safe procedure at any stage, it's still a more invasive procedure the further you go along.'

That's why 'the first thing these crisis pregnancy centres try to do is delay you,' Clarke continued. 'We've had clients who went to crisis pregnancy centres and were told, "We will help you arrange an abortion, you just sit tight and we'll call you when we've booked the appointment." Which they never do. One woman was delayed by nine weeks because they told her there were no appointments as Marie Stopes' mother had just died. That's how ridiculous they are.' (Marie Stopes was a twentieth-century reproductive rights campaigner. Her mother died in 1929.)

As well as slowing women down in relation to abortion, the trainer encouraged me to share information about emergency contraception. The focus on emergency contraception tracks back to strategies voiced by Agenda Europe – which seeks to ban emergency contraception except in cases of rape as a weapon of war – and Alliance Defending Freedom's intervention in the Hobby Lobby case. The latter sought to change the culture when it comes to how we think of contraception, including by blurring the lines between emergency contraception and abortion, and by suggesting there is a conflict of rights between religious freedom and healthcare.

The webinar's narration continued: '*Don't be intimidated or think you don't have anything to offer to callers asking about the morning-after pill. Just as you have something to offer callers asking about abortion, you have the same thing to offer these callers: information.*'

The information the trainer goes on to offer me is misleading, claiming 'callers asking about the morning-after pill most likely do not think of the morning after pill as a form of abortion or understand that it has an abortifacient effect'. This language is misplaced – the morning-after pill prevents a fertilised egg from implanting into the uterine lining. It is not an abortion. But what is even more problematic is that, rather than explaining I don't offer emergency contraception and ending the call, I'm told to offer the caller a pregnancy test to affirm she is pregnant.

This is where 'slowing her down' becomes urgent. There are two types of morning-after pill commonly on the market – one must be taken within seventy-two hours to work, the other within five days. A pregnancy test, as Heartbeat International explains in another webinar, 'Talking About Abortion', will only show a pregnancy after seven to ten days *at best*. The morning-after pill won't prevent a pregnancy after seven to ten days. Telling a woman to wait until she is sure she is pregnant is to saddle that woman with an unplanned pregnancy.

The training moves on to discuss how to deal with calls from the 'abortion minded', and I am instructed to refer to Heartbeat

International's 'Ten Point Health and Safety Checklist'. I'm told to tell my fictional caller that taking her through the checklist 'will make it a lot less likely for you to be hurt in the [abortion] process'. The implication that abortion hurts women is in itself a form of disinformation designed to prevent women accessing healthcare, discredit abortion providers and undermine the legal basis for abortion in most European countries.

This checklist is expanded upon during the second webinar, 'Talking About Abortion'.[36] Once again, the focus is on slowing the caller down by encouraging her to come to a centre for a pregnancy test or an ultrasound. 'Some people have admitted that personnel in their clinics perform abortions on women who are not pregnant,' the webinar explained. No evidence is provided for this claim. 'We can provide you with free and confidential pregnancy tests and ultrasounds. Would you like to make an appointment?'

The 'Ten Point Checklist' warns against the emotional complications that can arise from abortion, which I'm told to explain to my caller are 'more likely [if] ... you make the decision too quickly without time to consider all your options' or if you only consider the 'practical reasons, for example, financial problems, single parenthood, for having the abortion'. This is a form of disinformation: while of course some women will experience emotional complications following abortion, the UK NHS confirms that a woman who has an abortion 'is no more likely to experience mental health problems' than if she continues with her pregnancy.[37]

The trainer then moves onto the 'physical complications' of abortion, stating:

> *Statistically most abortions do not cause physical injury. However, statistically the chances of you getting pregnant might not have been great either. It is also becoming clear that more women are dying from legal abortion than we realised, because most abortion-related deaths are not reported as such.*

Again, no evidence is given for this claim. But linking abortion to death is becoming an increasingly visible tactic of the anti-abortion right. It groundlessly attempts to link the deaths of women following abortions to the procedure itself – chiefly by claiming life-threatening diseases or conditions are linked to abortion.

One of the most common forms of disinformation linking abortion to death are the false claims that having a termination can increase the risk of breast cancer and ectopic pregnancies. Both of these are life-threatening conditions and both can happen to women who have previously had an abortion. But they aren't *caused* by the abortion. The American Cancer Association says 'the scientific evidence does not support' any link between abortion and cancer risk.[38] The NHS debunks any link between abortion and issues in subsequent pregnancies, stating that 'having an abortion will not affect your chances of becoming pregnant and having normal pregnancies in the future'.[39] A US study into abortion and subsequent ectopic pregnancies also found little to link the two.[40] Another common claim is that abortions can cause infertility later in life – again, this has been roundly disproven by expert sources such as the NHS.

It is enraging that crisis pregnancy services exploit the very real health concerns women have about cancer and ectopic pregnancies in order to push disinformation and fuel their anti-abortion message. Like most of us, I know women who have endured life-threatening ectopic pregnancies, and cancer is something that impacts all of us, whether we have a diagnosis or love someone who has. Women's lives, fears and health concerns are not pawns in a game – they are real and serious, and deserve respect. That the anti-abortion movement treats these issues as bogeymen to scare women from accessing reproductive healthcare is, in my view, a calculated cruelty.

A further webinar, called 'Abortion, the Basics' (which was removed after I reported its contents in *openDemocracy 50:50*) expanded on the alleged complications explored in the 'Ten

Point Checklist', including sharing disinformation about cancer, death, 'handicaps in new born babies', PTSD, suicide, substance abuse, sexual dysfunction in both a woman and her male partner including 'homosexuality ... impotency, or addiction to pornography and masturbation'.[41] The webinar also claimed that having an abortion can make a woman more likely to neglect and abuse existing or subsequent children while providing no evidence for this deeply hurtful allegation.

The disinformation shared by crisis pregnancy services and the anti-abortion right are harmful enough on their own. But they have a deeper and more troubling aim: the claims they make about abortion providers, and about the mental and physical health impacts of abortion, are designed to change the laws around reproductive healthcare. This happens in two ways. The first is by increasing the legal burden on clinics and thereby making it harder to provide abortions; the second is by undermining the legal basis for abortion in countries such as the UK, Italy and other European nations.

In order to increase the legal burden on abortion providers, crisis pregnancy services first attempt to build an atmosphere of mistrust. For example, the claim in 'Talking About Abortion' that 'abortion providers are largely unregulated' – an irony considering the lack of regulation governing crisis pregnancy services – suggests that abortion providers are somehow nefarious, even criminal, and operate outside of clinical norms, in order to plant fear in women's minds and undermine the very notion of a safe, legal abortion.

The reality is very different. In England and Wales, the 1967 Abortion Act stipulated that terminations can only take place in clinical settings – so even if a woman was taking a pill for an early-term abortion, she had to take it in a doctor's office or a registered healthcare clinic. This was relaxed during the coronavirus pandemic to reduce pressure on the NHS, and the law was formally changed in March 2022, although not without a fight. Meanwhile, abortion providers in the US are subject to strict evidence-based rules that include federal workplace health and safety regulations. This is only right and proper. But increasingly, anti-abortion majority states started to use a tactic known as targeted regulation of abortion providers – so-called TRAP laws – leading to these services being strangled and shut down by the application of overly zealous rules and laws. The rules are not designed to promote hygiene, but to make it harder for women to access reproductive healthcare.

According to the Guttmacher Institute, most of these TRAP laws 'apply a state's standards for ambulatory surgical centers (ASCs) to abortion clinics, even though surgical centers tend to provide riskier, more invasive procedures and use higher levels of sedation. In some cases, TRAP laws also extend to physicians' offices where abortions are performed and even to sites where only medication abortion is administered.' Applying surgical hygiene standards to an office where a woman is having a consultation or being given a prescription for a pill is obviously unreasonable, and can require expensive renovations that many providers can't afford. The anti-abortion right claims this is all done in the name of patient safety, but the Guttmacher Institute has instead found that 'these laws endanger patients by reducing the total number of abortion facilities that are able to stay open under these financial and administrative constraints, thus making safe services harder to obtain'.[42]

In contrast, crisis pregnancy services are the wild west. In the USA, crisis pregnancy centres are protected by the First Amendment, with various lawsuits affirming their right to offer advice to women whether the advice is accurate or not. Even centres offering medical procedures such as ultrasounds are not required to comply to ASC standards, unlike abortion providers. While the UK's Department of Health and Social Care offers guidelines instructing that pregnancy counselling 'must be non-directive and non-judgemental and should not create barriers or delays', it's not clear how this can be enforced. Crisis pregnancy services that offer clinical procedures such as ultrasounds are regulated by the UK's Care Quality Commission, but this covers health and safety, not the content of advice offered.

Anti-abortion organisations such as Heartbeat International also undermine trust in abortion providers by claiming they are profiting from women's distress, following Agenda Europe in their focus on the *abortion industry* as the Goliath to the anti-abortionist's David. This is less of an issue in the UK where abortions are free on the NHS (for those who are entitled to NHS care – it took until 2017 before women and pregnant people in Northern Ireland were allowed to access free abortions, despite being UK citizens who pay National Insurance, and others with specific immigration statuses have to pay for healthcare). But even within the UK with its free healthcare, anti-abortion activists still depict abortion providers as an industry raking in profits from terminations. In an email, CBR UK Director Andy Stephenson asked me if I would only 'advocate for those with a financial interest in abortion [to] have exclusive access to women'.[43] If it means protecting women from lies and graphic imagery, then yes, Andy – yes, I would.

The idea that abortion providers are splashing around in cash extracted from vulnerable women is enforced by Heartbeat International. During the 'Answering Tough Calls' training, I was told 'to emphasise that you do not profit in any way from the decision she makes'. This suggests that anti-abortion groups are more trustworthy because they won't make money from giving a woman advice or, for example, offering a pregnancy test or ultrasound. The statement undermines trust by insinuating abortion providers are profiteering from women's health rather than engaged in caring for women. But once again, it's simply not true. Crisis pregnancy services have money and they make money. As we saw above, Heartbeat provides tens of thousands of dollars to its partners, and its total revenue in 2020 was over $6 million.

The most troubling tactic employed by the anti-abortion, religious-right crisis pregnancy movement is to try and undermine the legal status of abortion around the world. In the UK, they are aided in this aim by religious-right organisations who falsely claim that the majority of abortions taking place in Britain are illegal, by sharing disinformation that states abortion endangers a woman's physical and/or mental health. In the majority of European countries, abortion is available on demand in the early phases of pregnancy (although, as you saw above, many nations enforce counselling or a cooling-off period), and then permitted on health grounds during the second and sometimes third trimester. There are exceptions to this: abortion remains illegal in Poland, Malta and Andorra, and in Gibraltar it is only legal before twelve weeks in cases of risk to the mother's health. It is not available on demand in Britain, where a woman needs two doctors to confirm that continuing her pregnancy will have a negative impact on her mental and/or physical health. Switzerland and Luxembourg also require confirmation that continuing a pregnancy will negatively impact a woman's mental or physical health before she can be given legal permission for a termination. The key thing to note here is that in almost every European country, the threat to mental and physical health will, at some point during her pregnancy, become a key factor in whether or not a woman can have a termination.

The mental/physical health exception is now being used by UK groups including Christian Concern and the Christian Medical Fellowship (CMF) to undermine the legal status of abortion. They argue that most abortions taking place in Britain are criminal offences and use disinformation to suggest an abortion is more harmful to a woman's mental and physical health than continuing an unwanted pregnancy. CMF's head of public policy, Philippa Taylor, has claimed that women 'should be told there is a lack of academic studies showing any benefits from abortion – despite the fact that so many are carried out on the presumption that abortion reduces mental health risks'.[44] This is frankly nonsensical: the benefit of an abortion is that it ends an unwanted pregnancy, saving women from the mental and physical health risks of continuing with an unwanted pregnancy and being forced to give birth.

Christian Concern claims 'it is highly unlikely' that all abortions carried out in Britain 'fit the current regulations'. It shares disinformation that abortion is linked to poor mental health outcomes, which would therefore mean most abortions are not permitted under the 1967 Abortion Act. It goes on to claim that, as a result, 'most abortions in the UK are, in fact, illegal'.[45]

Meanwhile the crisis pregnancy charity Life, which was listed on Heartbeat's worldwide directory, has in the past published unsubstantiated links between cancer and abortion.[46] If this link could be proven – and it has been repeatedly debunked – it would risk the legal status of abortion in Britain. Life also questions evidence debunking links between abortion and subsequent poor mental health, saying 'it is not uncommon for women to carry the pain of their abortion with them for many years into their adult life'.[47] Both of these claims seek to undermine the legal basis for abortion in the UK by presenting abortion as more physically and emotionally harmful than pregnancy.

What my research into crisis pregnancy movements and anti-abortion disinformation revealed to me is that false claims about abortion's impact on women's mental and physical health are not only designed to deter women from having an abortion; they are also a tool to undermine its legal status. Heartbeat and its allies on the religious and far right want to hide that having a safe, legal termination is *almost always* less harmful to a woman's mental well-being than carrying an unwanted pregnancy to term. What's more, these organisations rarely mention how even a *wanted* pregnancy and childbirth are more dangerous to women's health and life than a safe, legal abortion. In the UK between 2016 and 2018, 546 women died in childbirth, the majority of them black and minority ethnic women.[48] Between 2015 and 2019 in England and Wales, three women died in cases where 'abortion was mentioned on the death certificate', and one was listed where abortion was 'the underlying cause of death'.[49]

An undercover investigation by Italian journalist Francesca Visser provides a fascinating and terrifying insight into how Heartbeat International's influence is spreading around the world, and exposes how the messages fed to me via the training webinars are being repeated every day to pregnant women in clinical settings.

Visser posed as a young woman with an unwanted pregnancy and went to the San Pio hospital in Benevento, Southern Italy.[50] Here she was met by volunteers from Heartbeat's partners Movimento per la Vita (Movement for Life). These partnerships are essential to the Heartbeat International model, providing the anti-choice movement with the chance to 'better serve women and families on every continent of the globe'.

Visser was told by the volunteers that having an abortion could cause 'post-abortion syndrome' – a fake condition linking poor mental health to abortion – and linked abortion to cancer. Unlike in the webinar I took, her volunteers put a number on the risk, telling her she had a 50 per cent increased risk of getting *brefleetwooast* cancer. There was no citation given. Visser visited a further five clinics, all repeating the same disinformation. She then called a Movement for Life centre in Vigevano hospital near Milan, where she was discouraged from seeking information from other sources and told to go to the hospital where she could discuss her options with volunteers based within the hospital's obstetric ward.

'Over the next hour and a half,' Visser explained, the volunteers 'pushed me to change my mind – using graphic language … and overinflated claims about abortion's health risks. Most of these claims were conveyed in the form of stories of women who they said suffered serious psychological, fertility and relationship issues after abortions.'[51]

All of these claims were used as talking points in the training webinars I completed. Further, the law in Italy is clear that in the first ninety days of pregnancy, women can access an abortion if 'continuation of the pregnancy, childbirth, or motherhood would seriously compromise their physical or mental health'. Falsely claiming that abortion causes physical and emotional harm to women is therefore a tactic to undermine Italy's law.

The crisis pregnancy movement is a strategy used by the coalition of the far and religious right to deny women's reproductive rights. It seeks to sow distrust about abortion providers, uses disinformation to manipulate women out of accessing abortions, and tries to undermine the legal basis of abortion by falsely linking it to serious health conditions. The movement also offers an example of how the strategies laid out by groups including Agenda Europe are acted out on the international stage, with crisis pregnancy centres co-opting women's rights language and portraying the pro-abortion movement as a money-making industry. Ultimately, the goal of denying women abortions tracks back to the overarching anti-abortion aim of forced pregnancy which traps women in reproductive labour and maintains an imaginary natural order.

4

The Allies: How (Some) Women Join The Far Right – From Trad Wives To Anti-Trans Activism

To achieve its white male supremacist aims, the far right needs women. It needs white women to recruit others to the cause, as well as to bring fascist ideas about sex, family and reproduction into the mainstream. More importantly, the movement urgently needs women's wombs as reproductive vessels to exploit for repopulation: in fascism, as Neocleous explains, 'biology is destiny. Where men are destined for war, women are destined for motherhood'.[1]

Alongside recruiting and exploiting women for their cause, the far right has formed a strange alliance with female anti-trans activists, some of whom claim to be feminists, in order to give a progressive polish to their anti-LGBTIQ campaigning. In order to attack LGBTIQ rights, the far right has adopted feminist talking points around protecting single-sex spaces, women's sports and the female identity, holding hands across the aisle with women it would traditionally consider to be the enemy. While far-right activists claim they care about women's safety, in truth its anti-trans work is preoccupied with entrenching gendered stereotypes in order to restore the fascistic natural order of female inferiority and male supremacy. Some gender-critical feminists have stood firm against the embrace of the far right. Too many, unfortunately, have been duped by a movement that fundamentally hates them.

According to philosopher Jason Stanley, 'in all fascist mythic pasts, an extreme version of the patriarchal family reigns supreme'.[2] Psychoanalyst Wilhelm Reich, in his *Mass Psychology of Fascism*, also recognised how fascism was the natural political form for the 'character type produced by the patriarchal family'. He continues to explain that, therefore, the 'potential for fascism thus existed in any country where a patriarchal family structure was dominant'.[3]

The fascist mythic past of patriarchal authority and women's subordination is brought to life in a subculture that calls itself trad wives or trad life – short for traditional – where women renounce the gains of feminism and instead embrace a role of obedience and subservience in relation to the patriarchal authority in the home (their husbands). In doing so, they hope to achieve adoration and reverence from their men, who view them as white goddesses vital to the recovery of the white race. Women are recruited into this movement by social media influencers who promote a traditional lifestyle via soft-focus shots of their homesteads, their children and their happy white families. White nationalist dating sites matchmake fascists who are committed to having children to 'secure the future of the white race' with those who have an interest in homesteading (the subject comes up *a lot*).

The far-right trad movement tells women that they can give up the stresses and strains of progressive, modern society which demands women 'have it all' and instead be worshipped and adored as the sacred womb. It positions feminism as harmful to women's happiness and portrays feminists as sluts who have lots of abortions, suffer from bad skin and hair, and are unhealthy and unhappy.

A popular trad wife meme on Reddit demonstrates how good, trad women and bad, feminist women are seen within the far right. A cartoon of a 'liberated feminist' shows a woman with punk hair and piercings, wearing a crop top. She's described as wearing 'tons of make-up because of low self-esteem'; she's 'chubby' from eating microwave meals; she 'sleeps around to improve her self-esteem but it only makes her feel worse'; and 'uses fake tanner so dark she looks Mexican'. In contrast, an illustration of the demurely clad trad wife holding a baby 'loves her natural face and only wears light make-up'; has a husband who 'works to support her staying at home and raising the kids'; has a 'slim figure from her healthy homemade meals and active lifestyle'; and sports a 'natural tan', because she spends a lot of time outdoors on, you've guessed it, the homestead. Crucially, unlike the liberated feminist who 'only sleeps with black men', the trad wife 'loves her family, race and country in that order', and is 'knowledgeable about her European roots'. All women have to do to achieve the health and happiness of the trad wife, the far right explains, is give up the rights won by feminism and, of course, have lots (and lots) of white babies.

The first thing you notice at far-right gatherings is that they are very white, and very male. The Patriotic Alternative's 2020 conference was no exception. It is the annual gathering of the far-right group founded by Mark Collett, formerly of the British National Party (BNP); its various branches across the UK take part in banner drops and leafleting actions, with banners emblazoned with slogans such as 'we will not be replaced'.

The 200 or so men at the event come in many varieties: the old-style skinheads who have come up through a long history of street violence and neo-Nazi activism; the grey-haired men who have shifted right from Conservative to UKIP to nationalism; the baby-faced YouTubers who tell their thousands of adoring fans that it's not racist to worry about replacement and love your white culture, while swapping vile racist slurs in private; the podcasters who bemoan women becoming too assertive and men becoming 'beta'. Many appear to have taken their fashion tips from men such as neo-Nazi leader Richard Spencer: smart shirts and blazers, their hair slicked back with a 1930s-style side parting. Others look more like hipsters, in skinny jeans, waistcoats, flat caps and beards – guys you'd expect to see in an East London bar rather than at a far-right meeting.

The keynote speaker is Jason Köhne, otherwise known by his avatar NoWhiteGuilt. Wearing a black blazer over a red shirt and tie, he interrupted his own speech to ask all the women in the room to stand up for a round of applause. There are some nervous giggles from the women – and then a lot of clapping from the men.[4]

The women in the audience stand out enough as it is: they're thin and blonde, and while there are elder stateswomen in the movement, many of them are young. Some are smartly dressed in LBDs with heels. Others wear the long dresses and flowing hair of trad wives. Tattoos or haircuts that are associated with being left wing are frowned upon – hair is dyed blonde here, not blue. As the women receive their praise, the men are looking at them. The women are also looking at each other – wary, unsure, in competition. In this patriarchal world, where success depends on male attention, it's not always safe to trust the women around you.

The clapping continues, as the men wonder if this will be the place where they meet a nationalist lady to marry and have kids with. They scan the women up and down, deciding. One woman shifts uncomfortably, the smile on her face strained. The trad wives, who are the Queen Bees of the movement, look at the other women with judgement. 'What's wrong with her?,' their eyes seem to say. 'Why isn't she married yet?' They watch, with an attitude that is both judgemental and riven with insecurity, as the men flock flirtatiously around the younger, twenty-something women in attendance. They know on some level those girls are at risk. But they don't want to speak up about the abuse of women in their movement. After all, it's an abuse they are suffering too.

'These men lovebomb you,' said Issy, a young woman who described to me the above scenes at the conference, which she attended when she was part of the far-right movement. She spoke to me across many interviews about her experiences and how she became disillusioned with the way the far right treated women. 'Then they attack you. It's an abusive relationship.'[5]

It's easy to see how the far right's adoration and applause promised to white women are incredibly potent and attractive. Who doesn't want to be celebrated simply for existing? Who doesn't want to be a goddess, especially when the alternative is working nine to five at a boring office or factory job, dating annoying men and having to juggle work, family and a million other responsibilities? Who doesn't want to be applauded, adored and revered? To be an ideal woman in the far right you don't have to fight or work or engage in difficult conversations – you get to be special just by having a functioning womb. You simply have to be, because your value exists solely by virtue of having a female body.

'They take things like motherhood for instance, and they make it political,' explained Seyward Darby, who examined the role of women in the US far right for her book *Sisters in Hate*. 'And when your body becomes a political force, that's potentially transformative for someone. That's a key thing to remember about the far right: that women's reproductive potential, their bodies, their aesthetics, become political.'[6]

The far right promises white women a privileged position in its movement. But the reality of being a revered body is that *you are nothing more than a body* – a reproductive vessel to exploit. As such, women hold a double role in the far right. Yes, they get to be the white goddess. But they also exist as objects which are only as valuable as their reproductive potential. The more I looked into the position of women in the far right, the more I was reminded of an Elizabeth Wurtzel quote: 'He puts her on a pedestal and she goes down on it'.[7] I share this with Issy, who agrees.

Because women's value to the far right is predicated on their reproductive potential, there is a fairly creepy obsession about women's age and fertility. Issy told me how men would refer to women over thirty as being an 'empty egg box'; they would mock women approaching thirty for getting old and 'running out of eggs'.

'You are seen as a breeding mule,' Issy explained. 'If a young woman was around, men would linger around her because she is young and fertile. Someone being thirty is an insult. Being childless is a slur. They ask – where's your baby, where's your husband?'

'There's a lot of mental gymnastics that goes on to be a woman that wants to have a voice and agency beyond motherhood in the far right,' explains Darby. 'There's a lot of self-deluding that goes on'. For trad wives, that self-delusion means women believing that going trad will give them the status of a goddess adored for her biological potential. But the price is high: women have to give up any autonomy at all in order to be accepted.

This was the origin story, as it were, for white nationalist and trad wife influencer Ayla Stewart, otherwise known by her social media avatar Wife with a Purpose. She describes herself online as a 'former SJW [social justice warrior] now #Tradlife ... Loving my #WhiteCulture is about heritage not hate'.

Stewart's fame took off when she set the infamous 'white baby challenge' on social media. 'As a mother of six, I challenge families to have as many white babies as I have contributed,' she declared. Her invitation to white women to match her fecundity was sold with cheery photos of herself with her children, and greeted with enthusiasm by male and female fans. Followers cheered her on to 'make white babies great again!'[8] On the Telegram channel, 'Opposing the Great Replacement', Stewart's call is echoed by a poster who says 'three children is said to be replacement rates, personally I want six. If all white nationalists have six, I think we can make a real difference.'

When Ayla Stewart launched her challenge, she was at the height of her powers in the white nationalist movement. Her traditional lifestyle and single-minded dedication to white motherhood was social media gold for the American far right.

She was such a star that she was billed to speak at the notorious Charlottesville rally where racists marched with flaming torches, chanting, 'Jews will not replace us!' One attendee killed Heather Heyer, a young woman taking part in a counterprotest. Stewart decided not to attend the event due to security fears.

But before she joined the far right, Stewart called herself a feminist.[9] How, then, did a young woman interested in feminism and human rights become the poster girl for a movement fuelled by racist misogyny, one that wants to reverse the progress she once celebrated and benefited from? It starts with a backlash against the demands put on women, by a false idea of feminism that demanded we *have it all.*

One of the tenets of feminist ideology is that women should have the freedom to control our own fertility: that we have the right not to continue an unwanted pregnancy; the financial security to give birth to wanted children; and a real, informed choice when it comes to working and childrearing. However, during the anti-feminist backlash of the 1980s and 1990s – a backlash fuelled by rampant neoliberalism – the idea of women having authentic choice when it came to reproduction and economic independence became reduced to a slogan: having it all. The soundbite told women they could choose to work *and* have a family. It wasn't long before the messaging around women's reproductive choices shifted from a focus on the social, political and economic support to raise children and work, to having no choice *but* to do it all. Laura Doyle – the author of a wannabe trad wives self-help manual called *Surrendered Wife* – explains it as 'I took feminism and twisted it into a belief that I had to do everything myself.'[10]

This was not a failure of feminism, although we could have done better to fight the orthodoxy that allowed 'having it all/ doing it all' to become the defining mantra of the movement. Feminism has always fought to open up spaces for women so that we can choose to have children, to work, and to live our lives on our own terms. But as neoliberal capitalism worked harder and harder to squeeze women's choices, and as hostile political forces sent conflicting messages to women about their roles as workers, mothers and wives, some women started to blame feminism for the challenges they were facing in trying to balance work, family and basic happiness.

Women who *didn't want* to have it all – who instead wanted to be a housewife and stay at home raising children – felt increasingly judged and sidelined by mainstream feminism. Again, this is an upsetting misinterpretation of what feminism is about: the objections to housewifery and childrearing came from challenging the belief that this is all women are good for, not that women who make those choices are wrong or deserve exclusion from the movement. Further, campaigns such as Wages for Housework advocated for women's domestic labour to be respected and renumerated, not degraded and despised. If anything, it was neoliberal capitalism that removed women's freedom to be a stay-at-home mum (who can afford to raise children on one income?). Particularly in the US, where the market-driven culture and lack of national healthcare demands mothers return to work almost as soon as their episiotomy stitches are healed.

This was the case for women like Ayla Stewart – women who, Seyward Darby told me, 'felt frustrated by what they saw as the unfair demands of feminism and the unfair demands of capitalism'. The attraction of the far right's idealisation of motherhood and promised adoration of its women, she explained, gives women 'this sense of – oh, here's a way I can feel powerful without having to engage with a lot of this stuff that I have found disillusioning or alienating'.

Where the left recognises that capitalism and patriarchy are to blame for the squeezing of women's choices and rights, the far right blames feminism. It positions feminism as the antithesis of what women want or need. The movement then recruits women by pointing the finger at feminism for any dis-satisfaction women may feel with their lives. No wonder, then, that white nationalist Lauren Southern – the blonde, red-lipped star of the international far right – claimed that feminism 'has caused a drastic decrease' in women's happiness.[11] She argues that while feminists and progressive movements criticise a more traditional and conservative past, they have replaced it with an era of 'selfishness' and 'narcissism'. Such language echoes the much maligned individualism of women attacked by proponents of the Great Replacement conspiracy theory, which chastises women for selfishly failing to fulfil their natural role of bearing children.

Southern told her followers that men are being taught to hate their gender, to 'grovel' to women and be 'weak', which, she says, makes neither men nor women happy. Women, by contrast, are 'being taught to work 9–5 and drink wine every night until their ovaries dry up' and are 'surprised when this leads to regret'.[12] Colin Robertson, a far-right influencer whose social media avatar is Millennial Woes, took to the stage at the Patriotic Alternative 2020 conference and echoed Southern's rhetoric. He complained that men were becoming submissive and women too assertive – saying women look for ways 'to break down her man' because she doesn't know 'how to submit'. This rejection of 'sexual dimorphism' which defines men as dominant and women as subordinate has led to a loss of attraction between men and women, and, he claimed, a lack of millennial sex.

It's easy to understand why angry white men hate the feminism that may have given them a female boss, or led to a woman saying no to sex they don't want to have. They see only that feminism has taken something away from them – they have lost economic or sexual power. But to make women hate feminism, women must also be persuaded they have lost out on something. This explains Southern's video which tells women that feminism has caused them to lose happiness, fertility and the love the of men. There's a historical precedent for this: Nazi ideologue Alfred Rosenberg called in 1930 for 'the emancipation of women from the women's emancipation movement'.[13]

The far right likes to claim that feminism judges women – that it is *anti-women* because it denies women the choice to be a stay-at-home mum. In contrast, the far right sells itself as being *pro-women*, because after all, these men just want to worship women's fertile bodies and look after their wives and daughters. Darby saw this in Stewart, who felt 'unfairly judged' – 'shunned, ostracised and called down' by women in the feminist movement who she believed were judging her approach to motherhood and marriage.[14] In contrast, the far right promised Stewart something very different: it told her she would be worshipped and celebrated as a mother and wife. Stewart's social media avatar is the giveaway: in the far right she can be a woman 'with a purpose'– and that purpose was to save the white race from the Great Replacement. Her fertile body, which she saw as being unfairly maligned by feminism, was now a precious resource. To embody this powerful force, she had only to keep on serving her husband and her race, simply by having children.

The paradox of adoration and exploitation in regard to white women's bodies reaches far back into the roots of white male supremacy. Political philosopher Angela Davis describes how, during the nineteenth century, the 'cult of motherhood was in full swing ... the perfect woman was the perfect mother. Her place was at home – never, of course, in the sphere of politics'.[15] The cult was, of course, highly racialised. According to Davis, 'white women were learning that, as mothers, they bore a very special responsibility in the struggle to safeguard white supremacy. After all, they were the "mothers of the race".' In contrast, she explains, 'judged by the evolving nineteenth century ideology of femininity, which emphasised women's roles as nurturing mothers and gentle companions and housekeepers for their husbands, Black women were practically anomalies'.[16]

Fast-forward seventy years from the end of slavery in the USA, and a similar dynamic was in play in Nazi Germany, where Aryan women were the focus of a nation/race-saving drive. Writing in a pamphlet in 1933, Paula Siber, acting head of the Association of German Women, explained how 'the highest calling of the National Socialist woman is not just to bear children, but consciously and out of total devotion to her role and duty as mother to raise children for *her people*'.[17] Like Stewart, Siber is calling for women to be wives with a purpose. This echoes Mussolini: biology is destiny, and a woman's destiny in the war is motherhood.

'It's this adoration you are being promised,' Darby explained. 'There's power in being adored and filling this role. It's also frankly easy because you are being told you are innately powerful. You don't have to do anything, you don't have to put yourself in uncomfortable situations or have conversations you don't like, you don't have to be engaged in politics, you don't have to be engaged in business, you just have to be exactly biologically what you are and fulfil that potential.'

It's clear how all of this fits into the fascist thought architecture. The far right hates feminism because it has destroyed the imagined world its followers feel they have lost: the fascist mythic past where men were superior and women were inferior. Further, the far right has to eradicate women's liberation because sexual and reproductive rights allow women freedom from male control, and freedom undermines fascism. Feminism is the enemy, because feminism has offered women a glimpse of freedom from patriarchal authority and male entitlement. Therefore, the far right needs to roll back women's liberation in order to restore the natural order and return to its fascist mythic past. It hopes to achieve this by telling women that the freedoms created by feminism are a lie, that women have lost out as a result of feminism, and that submitting to patriarchal authority is a woman's natural role.

The attack on feminism also allows the far right to achieve

a secondary aim in relation to women: to overturn gains made in protecting women and girls from gender-based violence. This aim came to light in the Trump administration's attack on violence-against-women laws, a stance that met the needs of his misogynist voters. Fascism designates women as male property. This means that, while individual members of the far right may not necessarily condone gender-based violence, they believe that it is a man's role to discipline and control women and children within the family unit (as well as to protect them). Feminism has sought to liberate women from such control, both through access to abortion and contraception, as well as through overturning laws that allow husbands to rape their wives and challenging male sexual entitlement to women's bodies.

The twisted messaging, though, presents this to women as an arrangement in their own interests, a way to ensure their health and happiness. As the messaging goes, men know what is best for women, who should submit to male authority if they want to be happy. This was Robertson's argument at the Patriotic Alternative conference: women must learn to submit and men must learn to dominate.

This is communicated to women via the trad wife community, which exhorts its members to be entirely pleasing and obedient to their husbands. The community rebrands domestic abuse as *discipline*, with women taught to accept physical, emotional and sexual violence as part of being a good wife. In being wholly submissive to your husband, the women are told, it is necessary to give up your right to consent and to respect his right to be violent towards you. An anonymous trad wife quoted in Julia Ebner's book *Going Dark*, gives tips to men about how to administer discipline to their partners. She explains:

Don't delay discipline any longer than is absolutely necessary. If you think she should be spanked for a sarcastic remark, it is infinitely more effective if you take her by the arm, and lead her to the bathroom, the bedroom, the garage, and administer the swats right then.[18]

Another woman posted that she was upset by her husband's violent behaviour. Rather than receiving support, she was quickly admonished and told 'in some more traditional relationships (but not all) the man disciplines the woman either physically (like spanking) or with things like writing lines or standing in the corner'.[19]

The prevalence of domestic abuse in far-right relationships was described to the *New Yorker* by a young woman calling herself Samantha.[20] She had been in a trad relationship with the head of the alt-right Identity Europa group, but Samantha had a job and has since left the movement. She described how, despite their relationship breaking down, he would not accept that she wanted to leave him. He refused to let her leave her apartment and threatened to doxx her (reveal publicly that she was part of a neo-Nazi movement).

Women in the subculture are encouraged to read Laura Doyle's *The Surrendered Wife* for tips on how to behave in a suitably submissive way. It's important to acknowledge that Doyle is not in any way associated with the far right, and her book is explicit that if a man is abusive towards his partner or children, or has issues with addiction, then she does not recommend 'surrender'. She is also at pains to point out that women who have experienced abuse should seek therapeutic support, and she encourages women to talk to their husbands about their trauma so they can move towards a healthy intimate life. But despite these sensible guidelines, it's clear why *The Surrendered Wife* has become something of a bible to women entering trad wife circles. Doyle advocates for strict gender roles within the household, extols the virtues of 'high gender contrast' and encourages couples to 'abandon the myth of equality.'[21]

This advice echoes Robertson's claims that a rejection of rigid and unequal gender roles is causing millennials to have less sex, and shows how far the trad wife subculture taps into the fascistic notion of a natural order. *Faux* evolutionary psychology is called upon to present traditional gender roles as natural, while gender equality is *unnatural*, a manufactured construct. Of course, there's a huge body of feminist anthropological work that demonstrates how little evidence exists for these so-called traditional gender roles – from historical matriarchal cultures to the obvious fact that women have always gone out to work. But for the far right, it's urgent to show that gender equality is a myth, so that inequality is accepted as natural. This positions feminism and women's liberation as something corrupt and perverse – reinforcing the satanic conspiracy theory that claims women's equality is devilish and unnatural.

Clearly, the trad wife subculture solves a major problem for the far right. It creates a space for women in a profoundly misogynistic movement, all while helping to achieve its anti-abortion, anti-feminist aims. Its hatred of feminism, fuelled by the fact that gender equality represents a loss of white male supremacy, positions the freedoms promised by women's liberation as harmful. Instead, its followers claim, women can find happiness by giving up their rights, giving in to patriarchal authority and devoting themselves to reproduction.

As described above, the far right deploys women representatives through its trad wives movement to win female supporters and thereby broaden its appeal. Likewise, more mainstream groups also need woman advocates to push forward their anti-abortion agenda. Traditionally they have put forward women such as the radical-right, anti-feminist activist Phyllis Schlafly – women who, in their twin sets and pearls, align closely to the trad wives model. These women see themselves as sacrificing their true desire to be a housewife in order to live in the public eye and fight for the traditional values of husband, hearth and nation; they claim to resent having to leave husband and children at home, but are compelled to do their duty to restore their subordinate place under patriarchal authority. These conservative women can be found in Schlafly's Eagle Forum, and in groups such as Concerned Women for America and the Independent Women's Forum. They have long been a successful force in bringing women to a cause that is antithetical to gender equality and their basic freedoms.

In recent years, however, the right has wooed a new set of female allies – women claiming to be gender-critical feminists who are ideologically opposed to trans rights. On the surface, this makes no sense. Feminism fights the male violence and patriarchal power that keep all women in a state of oppression and fear; it seeks to overthrow the gendered hierarchy that oppresses women, and supports the right to abortion and reproductive justice. It is pro-lesbian and challenges notions of compulsory heterosexuality. All these stances are anathema to a far and religious right that wants to ban abortion, remove protections against gender-based violence, and roll back LGBTIQ rights. But through their defence of sex-based rights for women, some self-proclaimed gender-critical feminists have found common cause with a religious right that wants to criminalise trans people and naturalise gender stereotypes as innate, fixed and biologically immutable.

The organisations that form part of the Council of National Policy network – such as ADF and Family Research Council – are financially and practically supporting anti-trans feminists in order to garner wider support for their own anti-women aims. As a result, some feminist groups and individuals have become a useful front for the radical and religious right, providing protective cover for the anti-abortion agenda and helping to deliver a new and unexpected support base. By getting into bed with the enemy, the anti-abortion movement can successfully deploy the Agenda Europe tactic of co-opting the language of its opponents and using it against them, in order to mainstream and achieve their aims. After all, the argument goes, how can organisations like ADF and Family Research Council be anti-women, when they are working with feminists who claim to defend women?

This sorry alliance began in 2016, when an unlikely name turned up in the list of funding recipients in Alliance Defending Freedom's tax form: the DC–based Women's Liberation Front (WoLF).[22] The radical feminist organisation had received a $15,000 donation from ADF for the purposes of 'general litigation'. The group, which claims to fight for women's rights and freedom of expression, is relatively small: it has fewer than 20,000 followers on Twitter and boasts of a campaign in which 10,400 women wrote to lawmakers. Its 2020 revenue was $263,901, the majority of which came from direct donations. In other words, WoLF might have remained on the margins, enjoying little cut-through – but through its alliance with radical and religious-right organisations, it has developed an outsized influence that has seen its members hosted on mainstream right-wing news channels such as Fox, testifying before Congress and enjoying a global reach through its campaigning in the UK and South Korea.

It would take a whole other book to explain the origins and intricacies of the row over trans rights that erupted among feminists in the mid-2010s. Put very, *very* simply, it started with discussions around the right for trans and non-binary people to self-identify as the gender of their choice without having to go through a painful, often costly, and sometimes cruel medical process to confirm their gender identity legally. The row evolved into the slogan 'sex not gender' – meaning that gender identity should be excluded from laws protecting women's sex-based rights.

In the UK, the issue was put under the spotlight when the Conservative Party announced a consultation to reform the Gender Recognition Act. The 2004 legislation stated that a trans person must jump through various medical hoops and psychological assessments to confirm their gender identity after a medical transition. It was a progressive piece of legislation when introduced (remember, only a year before Labour had repealed a law that banned the 'promotion' of LGBT lifestyles in schools), but by the late 2010s it was clunky, no longer fit for purpose, and caused unnecessary distress to trans people.

In the US, the row was prompted by a lawsuit filed by a young trans man named Gavin Grimm, who had sued his school arguing it was discriminatory that he was expected to use an 'alternative private' bathroom rather than simply using the boys' bathroom. This brings us back to that $15,000 donation.

In response to Grimm's suit, the US Departments of Education and Justice wrote a 'dear colleague' letter to schools, updating them on how to interpret the law designed to protect students from discrimination on the basis of sex in American schools in order to best support trans students. The letter asked that 'departments treat a student's gender identity as the student's sex for purposes ... This means that a school must not treat a transgender student differently from the way it treats other students of the same gender identity.'[23] Schools were told that gender identity should be treated as – and therefore protected as – sex in order to protect them from discrimination, so Grimm should be allowed to use the boys' bathroom and trans girls to use the girls'. WoLF filed a suit against the US federal government in response.

WoLF's objection to the letter is that it believes replacing sex-based protections with gender identity risks erasing rights and protections for women and girls, putting them at risk of harm. This is not, however, the concern that motivates the religious and far-right allies of these feminist groups. Rather, they are motivated by the desire to do away with the idea that gender is a construct, and that gender stereotypes are not innate, proposing instead that women and men should stick to their so-called natural roles in a natural order where women are inferior and men have authority.

WoLF's suit was in support of a New Mexico student concerned the letter would lead to girls having to share bathrooms with students who are biologically male. An email to the group's members called the ADF donation 'pretty darn phenomenal'. At the same time, WoLF also collaborated with the Christian-right group Family Policy Alliance (FPA) in a countersuit against Grimm's delayed suit. Explaining the alliance, FPA's director of policy Autumn Leva asked, 'How wrong does something have to be for a Christian family group, and a radical feminist group, to take their argument together to the Supreme Court?'

Ultimately the Education Department's letter to schools was rescinded under Trump as part of his administration's raft of attacks on women's and LGBTIQ rights. But WoLF's collaboration with the religious right did not stop there, including working with Family Policy Alliance and the CNP-linked, radical-right think tank Heritage Foundation to launch an anti-trans 'Gender Resource Guide' designed to 'respond to the unscientific and dangerous craze of "gender affirmation therapy"'.[24]

It's important to note here that radical feminist opposition and support for trans rights sits across a spectrum. The majority of feminists agree that trans people should be able to live and identify as they choose, free from violence and discrimination, with access to healthcare, work and all other human rights. Some gender-critical feminists have raised concerns, however, that allowing people to define their own gender could create a loophole for abusive men to identify as a woman in order to access female-only spaces, such as prisons and refuges. These are women who otherwise support trans people's right to identify how they choose but believe there is a risk of conflicting rights when it comes to protecting female-only spaces, women's representation in sport or all-female political shortlists. Their concerns about men exploiting the ability to self-identify aren't just unfounded fears – there have been a couple of worrying cases where violent individuals have identified as trans in order to be housed, for example, in a women's prison where they have sexually assaulted vulnerable women. The fact that men felt able to exploit such a loophole demonstrated how critical it is to take care when introducing any policy change. Careful consideration was required to ensure all women, including trans women, as well as trans men and non-binary people, were equally protected from male violence and exploitation, while easing the burden of the transition process at the same time.

It's also important to note that many gender-critical feminists in the UK have condemned alliances with far-right groups. The feminist campaigner Julie Bindel, who has worked for decades to support women who have been incarcerated after killing their abusers, 'despises their tactics', while the organisation Women's Place UK is categoric that the 'far right is not welcome here'.

Unfortunately, at the far end of the spectrum there are women who may or may not identify as feminists and who simply engage in transphobic rhetoric – deliberately misgendering individuals, claiming that trans women are men in dresses, accusing trans women of autogynephilia, and saying they are predatory.

In the last few years, the row has evolved beyond conversations about self-identity versus single-sex spaces, to the very meaning of what it is to be a woman. This leads to fights erupting over inclusive language, gender stereotypes, the definition of biological sex, the difference between sex and gender, and the importance of protecting sex-based rights and gender identity respectively.

It's this aspect which has led to some of the nastier opposition to trans rights voiced by those calling themselves feminists, who are seemingly willing to ignore the connections between women's oppression, reproductive capability (biological sex) and gender stereotypes (women should be pinned to reproduction because that's our natural role). In some corners, the row over protecting women's sex-based rights has evolved to meet a far-right imperative: that women's biology is destiny, and that destiny is reproductive labour. As soon as self-proclaimed radical feminist groups such as WoLF started to argue that men could not transition to be women and vice versa – and that to protect gender identity was to erase sex-based rights – the far and religious right were able to jump right in and agree, gaining feminist cover for their ideas. This is because the right absolutely does not want a world where gender is no longer fixed to biological sex, or where women and men can reject gendered stereotypes. They want to maintain the lie that gendered stereotypes are rooted in biology – and therefore that women's inferiority to men is part of the natural order.

The more I looked into the extremist allies backing some gender-critical feminists, the more convinced I became that there is no defence for feminists who choose to work with the anti-abortion, anti-LGBTIQ right. It is unacceptable to collaborate with those who seek to undermine women's human rights when it comes to sex, reproduction, and even protections against rape and domestic abuse. WoLF has attempted to defend its decision to work with organisations opposed to abortion by saying it's an 'effective tactic', that women feel abandoned by 'the Left' and 'conservative women are women'. Hands Across the Aisle – a group set up by radical feminists and a right-wing activist who compared abortion to the Holocaust – have also defended the strange alliance, with cofounder Miriam Ben-Shalom posting on Facebook that working with Conservative women was an opportunity to 'demystify' lesbians to the far right, and that her Conservative sisters have never 'called me names, threatened me, or otherwise been nasty'. But what about the nastiness of comparing abortions to the Holocaust? What about the threats to women's human rights? What about the name-calling against LGBTIQ people from men like the Family Research Council's Tony Perkins, who said in a 2011 speech that LGBTIQ people are 'intolerant, they're hateful, vile, they're spiteful ... To me, that is the height of hatred, to be silent when we know there are individuals that are engaged in activity, behavior, and an agenda that will destroy them and our nation.'[25]

All of this is much, much nastier.

Some gender-critical feminists who don't go so far to defend the alliances have expressed either genuine or feigned surprise that 'Christian Conservative' groups are working with women on this issue.[26] Too many have failed to ask *why*. Well, I have bothered to ask why, and to me the answer is clear: the right's endorsement of 'sex not gender' all links back to its theory of the Great Replacement, the threat that women's bodily autonomy poses to white male supremacy, and the need to assert control via exploiting reproductive labour in order to treat women as wombs of the nation.

When ADF, the Family Research Council, the DeVos family, Concerned Women for America and other conservatives promote men being male and women being female, their goal is to naturalise gendered stereotypes about men's and women's behaviour – and, more crucially, their *status*: they want to naturalise men's supremacy and women's inferiority. If women's perceived inferiority to men is a gender stereotype and *not* a biological fact, then it can be changed. The foundation of the far-right theory crumbles, along with any claim for (white) male supremacy.

Women's oppression is historically rooted in biology: women experience oppression as a class because of our perceived reproductive capability and the need of patriarchal capitalism to exploit women's reproductive labour and entrench nationalist, male power. Abortion bans and restrictions enable that exploitation of women's perceived or actual reproductive capability. This oppression is justified by enforcing gender stereotypes, for example, that women are *naturally* more caring and nurturing than men and therefore *better* at being in the domestic space raising children. Throw in a bit of evolutionary psychology and you have an ideological framework to explain away women's subordinate role to men. That same fascistic notion of nature fixes female inferiority to men (and black people to white people, etc.).

The existing gender paradigm that proposes female inferiority and male superiority is deeply threatened by feminists and LGBTIQ people who say biology isn't destiny and you can express your gender identity however you want, whatever reproductive organs you were born with. This approach demands that we recognise women's inferiority as a social and political fiction rather than as a scientific fact. Recognising that it is gender, not sex, that dictates women's subordinate status in the patriarchal hierarchy is to recognise that humans have the potential to change society to be more equal – and it allows society to change human nature too.

This is not to claim that the right's attacks on trans people are simply a diversion from its deeper goal of attacking women in general; nor is it to distract attention from the horrific suffering and harm the LGBTIQ community endures at the hands of the far and religious right, which is clearly motivated by hatred or disgust of LGBTIQ people. But the stem of that hatred is shared: LGBTIQ people challenge heteronormative male supremacy and male power, just as reproductive rights do. The far right wants to retreat to a fascistic mythic past where LGBTIQ people don't have the right to exist – its anti-humanism informs its hatred and disgust. The attacks on trans rights are acted out by eroding legal protections based on gender, which in turn dovetails with the attack on reproductive and wider sexual rights.

To see how far the right has gone with this issue, just look at what Alliance Defending Freedom wrote about the bill that led to Texas banning abortion after six weeks. It mocks how a subcommittee titled 'Protecting Roe: Why We Need the Women's Health Protection Act' referred in a meeting to a 'person who is pregnant'. ADF wrote how 'despite claiming to be a Bill that protects women's health, the WHPA includes gender-neutral language when referring to women ... How can one claim to protect women while refusing to acknowledge that women exist as a category?'[27] Of course, women comprise the category whose rights ADF helped to cruelly rip to shreds. But hey, at least they know what a woman is! How else would they know who isn't deserving of human rights?

WoLF's aims clearly do not always tally with the aims of its far-right allies. But by holding hands across the aisle they are providing cover for the right to attack women's and LGBTIQ rights, helping win them support across a new, left-leaning and feminist coalition. Their support allows for ADF to justify its attack on women's rights. They are fulfilling the role, too, of what feminist writer Ariel Levy described as the 'the loophole woman'. 'It can be fun to feel exceptional – to be the loophole woman, to have the whole power thing, to be an honorary man,' Levy wrote in 2006. 'But if you are the exception that proves the rule, and the rule is that women are inferior, you haven't made any progress.'[28]

In the case of WoLF and its feminist colleagues, the analogy still works. You can share a platform with the right. You can nod along to their hate. But ultimately, you will always and only ever be a woman to the men who inhabit its leadership – and as such you will always be (innately) inferior. They will use you and they will always despise you. They will come for your rights too, in the end.

5

The Money: Who Is Funding
The Anti-Abortion Right?

So far, we have established the pipeline through which fascistic ideas about women's bodies travel from the extremist fringes to mainstream governments – with the far right on the streets and in the online forums, the legal networks in their suits, and the politicians in the voting lobby. Fascist ideology, fuelled by racist conspiracy theories, raises fears of a white genocide, and argues that it must be prevented through a race war, with white women's role being to make white babies. Networks such as Agenda Europe and the Council for National Policy put a respectable gloss on fascistic notions of the natural order and propose strategies, tactics and networked support to achieve anti-abortion aims. These strategies and tactics are then put into action by organisations including CitizenGO and Alliance Defending Freedom, which mainstream opposition to abortion through legal cases, petitions, grassroots campaigning and lobbying – as well as by putting their men in positions of power and influence in international bodies, such as the United Nations and Parliamentary Assembly Council of Europe (PACE). From here, they can pressure mainstream governments and politicians to enact their agenda. But where does all the money for these organisations, public-facing campaigns, expensive legal cases, and on-the-street activism come from?

The funding stream for the anti-abortion right, it turns out, is a pipeline of its own, moving from wealthy foundations to on-the-street campaigners. We will look at three pots of spending: European foundations and organisations spending money on anti-gender campaigns within the region; funding from Russia into Europe; and funding from the United States. You'll meet individuals who have been indicted by the FBI; Conservative Party donors who take their riches and anti-rights agenda to the UK government; US politicians; European aristocrats hoping to rebuild a fascist mythic past where they can reign supreme; and Russian oligarchs who fund anti-rights movements in order to disrupt post-war European unity and amplify Russian influence.

Tracking the funding of anti-rights movements is, for an investigative journalist like me, interesting in and of itself: following traces of dark money and unearthing surprising names is always a fascinating exercise. But more importantly, understanding how the anti-abortion agenda is funded helps to make the case that this is a highly organised movement: far from being a motley crew of fringe groups, it is an expertly networked and strategically competent operation. It also helps us to clarify how far-right attitudes towards abortion are going mainstream. Wealthy people don't like to waste their money (although the questionable decor choices of oligarchs and billionaires may suggest otherwise). That they are choosing to invest in a global movement to roll back human rights tells us something important: far-right ideology has brought together the elite and the mob, with business billionaires and aging aristocrats offering financial backing to the ideas expressed by conspiracists on the dark web.

The first stop on our adventure is Europe, where I live.

There has been a tendency when looking at anti-gender funding to position Europe as a put-upon victim of malign forces in the US and Russia. This is wholly inaccurate. When it comes to raising money to ban abortion, Europe is doing quite well on its own, thank you very much! As founder and director of the European Parliamentary Forum for Sexual and Reproductive Rights Neil Datta told me, 'The anti-gender movement is very much a domestic phenomenon. Americans

have a distinct role. But it's not just a foreign intrusion on inno-
cent Europeans who would otherwise be nicely progressive.'[1]

Out of $702 million spent by fifty-four organisations on
anti-gender movements between 2009 and 2018, a total of
$437 million originated within Europe, according to research
carried out by Datta.[2] Those funders include religious foundations, economic elites such as wealthy businesspeople, and
foundations established by aristocrats. Because this is Europe,
those aristocrats descend from the families who once ruled the
region – from the Habsburg dynasty to the descendants of the
German Kaiser. They meet at Agenda Europe summits and at
the annual World Congress of Families; they have offices within
the political decision-making centres of the region such as Brussels and Geneva; and they fund anti-gender political parties,
activists, public-facing campaigns and legal cases.

As described in the preceding chapters, at the heart of
Europe's anti-gender movement is CitizenGO, an organisation
that is networked with US, Latin American and African organisations as well as within Europe. Understanding the financial
backers of CitizenGO can help us map the money men and
women in the region, due to the campaigning organisation's
connections to Agenda Europe, Spain's far-right Vox party, the
One of Us Initiative, and influential anti-gender actors such
as Brian Brown and Alexey Komov at the World Congress of
Families.

Combined with Hazte Oír, CitizenGO spent a total of $32.7
million on its anti-gender activism in Europe between 2009
and 2018.[3] Its publicity claims that it is 'completely financed
by small online donations arranged by thousands of citizens
from all over the world'. In 2021 it raised $4.9 million from
donors – nearly double its 2019 revenue of $2.7 million.

Founder Ignacio Arsuaga has always said neither Hazte
Oír nor CitizenGO get funding from US groups as '99% of
HazteOír's €1.9 million ($2.5 million) annual budget comes
from donations from Spanish citizens. CitizenGO has been

raising €30,000 to €40,000 (roughly $40,000 to $55,000) each month from the 1.2 million members it's signed up worldwide since its October launch.'[4] This insistence from CitizenGO that it is funded by the grass roots is crucial to its campaigning strategy, and to our understanding of how far-right objections to abortion move into the mainstream. First, the idea that the anti-abortion movement is funded by €5 gifts from humble supporters taps into the Agenda Europe strategy of positioning the anti-gender movement as David to Abortion Industry TM's Goliath – with the latter presented as a well-funded satanic behemoth set to crush the wishes of its good, God-fearing opponents. Second, by pointing to thousands if not millions of small individual donations, CitizenGO can claim to represent the silent majority, arguing that opposition to abortion and LGBTIQ rights is the mainstream view being ignored by pro-abortion elites in the European Union and/or national governments.

CitizenGO also, however, benefits from elite donations. While it is true that it receives many individual gifts from the public, it has also been supported by major donations from wealthy and influential businesspeople. A leaked document revealed that Eulen's David Álvarez donated €20,000, while Isidoro Álvarez, founder of El Corte Inglés, and businesswoman Esther Koplowitz gave €10,000 each.[5] Data collected by Neil Datta revealed how Juan-Miguel Villar Mir, a member of the fifth-wealthiest family in Spain, is a backer; he also lists José Luis Bonet Ferrer, from the family behind the Cava brand Freixenet.[6]

What's more, far from growing from the grass roots, research published by Neil Datta in a report titled *Tip of the Iceberg* exposed how CitizenGO raised seed money worth up to $600,000 from 'generous entrepreneurs and citizens' support'.

'To set up the technological infrastructure to have CitizenGO, that took a certain amount of money to pay for that,' Datta explained during our chat. 'You need first the technological infrastructure to start generating these petitions and then you can start hoovering in the money.'

In 2018, the French television channel Arte revealed how CitizenGO had launched a fundraising drive to target possible donors. Arsuaga sent out a business plan outlining his aims:

CitizenGO will produce a social benefit that we trust will impact on human history. Abortionists, the homosexual lobby, radical secularists, and champions of relativism will find themselves behind CitizenGO's containment wall. The platform will not only denounce the manoeuvres against freedom, but will also mobilise public opinion in nations around the world, and will be able to influence the decisions of politicians and businessmen.[7]

'You take a look at who he sent those letters to ... and then you compare that with the board membership,' Datta told me. 'There's a correspondence – Brian Brown, Luca Volontè. He had also written to a bunch of people in the Holy See, state secretaries for the Vatican. We know that one of the people on the board called Dr. Garcia Jones happens to be the Human Rights adviser to the Holy See to the Organization of American States. So it looks like he got lucky with almost every donor he wrote to, to be supportive in some way.'

Brian Brown is a crucial link in the anti-gender chain. A board member of CitizenGO, he's best known in the US for setting up the National Campaign for Marriage, which fought equal marriage rights for same-sex couples. He's also the president of the World Congress of Families – an annual event that provides networking opportunities for anti-abortion extremists, their mainstream peers and leading politicians, and he has attended Agenda Europe summits.[8] In 2021, he travelled to Georgia (the country, not the US state) to support far-right actors intent on rolling back LGBTIQ rights. Speaking alongside the ultra-nationalist politician Levan Vasadze, Brown said that LGBTIQ activism will 'undermine your freedom ... undermine your church [and] will undermine your country'.

He also engaged in antisemitic conspiracy theories against the billionaire philanthropist George Soros, claiming that 'liberals' are trying 'to use their power and money and wealth to tell countries around the world that they must do what liberalism says they must do'.[9] His speech was given a week before Georgia's beleaguered Pride march, which had been cancelled two years earlier due to security concerns. The 2021 Pride march never went ahead either. What should have been a day for celebration descended into terrifying scenes of street violence, as anti-gender protesters gathered on the streets of Tbilisi to harass, threaten and physically attack the LGBTIQ community.

The violence started early. Far-right and anti-gender protesters arrived at the Tbilisi Pride office, smashing windows, plant pots and shouting homophobic abuse. From there, they moved to the offices of liberal activist group the Shame Movement, wreaking destruction as they went. As the day continued, so did the violence. It was still only early afternoon when one protester drove a scooter into a crowd of journalists in broad daylight. By the end of the day, fifty-three journalists had been injured along with two civilians – including a Polish tourist the mob accused of being gay.

The Georgian Orthodox Church was the primary organiser of the violent counterprotest, although its ruling patriarchate body asked for protestors to remain peaceful. In one of the day's most shocking scenes, an Orthodox priest was photographed holding a journalist in a headlock. The incumbent of the patriarchal throne, Reverend Shio Mujiri, warned the LGBTIQ community that 'no matter how many times there is an attempt to hold such an event, our nation will always unite against it'.[10]

The scenes at Tbilisi Pride are the real-world consequences of the hate peddled by men such as Brown. The street violence and intimidation show us that the anti-gender movement is not working in hypotheticals or with abstract concepts; they aren't debating rights in their secretive summits as some kind of thought exercise. Rather, they are using their money and power to sow division and foster hatred. That, in turn, leads to people bloodied and beaten on city streets, to women dying in hospital beds having been refused treatment, and to women and girls forced to endure violence and degradation in the patriarchal family home.

That's why it's so important for us to understand how the influence of Brown and his allies works – including how they use their wealth to spread their agenda across Europe. Brown's backing of CitizenGO goes beyond board membership. A report by *openDemocracy* found that CitizenGo gets advice 'every couple of months or so' from a 'senior expert' in fundraising and technology who is 'paid by Brian Brown'. The expert was Darian Rafie, Brown's partner at an American organisation called ActRight which self-defines as a 'clearing-house for conservative action', and which helps conservative campaigns out with advice on how to do petitions and email lobbying.[11] Along with Rafie's support, *openDemocracy* reported that it 'understands paid for a CitizenGO staff member in 2013, a claim that Rafie did not deny in email comments'. Research by Neil Datta revealed how CitizenGO had a contract with ActRight regarding financial support. It states, 'ActRight will support CitizenGO (member of ActRight Global) with an annual amount of 50K US dollars, via a direct contribution.' The contract also confirms that 'Brian Brown will seat [*sic*] on the CitizenGO board of trustees.'[12]

Brown's involvement tells us something significant about how money operates in the anti-gender movement. It is international, it is networked and it relies on global wealth to carry its extremist ideology about women's bodies into the mainstream.

Much of the anti-gender activism in Europe is paid for by individual foundations, often linked to mainstream politicians, wealthy business leaders, or the scions of Europe's old aristocracy – at least some of whom have historic links to the Nazi, fascist and Falangist regimes of the twentieth century.

While anyone whose grandparents or great-grandparents lived in Europe during this period will have a connection to the Second World War, Datta explained to me that a lot of these influential families in the modern anti-gender movement 'played very dodgy roles in the Second World War, and also during the illiberal regimes of the Mediterranean countries'.

Italy's Fondazione Vita Nova, the Spanish Fundació Pro Vida de Catalunya, and the Fundación Valores y Sociedad (run by former People's Party politician Jaime Mayor Oreja) all helped to raise €150,000, for example, to fund the One of Us campaign.[13] As described above, One of Us sought to undermine pro-abortion, pro-LGBTIQ and pro–sex education initiatives in the European Union, and was cited as a model of successful campaigning by Agenda Europe. The movement began life as a million-signature petition, before becoming an NGO in its own right in 2014 and becoming entangled with France's Fondation Jérôme Lejeune, which took on an administrating leadership role. The foundation has spent $120.2 million on anti-gender activism between 2009 and 2018, including litigation and public campaigns. It recently opened offices in Argentina and the USA, and was linked to the homophobic La Manif pour tous organisation in France. Another major promoter of the One of Us campaign was Germany's Foundation Yes to Life, set up by the late Countess of Westphalia – one of many examples of Europe's old aristocracy pouring their ancestral wealth to attempts to roll back women's and LGBTIQ people's rights. In total, the financial weight of One of Us between 2009 and 2018 was $31.5 million.[14]

The Countess of Westphalia was not the only German aristocrat funding anti-gender activism. Both The Foundation for Family Values (Stiftung für Familienwerte) and the European Family Foundation have old-money links. The latter was established by Count Albrecht Graf von Brandenstein-Zeppelin, while the Foundation for Family Values is funded by a range of aristocratic Germans.[15] Another German aristocrat, Princess

Gloria von Thurn und Taxis, donated to the World Congress of Families, and has supported Trump's far-right former adviser Steve Bannon with his (failed) European projects.[16]

That European nobility want to spend their ancestral fortunes on campaigns to undermine women's reproductive and sexual freedoms is no surprise: this is a demographic that wants to restore a natural order rooted in the fascist mythic past, when the old families reigned supreme. After all, the wealthy benefactors of the anti-gender movement are those whose ancestors once ruled Europe – who had vast influence over millions of people's lives and who saw their land and wealth as their God-given right. Even when aristocratic influence was waning after the First World War, the old aristocracy was partly protected by the fascist, Nazi and Falangist regimes. It doesn't take a genius to understand why landed gentry would side with the far right against socialist and communist movements sweeping across Europe after the First World War. These were movements that wanted to end the exploitation of labour and property rights that enriched the aristocratic class. Further, the aristocrats' time in the sun was an era of rampant colonialism and unchallenged white supremacism. Aristocratic families made their wealth from the exploitation of others; they were told their right to do so came from God; and during their heyday white male supremacist rule went unquestioned. Those who did question this inequality suffered the consequences.

'You have these foundations,' Datta told me. 'And then they're all married to each other. They then fund different things. What it means is that we have an ecosystem in Europe, which is very similar to what Jane Mayer described in the United States with her book *Dark Money*. So we're not more virtuous than the Americans, we have these people.'

This desire to create a fascist mythic past is best illustrated by the Oldenburg dynasty and the Tradition, Family and Property (TFP) organisation – a global anti-rights initiative that seeks to build alliances and share tactics to bolster the far right, including political parties. Duke Paul of Oldenburg is TFP's representative to the European Union and heads up the Brussels Bureau of its Pro Europa Christiana federation. This umbrella group's 'goal is to defend the Christian roots of Europe and particularly what Pope Benedict XVI called the "non-negotiable values," that is, the right to life from conception to natural death, the sacred character of the family founded on marriage (between one man and one woman) and the right of parents to raise their children without undue interference from the State'. Originally a Catholic sect that emerged in Brazil, its influence 'withered away from Latin America', and now 'TFP is an active European network with positions against sexual and reproductive rights (SRR) among its priorities'.[17]

The organisation's purpose is in the name – it does what it says on the tin. It wants to defend tradition, as defined by the historical primacy of the Catholic Church over the secular state; it also opposes progressive movements within the Church. It's commitment to family means the married heterosexual unit as per the far-right ideal of the natural order and patriarchal authority in the home. Its approach to property involves defending 'inherited wealth and privileges; it opposes the notion of socio-economic equality, which it considers dangerously Communist'.[18] Importantly for our understanding of the aristocracy's attraction to the fascist mythic past, it calls for the return of outdated aristocratic structures and analogous traditional elites. For this reason, it counts among its backers Austria's baronial Tschugguel family, Italy's Marquis Coda Nunziante, the imperial family of Brazil, and the Oldenburgs themselves, according to Datta's research.[19]

Having spread across Latin America in the 1960s, TFP appeared in Europe in the 1970s, but it was not until the twenty-first century that the organisation really took hold in the region. In 2008 it built offices in Brussels, where Duke Paul of Oldenburg is based. The duke explained in a 2012 interview how TFP supports 'the formation of conservative coalition networks in several areas: right to life, family, religious values etc ... Since our center is spacious, we are facilitating meetings and gatherings of leaders and grassroots to forge common strategies and create some synergy.'[20]

In that same 2012 interview, Duke Paul condemned abortion and equal marriage. He shared quotes from a lecture hosted by his organisation and given by European MP Magdi Cristiano Allam, who had said, 'while moderate Muslims do exist, as a religion Islam is always radical'; and warned that if European leaders do not change their attitude, Eurabia – Islamic Europe – will very soon become a reality.[21] Duke Paul also claimed that 'the EU provides legal cover for the feminist and homosexual lobbies' agendas', and praised CitizenGO's Ignacio Arsuaga. This is unsurprising in light of Duke Paul's background: his cousin Beatrix von Storch is the deputy leader of the German far-right AfD party, and highly influential in the social conservative movements in the country; her maternal grandfather was the finance minister in the Nazi regime.

Like CitizenGO and Hazte Oír, TFP runs social mobilisations to attack abortion and LGBTIQ rights. It develops policy and legislative campaigns that seek to undermine left-wing political parties and governments – as well as directly influence national laws. Finally, as with Agenda Europe, it seeks to infiltrate decision-making spaces, including in nation-state parliaments. The fact that TFP aims to restore the aristocracy in Europe, and therefore gets funding from the nobility to make its conspiracist, anti-abortion agenda a political reality, demonstrates how fascistic notions of the mythic past and the natural order drive elite opposition to reproductive and sexual rights that then reach into the mainstream.

Its shadowy nature means Agenda Europe's funding sources are difficult to trace. The make-up of programmes and the participants in Agenda Europe's annual summit can provide some clues, however, as some participants appear to be invited because of their connections to potential donors.

Datta's research uncovered, for example, how Vicente Segu attended Agenda Europe's 2013 London summit. Segu helps to manage the fortune of Mexican billionaire Patrick Slim Domit's fortune, who is a key funder of anti-gender activism. Representing the aristocrats at the 2013 London summit were Archduke Imre and his wife, Archduchess Kathleen, scions of the Habsburg-Lorraine dynasty who once ruled Europe and now extend their patronage to a range of anti-rights initiatives. Also present was Oliver Hylton, asset manager to UK Conservative donor Sir Michael Hintze, an Australian banker who was knighted by former prime minister David Cameron; Hintze has also donated directly to former prime minister Boris Johnson, who added him to his resignation honours list after he left Downing Street, is close to anti-abortion Conservative MP Liam Fox and connected to a climate change–denying think tank. Luca Volontè, whose Novae Terrae Foundation is a big funder of anti-gender projects, attended the 2014 summit. Austria's manufacturing Turnauer family, who are linked to the far-right Freedom Party of Austria, has also been identified by Datta as being linked to Agenda Europe.[22] Another source of support is in-kind funding – for example from CitizenGO's Arsuaga, who is crucial to Agenda Europe's operations. Arsuaga brings expertise on crowdfunding and digital campaigns, with Ellen Rivera describing his and Hazter Oír's role in Agenda Europe as 'implementing Agenda Europe directives locally'.[23]

While the majority of anti-gender funding comes from private wealth, there are examples of anti-gender organisations receiving state support, too. Spain is particularly guilty of state-sponsored anti-abortion disinformation delivered by crisis pregnancy centres. The REDMADRE network offers crisis pregnancy services to women, warning them that abortion leads to serious consequences, and women who have terminations endure 'torturous journeys'. It received almost €1.2 million from the Spanish government and local public bodies between 2014 and 2018. Other anti-abortion groups in receipt of Spanish public funds include the Pro-Life Federation, which tells women not to 'make a hasty decision ... calm down'. The federation represents thirty-four organisations, ten of which are listed in Spain's national subsidy advertising system, receiving €182,000 between 2014 and 2018.[24]

Malta, where abortion is illegal, is another nation where state money funds crisis pregnancy services and disinformation. In July 2020, the Maltese government gave a grant worth €130,000 to the Life Network to support its counselling.[25] The Life Network shares disinformation about reproductive health and was one of a network of anti-abortion groups to claim falsely that the morning after pill destroys a fertilised egg and therefore constitutes an abortion.[26] In Slovakia, where abortion is legal but under constant attack by far and religious-right politicians, the Ministry of Labour, Social Affairs and Family provides state subsidies to anti-abortion organisations such as Ano Pre Zivot, Forum Zivota and Alexis.[27] The groups all provide abortion counselling in a country where women must undergo mandatory counselling before accessing an abortion. This means that these organisations are not only getting state money to spread their agenda, they are also capitalising on laws that restrict access to abortion.

European Union funding is also benefiting anti-abortion actors in Slovakia: Forum Zivota receives money from both the European Social Fund and the European Regional Development Fund for its crisis pregnancy centres.[28] Even the UK is not immune: the charity Life received £250,000 from the so-called 'tampon tax' – money raised from VAT charged on period products that the UK government then awarded to charities working on women's issues. As mentioned in the previous chapter, Life has shared disinformation about the health impacts of abortion; the organisation was prohibited from spending the grant money on publicity or on its controversial pregnancy counselling and education services.

That some crisis pregnancy services operate within clinical settings raises additional questions about funding and whether they are in receipt of money from national healthcare budgets. When anti-abortion actors are supported by the state or by European Union funds, their messaging and aims have become mainstream. It's one thing for extremists with neo-Nazi links to fund activism that attacks human rights – but when the state is doing so, it sends a clear message that anti-abortion propaganda is acceptable, that spreading this ideology should be funded by taxpayers and that disinformation should be treated as equal to legitimate healthcare.

The money fuelling Europe's anti-gender activism challenges the stereotype that money for anti-gender activism in Europe comes from outside the region. Instead, it is a rich, networked movement bankrolled by local business elites, US activists and a regional aristocracy that want to reinstate aristocratic power.

All this shows how the pipeline from extremism to the mainstream is paid for, and why: wealthy people don't invest in causes they don't support. At the same time, the success of the anti-abortion movement in normalising its agenda allows it to benefit from taxpayer funding to push its harmful aims, showing once again how far-right ideology about women's bodies has become the mainstream.

While it is true that Europe is doing a good job of funding its own anti-gender movement, significant amounts of dark money from the Russian Federation are also playing a role in undermining abortion rights in the region.

At least $186.7 million of funding came into Europe from Russian oligarchs between 2009 and 2018.[29] This figure is a minimum, because it is difficult to track just how much money is flowing out of the Russian Federation and into Europe's far-right and anti-gender activism. Some of the money is simply too dark to trace – funds channelled through the state, for example, or sent via laundromats (financial vehicles set up by a bank or a financial services company to help clients launder money, hide ownership, evade taxes or currency restrictions and even to embezzle or move money off shore) – while the sanctions imposed on Russia since 2014 have created additional challenges in tracking its financial influence.

As with funders within Europe, Russian donors to anti-gender movements share far-right and fascistic ideas about women's bodies and LGBTIQ rights; they are driven by a desire to restore a fictional natural order and return to a fascist mythic past. Reproductive and sexual rights are often articulated as an attack on Mother Russia: the fascist mythic past Putin and his anti-gender allies wish to resuscitate dates from the tsarist period of imperial power and patriarchal authority over the family (the Bolshevik revolution legalised abortion and made divorce easier to obtain, and its criminal code did not include a law against homosexuality – much of this was reversed under Stalin).

Russian influence in Europe has another goal: to sow discord and instability in fragile and emerging democracies, using abortion and LGBTIQ rights as a wedge issue. This is especially true in former communist countries where there is a growing split between young, city residents who consider themselves European and progressive and older, anti-EU, rural populations who are turning east. Russia is waging a culture war against the West, using disinformation to foment division and unrest. For this reason, Russian money also tends to find its way to anti-European, anti-gender politicians – from Trump to Salvini to Le Pen – attempting to weaken European solidarity and influence.

I'm writing this as Russian forces invade Ukraine, after months of rising tensions. Ukrainian men and women are on the streets defending their cities; families are desperately trying to get on trains, buses and into cars to escape over the border; babies are being born in makeshift shelters; and both Ukrainian and Russian fighters are dying in battle. On day two of the invasion, I investigated the far-right reaction to the invasion across Europe and found what I had expected: that the far right were supporting Putin over the Ukrainians, and praising his anti-LGBTIQ, anti-women's rights stance. Just as the US Red Pillers saw Trump as the alpha male set to win the war on men, the European far right admires Putin because he has banned what they consider to be gay propaganda, and has effectively decriminalised domestic abuse. He's creating the fascist mythic past they desire with his backlash against reproductive and sexual rights – and his military aggression maintains the desired state of constant war.

The Russian Federation uses anti-gender actors as a way to exert power across the region, and as pawns in its war of influence against the West. No surprise, then, that one of the two major oligarchs responsible for most of Russia's anti-gender funding in Europe is Konstantin Malofeyev, the bearded billionaire considered by US intelligence to be President Putin's right arm for operations of political interference in Europe. He was indicted by the FBI following Russia's invasion of Ukraine.

Malofeyev presides over a vast disinformation empire that includes charitable foundations, TV channels and think tanks. He's also closely connected to the Russian Orthodox Church and the Russian duma, and to Putin himself. His far-right TV channel Tsargrad TV employed Aleksandr Dugin, the far-right philosopher known as Putin's Rasputin, who believes that modernity should be reversed and Russia should rebuild its Tsarist Empire, including by invading Ukraine. The channel attracted extremist and conspiracy theorist Alex Jones.

Malofeyev's network also includes the Katehon think tank, the International Agency for Sovereign Development (IASD), the Double-Headed Eagle Society, the Nobles Society and the St Basil the Great Charitable Foundation. Through these entities, Malofeyev seeks to influence and fund the US Christian Right and far-right political actors and parties across Europe, as well as Agenda Europe, CitizenGO and the World Congress of

Families – and he is linked to all these organisations via Alexey Komov, his employee at the St Basil the Great Charitable Foundation. Komov, as outlined in previous chapters, was formerly a CitizenGO board member, Agenda Europe summit attendee, Russia's representative at the World Congress of Families and Malofeyev's man in Europe.

As well as funding foundations and networks, Malofeyev has been linked to financial support for far-right political parties across Europe, including the far-right Rassemblement National in France.[30] In the 2014 European elections, two French MEPs – one who had attended the World Congress of Families and the other linked to extremist Catholic group Opus Dei – negotiated Russian loans for the party worth €11 million. Malofeyev then helped Jean-Marie Le Pen channel the loan into his election campaign; Le Pen was leader of France's Front National at the time; now rebranded as Rassemblement National, the party is led by his daughter Marine Le Pen. In return, Rassemblement National intensified its pro-Russian lobbying in the European Parliament. In recent years, the party has become more engaged in culture war issues, having previously focused on Islamophobia and immigration. Issues such as LGBTIQ parenting and inclusive sex education have increasingly formed part its electoral pitch, with some MEPs expressing solidarity with homophobic movements such as La Manif pour tous.

Another oligarch of interest is railway magnate Vladimir Yakunin. Like Malofeyev and Komov, Yakunin has links to the World Congress of Families: his wife Natalia Yakunina has spoken at the events as part of her role within the Sanctity of Motherhood Foundation. Yakunin was tipped as a potential successor to Vladimir Putin – although Putin's law that secures his power until 2036 might mean Yakunin missing out, as he'll be eighty-eight years old by then. He is credited with contributing to the socially conservative turn Putin's regime has taken, through his commitment to anti-abortion, anti-LGBTIQ activity and his closeness to the Russian Orthodox Church. Yakunin believes that post-Soviet Russia has lost its way when it comes to morality and tradition, and his influence spreads via his Endowment Fund Istoki, the Sanctity of Motherhood Foundation and his Dialogue of Civilizations Research Institute. The latter organises annual forums that attract anti-gender actors and promote an Orthodox, socially conservative view around women's and LGBTIQ people's rights.

When sanctions against Russia meant the World Congress of Families had to cancel its 2014 Moscow event, Yakunin stepped in to sponsor many of its participants and help fund a rebranded congress, the Large Families and Future of Humanity Forum. This was definitive proof of financial links between Russian and western anti-gender actors, including civil society organisations, parliamentarians and ministers.

Leaked documents reveal how sponsored participants on the forum's guest list included Hungary's Minister of Family Affairs Katalin Novák, French MEP Aymeric Chauprade and former vice-speaker of the Greek parliament Maria Kollia-Tsaroucha – as well as representatives from Human Life International, the World Congress of Families, Croatia's Family Centre, Italy's Pro Vita e Famiglia Onlus and CitizenGO.[31] Representing Ireland was Patrick Buckley from the Society for the Protection of Unborn Children (SPUC), and batting for the UK was Ben Harris-Quinney of the Bow Group, which describes itself as 'the World's oldest conservative think tank'. The latter counts a range of UK Conservative Party grandees and influential MPs in its network: patrons include prominent Brexiteers Sir John Redwood and Sir William Cash, as well as Conservative peers Lord Tebbitt and Lord Lamont. Anti-abortion, anti-LGBTIQ and Brexit Party MEP Anne Widdecombe is also a patron. Harris-Quinney is additionally linked to the Leadership Institute. He spoke at a 2012 event the institute hosted in Wellington College, UK, when the agenda included how to write successful direct marketing fundraising letters and social media campaigns. Running the 'Fundraising as Relationship Building' session at the Leadership Institute event was Matthew Elliott, of Brexit campaign group Vote Leave.[32]

It's worth taking a moment to consider the name of the forum: Large Families and the Future of Humanity. This focus on large families stems from the same natalism that underpins the trad wife movement and the Great Replacement conspiracy theory. The presence of so many elected politicians at the forum, mingling with representatives from extreme anti-abortion groups and right-leaning think tanks, shows how the belief that humanity is threatened by white women failing to produce enough children has moved out of the shadows and into the mainstream.

Yakunin's influence represents a respectable, soft-power version of the Kremlin's geopolitical diplomacy. Here, gender plays a central role in defining traditional civilisations epitomised by whiteness, church and family, as distinct from western civilisation, which is seen as corrupt, feminist and European. This is a regime, don't forget, that wants to create a fascist mythic past based on an idealised Mother Russia – a tsarist time before abortion, divorce and LGBTIQ rights, not to mention workers' rights, protection for Jewish people and peasants' land rights, as well as the liberation of colonised regions such as Finland. Through events such as the forum, and through Malofeyev's extensive charitable and media networks, fascist thought architecture around reproductive and sexual rights can infiltrate mainstream politics and think tanks.

Steve Bannon, Trump's former chief strategist, once wrote that the way to fuel division and distrust, and draw people towards the far right, was to 'flood the zone with shit' – to spread disinformation, lies and rumours, and destroy any notion of objective reality and truth. When it comes to Russian money and the influence war, this is the goal of funding anti-gender, conspiracist and far-right movements. When armies of bots and disinformation agents post about white genocide and satanic abuse, stoke division between metropolitan elites and traditional values, the goal is to create enemies of so-called cultural Marxists – feminists, Black Lives Matter activists, LGBTIQ people and Jewish people, so that white male supremacists can reap the rewards of power and control.

The third major funder of anti-gender activism in Europe is the US, from where at least $81.3 million of dark money was channelled across the Atlantic into European organisations between 2009 and 2018.[33] As with money coming into Europe from the Russian Federation, the sum is likely to be higher: one of the largest donors in this period was the Billy Graham Evangelistic Association, which spent nearly $24 million in the region between 2009 and 2014; it then changed its tax status so it no longer had to report its regional spending. The second-biggest spender is Alliance Defending Freedom and its European branch ADF International, at $23.3 million, followed by the American Center for Law and Justice (ACLJ), which has European (ECLJ) and Slavic (SCLJ) arms, at $15.7 million. Other big US funders, listed by Neil Datta, are the Federalist Society ($5.9 million), Human Life International ($4 million), the Cato Institute ($3 million), the Acton Institute ($2.3 million) and the Leadership Institute ($1.4 million).

These radical and religious-right organisations spend their money in Europe in order to change its culture and challenge its laws, as demonstrated in the previous chapter. For example, the Alliance Defending Freedom in the US donated £324,000 to ADF International (UK) in 2020 – 62 per cent of its total income for that year. The grant helped to fund its actions against buffer zones around abortion clinics and its research into freedom of speech culture on campuses – research that was quoted in a UK government white paper on education. Money tracks influence, after all. Another source of funding to Alliance Defending Freedom's activities in Europe is via anonymous donors to the National Christian Foundation. The latter's European spending footprint was $1.57 billion between 2009 and 2018.[34]

Similarly, the ACLJ channels $1.2 million annually to its European arm, the ECLJ. The ECLJ has used that money to campaign for more restrictive abortion laws in Poland and to challenge the sex education curriculum in France. The Templeton family via its Templeton Foundation has a European spending footprint of $1.6 billion, primarily channelled to an organisation called the Acton Institute, which declares on its website that it offers grants through a 'voluntary family planning scheme' for 'research and programs that affirm the value of human life from conception until natural death'.

Much of the money coming into Europe arrives via an entity called the Donors Trust, which, as a donor-advised fund, has no legal obligation to declare its donors. It is generally understood, however, that the donors to the trust include the disaster-capitalist oil-and-gas billionaire Koch Brothers, the Robert Mercer family and the DeVos family. The latter, who contributed $1 million to the Donors Trust in 2009 and $1.5 million in 2010, are motivated by extreme religious-right beliefs which they export into Europe through their family foundation.[35] Betsy DeVos was education secretary under the Trump administration, where she waged war on publicly funded schools in favour of religious schools. She also narrowed the definition of sexual harassment in Title IX, the law that protects against sex discrimination at federally funded schools, while expanding the rights of those accused of sexual misconduct. The move was praised by men's rights activists but provoked concerns from feminists who worried the changes would make it harder for victims to come forward following harassment or assault.

This anti-feminist, anti-state school stance is no surprise given the DeVos family's history: they are devout members of the Dutch Reformed Church, which, claims the writer and *New Yorker* journalist Jane Mayer, has become a vibrant centre for the vitriol of the Christian right. According to her book *Dark Money*, members 'crusaded against abortion, homosexuality, feminism and modern science that conflicted with their teachings'.[36] Meanwhile, writer Anne Nelson describes how the DeVos 'dynasty spent a king's ransom on political operations', including through the family's donations to Alliance Defending Freedom. 'As fundamentalists,' Nelson continued, 'they invested in campaigns against gay marriage and abortion rights', and had an 'abhorrence of homosexuality and abortion rights'.[37] The DeVos family (whose net worth is $5.4 billion) uses its riches to fund organisations and actors working to ban abortion and overturn LGBTIQ rights around the world – spending vast amounts of money to turn its extremist ideology into political reality and export the US anti-abortion agenda into Europe.

Of course, the US anti-gender billionaires don't only spend money across the Atlantic. They also splash their cash to support the anti-abortion movement at home. The DeVos family, for example, has provided funding to the Council for National Policy, and to its members: between 1999 and 2001 the family's foundation donated $275,000 to CNP-linked Focus on the Family.[38]

The latter organisation has been widely criticised for its homophobic and transphobic views. Its founder, James Dobson, was close to Trump, taking part in a 2018 evangelical leaders event organised by former presidential candidate Ben Carson working in conjunction with other organisations such as the Family Research Council. During the event, Trump called religious liberty 'the No. 1 question', and promised to appoint anti-abortion Supreme Court justices.

Betsy DeVos's parents, the billionaires Edgar and Elsa Prince Broekhuizen, have also funded Alliance Defending Freedom, the Leadership Institute and the Acton Institute. The Prince Foundation's European spending amounted to $49.8 million between 2009 and 2018.[39]

The money pouring into the anti-abortion movement from religious and radical-right billionaires has always helped to challenge pro-abortion laws and introduce restrictions such as the so-called Partial-Birth Abortion Ban. But in 2016, the election of Donald Trump gave the anti-abortion movement a new opportunity for mainstreaming its agenda in Vice President Mike Pence, a man described by Trump as being 'straight out of Central Casting'. A conservative evangelical Christian, Pence had long harboured hopes of overturning *Roe vs Wade*; he and Trump made the perfect political marriage of convenience, until 6 January 2021 when Trump ripped Pence apart for failing to support the coup attempt. Pence was Trump's ticket for attracting the religious-right vote; Trump was Pence's ticket for achieving a ban on abortion.

According to the journalist and historian Anne Appelbaum, writing in the *Atlantic*, Trump provided Pence with a 'biblical moment' to fulfil his desired policies – to ban abortion, to roll back LGBTIQ rights and to protect whiteness in America. Appelbaum describes how a former member of the Trump administration said Pence believed that 'we are approaching the Rapture, and this is a moment of deep religious significance'.[40] He was joined in this belief by Secretary of State Mike Pompeo and Attorney General William Barr.

Defining Trump's election as a moment of religious significance gave these deeply Christian men the excuse they needed to buddy up with a leader who couldn't name his favourite bit of the Bible. Allying with Trump, they argued, was their way to save America from a perceived apocalypse: he would appeal to both a plebeian far-right base and the right-wing millionaires who had made their money through the exploitation of people and natural resources. Bringing together these two seemingly disparate groups gave the religious right the voters it needed to win the election and push through an anti-abortion agenda. Trump could bring together the elite and the mob, raking in the votes of extremists, misogynists and sleazy moneymakers who were happy to swap tax cuts for the destruction of human rights and environmental protections. The relationship was useful to Trump, too. An adulterous, sexually incontinent, three-times-married man with dodgy financial links would otherwise have been a hard sell to the religious right. Pence helped Trump to attract the evangelical vote, creating the electoral coalition they needed to beat all expectations and win in 2016.

With the election won, Pence and his allies moved into the next phase of their plan to ban abortion in the US: to create a Supreme Court with a conservative majority that would succeed in overturning *Roe vs Wade* within a mere six years of the 2016 election. Becoming a Supreme Court judge is a lifetime appointment, and in order to ensure the religious right's legislative goals are passed, it needs at least five conservative-minded judges on the benches. For this reason, significant campaigning and funding went into making sure anti-abortion lawmakers were promoted to the court. Spearheading these efforts was Leonard Leo, vice president of the ultra-conservative, anti-abortion Federalist Society, a group of conservatives and libertarians who aim to reorder priorities within the legal system to emphasise their own ideas of individual liberty, traditional values and the rule of law.

Leonard Leo temporarily gave up his vice presidency of the Federalist Society in order to assist Trump's attempts to overturn the 2020 election results; but even before that, he had exerted significant influence over Trump's judicial nominations, including his Supreme Court picks. By one count, an estimated 85 per cent of Trump judicial nominees are or have been affiliated with the Society.[41] This was certainly the case in the Supreme Court, with Leo supporting moves to stack the benches with judges amenable to the society's anti-abortion goal of overturning the legal basis for statewide abortion in the US. According to conservative activist Edward Whelan, 'no one has been more dedicated to the enterprise of building a Supreme Court that will overturn *Roe V. Wade* than the Federalist Society's Leonard Leo'.[42]

Leo controls a fundraising entity known as the 85 Fund, which financially supports a range of anti-abortion, pro-Trump, radical-right and far-right organisations, including his Federalist Society. It helped to fund the Judicial Crisis Network, another legal charity linked to Leo, which in 2016 campaigned to block Barack Obama from nominating a Supreme Court justice as he was leaving the White House. Leo was aided in this by Senate Leader Mitch McConnell, who claimed it would be wrong for an outgoing president to nominate a judge to the Supreme Court, and that this should instead be left to the incoming President Trump. This led to the appointment of conservative anti-abortion judge Neil Gorsuch once Trump had taken office. Leo served as the effective subcontractor for Gorsuch's nomination, having successfully helped to appoint conservative judges John Roberts and Samuel Alito under George W. Bush.

Similar scenes took place when Anthony Kennedy retired from the court and the anti-abortion judge Brett Kavanaugh was nominated to take his place: the network around the 85 Fund, the Federalist Society and the Judicial Crisis Network pushed successfully for the controversial nomination. After the death of pro-abortion justice Ruth Bader Ginsburg in September 2020, Leo and his colleagues began to promote the nomination of anti-abortion judge Amy Coney-Barrett. Her appointment was controversial, not least because it came in the run-up to an election – with McConnell reversing his former stance: having blocked Obama nominating a judge at the end of his term, he supported the campaign for Trump to put his choice on the court despite the imminent election.

The 85 Fund donated significant sums to far-right and right-wing anti-abortion groups that backed Barrett's confirmation, including Turning Point USA ($2.7 million), Job Creators Network ($500,000), Independent Women's Forum ($310,000), the Susan B. Anthony List ($175,000), Concerned Women for America ($100,000), Faith and Freedom Coalition ($100,000) and Heritage Action for America ($50,000).[43] The campaign was successful and Amy Coney-Barrett took her seat on the Supreme Court, creating an anti-abortion majority which has had devastating consequences for reproductive rights ever since.

Leo's 85 Fund receives some of its income from the Donors Trust. Although little is known about the trust's backers, it's understood that one of the big funders is the Koch Foundation, the charitable arm of the Koch brothers' vast fortune. The Koch family made its money in oil and gas, and has spent the last fifty years funding radical-right causes which seek to remove workers' rights, environmental protections, checks and balances on electoral politics and human rights legislation. Their *bête noire* is environmental legislation that seeks to reduce the impact of fossil fuels on the climate. The Koch-backed advocacy group Americans for Prosperity supported the nomination of climate-crisis denying judge Coney-Barrett[44], who during her confirmation hearings refused to say whether she accepts the science around climate change. Because most far and religious-right actors hold both anti-abortion and anti-tax/climate-crisis-denying views, funding one cause invariably means funding the other.

Digging a bit deeper into this crossover reveals something interesting about the evolving nature of the Republican Party since the ruling on *Roe vs Wade* in 1973, and the contradictory role abortion plays in conservative politics. Disaster capitalists such as the Kochs support right-wing politicians and judges who share their neoliberal creed: freedom to destroy the environment, exploit their workers and make as much money as possible. This is the low-to-no-tax, deregulatory, small-state ideology where minority interests of the wealth and property-owning class trump the interests of the majority – an ideology that came out of the Virginia school of economic thinking in the 1950s and was picked up by the Chicago school and its push for deregulation in the 1970s. While the left wants a big state, high taxes, high regulation and majority rule, the right wants the opposite. Small-state minority rule will protect their wealth and their means of extracting wealth.

At the same time, the right is determined to create a government small enough to fit into a woman's womb. How can they claim to be in favour of freedom when they want to deny women the freedom to control their own bodies and fertility? The answer is simple and depressing: greed for power.

The radical right and the Republican Party's aims are generally antithetical to the desires of the mainstream electorate. Funnily enough, most people quite like the rule of the majority: they like having rights in the workplace and don't like to be poisoned by the water they drink or the air they breathe. In order to win electoral support for a neoliberal economic agenda, therefore, the Republicans turned to social conservatism as an effective weapon to bring in the votes. After *Roe*, they allied themselves with evangelical opposition to abortion and LGBTIQ rights, with even formerly pro-choice leaders declaring their opposition to abortion. It was, after all, Ronald Reagan who liberalised abortion law in California before becoming the figurehead for anti-abortion voters in the 1980s; Trump too once claimed to be pro-choice.

The Republican right has been able to merge various notions of freedom in the public's imagination, starting with the claim that human rights campaigners are trying to remove the freedom to disagree with abortion or LGBTIQ rights. From there, the right has claimed that these campaigners are cultural Marxists, intent on forcing a belief system on unsuspecting white American men – that they are threatening the freedom to make money, to drive a diesel car, go on multiple long-haul flights every year, smoke cigarettes, and so on. This positions the left as being anti-freedom, while the right is celebrated as pro-freedom. The right used this dichotomy to create a political platform that appeared to stand up for the freedoms of the work-a-day traditional man, while offering their radical-right financiers the economic freedoms they urgently desired.

If you think back to the definition of fascism at the start of this book, the American right has offered its supporters a glimpse of freedom – the freedom to disagree with abortion and LGBTIQ rights. But that glimpse has evolved into a fear of freedom – the fear that women and LGBTIQ people were exerting reproductive and sexual autonomy outside of patriarchal control.

Some neoliberal, climate-destroying, libertarian billionaires are clearly and openly anti-abortion. But the truth is, we simply don't know if all the moneymakers dictating right-wing Republican policy share these anti-gender views, or even care about the issue. For many of these libertarian billionaires, an anti-abortion stance may well be more cynical. The historian Nancy MacLean argued in her book *Democracy in Chains* that the radical right needs a popular base to succeed in building its economic and political vision, and that it has achieved this by pulling in 'the vast and active conservative grassroots base by identifying points of common cause. After 2008 [the radical right] adopted more and more the mantle of conservatism'. This, she explains, represented cynicism from economically right-wing actors who sought to 'make peace – at least in the short-term – with the religious right, despite the fact that so many libertarian thinkers ... were atheists who looked down on those who believed in God'.[45]

As we have seen, it's dark money from Europe, Russia, and the United States that funds anti-abortion activism across the West, and that uses its influence to place extremists into positions of institutional government power, as in the US Supreme Court. That wealthy people are willing to spend their fortunes on anti-abortion extremism tells us something concerning about the mainstreaming of this ideology: this cause is now understood as a worthwhile investment with the possibility of future returns. Further, the dark money spent on the anti-abortion movement represents an agreed alliance between libertarian disaster capitalists and far-right and evangelical extremists, providing a support base for neoliberal economic policy by destroying reproductive and sexual freedoms – that is, those who already have power and money are using women's bodies to get more of both.

6

The Politicians: How The Far Right Influences Governments Around The World

The success of the spending spree described in the previous chapter is manifest in the number of western political leaders now launching attacks on reproductive rights in country after country, using far-right conspiracy theories and disinformation to initiate their natalist and racist policies. Far-right ideas on reproductive and sexual rights have travelled the pipeline: developed on the extremist message boards, laundered by respectable organisations, funded by billionaires and lobbied to mainstream parliaments, where they eventually emerge as government policy. From Hungary to Spain, Germany to Greece and Italy, the far right is succeeding in getting its anti-gender policies written into political manifestos and law. These parties and their leaders adopt the extremist rhetoric of a demographic winter arising from low birth rates and rising immigration. Taking their cue from the conspiracy theories and white supremacist memes that circulate around the internet, they promise to resolve this perceived population crisis by melding anti-immigration policy with natalist initiatives to exploit women's reproductive labour. These are nationalistic party leaders who, according to *openDemocracy* editor and journalist Peter Geoghegan, 'are using the language of religion and identity to pursue culture wars characterised not only by racism but by sexism, homophobia, and aggressive anti-environmentalism'.[1]

In this chapter, we will visit European Union member states where the far-right attack on reproductive rights has travelled from extremist corners into government policy, before doing a deep dive into the anti-gender agenda in the UK. Those five countries are Hungary, Poland, Italy, Spain, Slovakia and the Netherlands – although the trend can also be seen in Greece, Germany, France and other nations. In Hungary, the Netherlands and Italy, far-right leaders are using Great Replacement rhetoric to promote natalist and anti-immigration policies, while adopting the far-right tactic of positioning the pro-abortion movement as a Goliath attacking traditional, Christian, western values. Poland – which has among the most draconian anti-abortion laws in Europe – provides an example of an effective far-right takeover of judicial and governmental powers in order to introduce extreme anti-gender policy. Both Spain and Slovakia demonstrate how far-right actors are influencing mainstream politicians to adopt anti-abortion, anti-gender policies in order to secure their own political success, moving the Overton window – the spectrum of ideas on public policy and social issues considered acceptable by the general public at a given time – further to the right. Finally, this chapter will look at the UK in more detail, and how it is attacking equalities in a so-called war on woke that undermines women's and minority rights. This section will explore the close relationship between the British and the American radical right when it comes to economic issues –and ask how easy it might be for them to mirror each other on social and cultural issues too.

'The primary objective for anti-gender actors in Europe is a normative agenda of changing laws,' Neil Datta told me. 'What we are now seeing across many more countries is the same anti-gender actors forming an important constituent part of the new alt-right, far-right populist political parties. You have this with Spain in Vox, you have a similar entryism in Germany with anti-gender actors using Alternative für Deutschland as their primary vehicle. Similarly, we're seeing the established far-right parties, Lega in Italy and Rassemblement National in France, experimenting with anti-gender social conservatism. It's not really in the DNA of the party. They've never been that socially conservative or Christian. But they're trying this now.'²

The trend is epitomised by Hungary's authoritarian Prime Minister Orbán, who has instigated a range of far-right, anti-gender policies while attacking migrant people seeking asylum as part of his stated aim to build a 'Christian Hungary in a Christian Europe'. This is the far-right Great Replacement conspiracy theory going mainstream: neo-fascist ideology shaping government policy. As the researcher and writer Julia Ebner explains in her book, *Going Dark*, an account of going undercover at far-right meetings including in Hungary, 'we have entered a new era of extremism. What was once fringe is now mainstream. Slogans of the extreme right have made their way into official campaign posters and election manifestos.'³

Hungary's capital city Budapest is famed for its historic riverfront buildings, its bridges and its spas where you can wile away an afternoon forgetting geopolitics and relaxing in the steam. I spent a freezing weekend there in 2010, eating chimney cakes, enjoying the sixteenth-century spas, and watching, fascinated, as men on horseback dressed in the national colours of red, white and green mingled with traditional musicians outside the imposing parliament building, ready to perform for Revolution Memorial Day. The day commemorates the 1848 revolution when the Hungarian people fought for independence from the Austrian Empire.

Seven years after my trip, the city became ground zero for the Christian far right when Brian Brown's World Congress of Families rolled into town, bringing with it delegates from across the globe eager to indulge in anti-abortion, anti-LGBTIQ discussions, as well as networking and agenda-building. Present at the event were individuals linked with Agenda Europe, including Ignacio Arsuaga, Sophia Kuby and Luca Volontè. The keynote speaker was Viktor Orbán himself.

A review of every WCF programme since 2004 reveals just how mainstream this anti-gender movement has become. The annual congress sees think tank staffers, prime ministers and anti-gender activists – including those from the UK – come together for sessions exploring 'international pro-life initiatives'; 'beyond abortion: how pro-life values affect all of life'; 'the distinctive role of mothers and fathers in families'; and 'the porn pandemic' (these were all session titles at the 2015 Congress in Utah; another featured famed movie producers such as *Jurassic Park*'s Gerald Molen who trained delegates in using Hollywood techniques to tell their stories). This isn't the preserve of cranks and the mob – although they are present too – it also involves the elite. Dozens of European politicians – including mayors, governors, MPs, ministers, ambassadors and heads of state – have spoken at the event over the past two decades, almost half of whom are members of far-right parties in Hungary, Italy, Poland, Serbia and Spain. Significantly, the majority of these leaders only started taking part in the congress in recent years, suggesting that the mainstreaming of its agenda is growing apace.[4]

Orbán's decision to appear as the keynote speaker sent a clear signal to the global far right. Here was the head of a European Union member state, an elected prime minister, standing on a stage that had previously been occupied by cranks, criminals and conspiracy theorists. He was telling them what they wanted to hear: that European elites were pushing replacement, and that pro-birth policies combined with violent anti-immigration were the solution to all their fears and anxieties. His speech culminated with a plan to set up a think tank to address what he claimed was the biggest issue facing Europe: white people not having enough children.[5]

In the years before and since 2017, Hungary has become increasingly hostile to abortion rights, single parents and LGBTIQ people, while its treatment of people seeking asylum has been internationally condemned.[6] Taking an antagonistic stance towards the progressive values he associates with the EU, Orbán has launched an all-out assault on human rights and equality: he has closed down gender studies courses; rewarded his allies with big-money contracts; threatened NGOs; shut up the independent media and gave TV channels and newspapers to his allies; supported antisemitic dog-whistle campaigning against the liberal-leaning philanthropist George Soros; and weakened judicial independence – tactics also used by Poland's authoritarian leaders. As he consolidated his grip on power after winning the 2010 election, the bullish prime minister turned Hungary into a European centre for far-right policy-making and activism. Generation Identity activist Tore Rasmussen boasted, 'The only place I go for vacation is Hungary these days. Because I only give money to free nations.'[7] Knights Templar International were so impressed by Hungary's swing to the far right, they set up shop there, before being banned from the country for allegedly joining Serb nationalist paramilitary groups.[8] The Hungarian shift towards authoritarianism and demagoguery has also been pronounced enough to draw censure from the European Union (EU), leading to an attempt in the European Parliament to trigger Article Seven and suspend the country's voting rights.

Two years on from Budapest's WCF, in 2019 Orbán was once again greeted with rapturous applause by an audience keen to hear more about how his natalist policies could defeat Europe's so-called demographic winter. This time the setting was the Third International Demography Conference in Budapest, where he laid out the motivations and justifications for his government's attacks on immigration and progressive politics. He argued that white, Christian Europe is threatened by immigration and must be defended by turning women's bodies into the womb of the nation.

'Political forces,' Orbán said, 'want to replace the white European population with "others" ... If in the future Europe is to be populated by people other than Europeans, then we will effectively be consenting to population replacement: to a process in which the European population is replaced.'⁹ This speech was the moment when the Great Replacement conspiracy theory explicitly entered mainstream political discourse in Europe. It was the endgame following nearly a decade where, at every step, Orbán's assault on democratic norms had been underpinned by two beliefs: immigration threatens a white Christian Hungary; and so-called gender ideology undermines the traditional Hungarian family that in turn protects a white Christian Hungary. Both immigration and women's/LGBTIQ rights are seen as an attack from outside forces, values being imposed on Hungary by western liberal elites and the EU. The pincer threat of gender and migration, he claims, must be defeated to maintain 'a Christian Hungary in a Christian Europe'.¹⁰

To understand the roots of Orbán's embrace of the Great Replacement theory, and his dedication to re-Christianising Europe via (ethnic Hungarian) women's wombs, it's important to acknowledge two things. The first is the crisis of identity that gripped Eastern Europe at the end of the Cold War, and how that inspired a desire to return to a fascistic mythic past based on Hungary's historic military might – Orbán has spoken of recreating Hungary to be 'how we became eleven hundred years ago here in the Carpathian basin'.¹¹ The second is what was happening in Europe over the five years leading up to the 2019 demography conference.

The collapse of the Soviet Union was, political theorist Francis Fukuyama famously wrote, the 'end of history'. It was supposed to be the end of ideology, as neoliberals such as Fukuyama argued that a society structured around a capitalist, market-driven liberal democracy had been proven as the only rational approach. Countries emerging from the Iron Curtain were therefore encouraged, even coerced, to imitate those in the West. To be a forward-looking nation meant adopting the economic and social structures of Western Europe and the USA. This worked ... for a while – and some good came out of it.

For example, one of the driving forces behind the legalisation of abortion in Romania was to shift away from the horrors of dictatorship and towards becoming a liberal western state. Under Romanian communist dictator Nicolae Ceauşescu, abortion and contraception were criminalised, leading to the deaths of at least 10,000 women (it is believed the true figure is much higher). The exact opposite happened in Poland: abortion had been allowed under communism but was criminalised after independence.

There was just one problem. Fukuyama had called it wrong: this was not the end of history. The existing model would not and could not last forever. There was nothing special about this model that made it different to others that had burnt out too; worse, there was no end of ideology – not when the neoliberal model was as ideological as those that had come before. In 2008, the global financial crash smashed up the old certainties, and suddenly the policy of western imitation was no longer delivering.

Even before the crash, some East European citizens and leaders had started to feel that rather than retrieve their identity from communist rule, the post-1989 world order had instead led to another identity and system being imposed on them: this time by the EU. At its most extreme, people felt they had left one supranational bloc controlling their every move, only to replace it with another. This fuelled a deepening resentment, according to political scientist Ivan Krastev, chairman of the Centre for Liberal Strategies in Sofia, Bulgaria, and Stephen Holmes, Walter E. Meyer professor of law at New York University. They explained how 'the attempt to democratise formerly communist countries was aiming at a kind of cultural *conversion* to values, habits and attitudes considered normal in the West'. Such 'political and moral "shock therapy" put inherited identity at risk'.[12]

These conflicts of identity became a breeding ground for resentment that was easily exploited by Orbán. He developed a populist message that the West was failing due to low birth rates and high levels of immigration – and worse, it was taking Hungary down with it. He claimed that Hungary's traditions were under attack and that Europe's Christian population was at risk of replacement. To get this message across, he invoked the fascist mythic past of Magyar warriors living 1100 years ago, claiming that Hungary had once been a great, brave and pioneering nation – all values which were being crushed by the liberal elites in the EU. At the same time, he captured 'the public's imagination by denouncing the universalism of human rights and open-border liberalism as expressions of the West's lofty indifference to their country's national traditions and heritage,' wrote Krastev and Holmes.[13] Orbán sought to reassert those national traditions, and reclaim the spirit of those ninth-century Magyar warriors – a native Hungarian spirit he alleged was being suffocated by western cultural imperialism.

The disillusionment with western democracy was the first favourable condition for Orbán's anti-gender revolution. The second was the Syrian refugee crisis of 2015. This humanitarian disaster which led to horrific death and suffering gave his government the backdrop it needed to persuade the electorate that Hungary was both under attack by outside forces hostile to the nation's tradition, *and* being forced to adopt unpopular policies by a European leadership that did not care about their values.

On 3 September 2015, Britain's *Independent* newspaper published a front-page photo of the body of a little boy, only two years old, lying still and lifeless on a Turkish beach. His name was Alan Kurdi. The journalists explained that they had debated whether to run the picture, but decided the image was justified to show 'the desperate situation facing many refugees' – a situation often forgotten among 'glib words about the "ongoing migrant crisis".'[14]

The response to the crisis had been sluggish and lacklustre. That started to shift when Germany's centre-right Chancellor

Angela Merkel announced her country would open its doors to a million refugees. Even Britain, with its increasingly hostile attitude towards migrant people, vowed to do more (a vow that was quietly shelved in a Brexit-related vote in 2020 – that year the UK resettled a paltry 353 refugees). In response to rising numbers of people arriving into the region – often via Eastern and Central European countries including Hungary and Greece – the European Commission presented proposals to reform the Common European Asylum System (CEAS) in 2016, including a reform designed to better allocate asylum applicants among EU countries. However, member states failed to reach an agreement on the proposals about how to share responsibility.

If Germany's response was to open its doors, in Orbán's Hungary the reaction to the refugee crisis was very different. The prime minister refused to go along with reforms to the CEAS and instigated a crackdown on families seeking asylum who, due to the routes from the Middle East into Europe, often ended up having to pass through the country. He declined to take part in the European Union's 2015 Refugee Resettlement Programme and attracted international censure for his regime's often aggressive and brutal treatment of those crossing the border into Hungary. In more recent years, he sought to criminalise NGOs for helping asylum seekers and in 2020 used the coronavirus as a cover to suspend asylum rights.

The reasons for Orbán's political response became clear in an interview with the German newspaper *Bild*, where he explained: 'we don't see these people as Muslim refugees. We see them as Muslim invaders.'[15] Following a 2021 meeting with UK Prime Minister Boris Johnson, Orbán clarified those remarks in response to questions from journalists about his comments, saying how Muslim families seeking asylum 'just destroyed the border and marched through the country. In Hungary, we call that an invasion.'[16] His words demonstrate how he succeeded in evoking the fascist mythic past in order to attract a right-wing populist base by presenting Hungary as being invaded by hostile forces. This came with a promise to his voters that only Orbán could channel the spirit of those Magyar warriors, protect Hungary's border and defeat the enemy – whether that was Syrian refugees or Merkel herself.

In the years following the 2015 crisis, Orbán continued to expand on far-right themes that Europe was being invaded; that white Christian people were being replaced; and that the attack on his people was being allowed with a wink and a nod by European Union elites. But alongside the anti-migrant rhetoric and policy was a growing emphasis on natalism and the responsibility of ethnic Hungarian women to have more children to reverse replacement. Too many European leaders, he explained in a 2018 speech, believe that 'for every missing child, there should be one coming in and then the numbers will be fine. Hungarian people think differently. We do not need numbers. We need Hungarian children.'[17] In 2019, he elaborated on this argument: 'we must reject the argument that on a global scale migration can solve the problem of population decline in Europe. There are political forces which, for a variety of reasons, want to see population replacement.' This was a clear attempt to mobilise a far-right following. His aim was to whip up fear in his voting base that European leaders were conspiring to create what he called in 2018 a 'new, mixed, Islamised Europe' designed to threaten Hungary's way of life.

Orbán was repeating the conspiracy theory shared by, among others, CBRUK's former director Wilfred Wong, Ordo Iuris–linked Duchess de Frankopen and TFP's Duke Paul of Oldenburg, who quoted an MEP warning that Europe could become 'Eurabia'. These activists and their allies claim the EU intentionally encourages Muslim communities to migrate to the Global North and de-Christianise society. The duchess claimed in her pro-Brexit book that 'the EU planned and encouraged the migrant invasion from North Africa for the past 12 years ... another wave will come from Azerbaijan, according to secret

EU plans'.[18] American TV presenter Tucker Carlson, in a monologue delivered in 2019, added an antisemitic dog-whistle to this conspiracy theory – calling a reliance on migration rather than native birth rates to maintain population 'the George Soros way'.[19]

As Orbán ramped up the Great Replacement rhetoric and launched repeated attacks on Muslim migration, ministers started to link women's right to safe, legal abortion to a decline in Hungary's population and, with it, the threat to a white Christian Hungary by 'Muslim invaders'.[20] Their aim was to use fears around immigration to incentivise women into having babies, while also connecting progressive, pro-choice values with an EU-linked threat to Hungarian values and nationhood. The approach was summed up in an academic paper written by Minister for Human Capacities Dr Miklos Kasler, who wrote: 'To this day six million abortions have been performed, thereby causing one of the worst demographic disasters of the Hungarian nation. If it had not been so, there would be over 20 million ethnic Hungarians in total.'[21] His comments foreshadowed those made by Republican Congressman Steve King, quoted above, about US replacement.

While abortion remains legal in Hungary, a change to the nation's constitution shortly after Orbán came to power defines life as beginning at conception. Inserting statements about the protection of life into nations' constitutions is a key tactic of the anti-abortion right. Used successfully in Ireland in the 1980s, it is designed to facilitate subsequent attempts to criminalise the procedure. The law also allows hospitals to refuse women an abortion, forcing them instead to undergo mandatory counselling and a three-day cooling-off period before a termination. Pressure is put on clinics offering terminations to deter women from making the decision to end a pregnancy.

Alongside the constitutional change, Hungary's Fundamental Law document is revealing on the state's approach to family and family policy. The 'Foundations' section, Article L, states:

Hungary shall protect the institution of marriage as the union of a man and a woman established by voluntary decision, and the family as the basis of the survival of the nation. Family ties shall be based on marriage and/or the relationship between parents and children.

Hungary shall encourage the commitment to have children

The protection of families shall be regulated by a cardinal Act

Inserting a definition of family and marriage that valorises heterosexual relationships in the constitution is an Agenda Europe strategy, and one that has been successfully employed by the Christian far right for many decades. It smooths the path for regressive legal changes that overturn women's and LGBTIQ people's human rights.

In practice, Article L is expressed by two policy programmes. The first is an all-out assault on the LGBTIQ community that includes a ban on gay couples adopting children and a ban on the legal recognition of trans people. Objects as harmless as a children's book featuring gay characters have been banned – one government minister ripped up a book on TV in a move that echoed the Nazi book burnings of the 1930s. Media law in Hungary now includes a clause that effectively outlaws any expression of support for the LGBTIQ community – demanding instead that public service broadcasting should promote 'respect for the institution of marriage and family values'. Media personalities who express solidarity with LGBTIQ people, including prominent national football players, have lost their jobs.[22] Unsurprisingly, anecdotal evidence suggests that the hostile legislation and media coverage has caused an increase in hate crimes against the community.

Alongside the state-sanctioned discrimination against rainbow families is the promotion of heterosexual marriage and childbearing among ethnic Hungarians, epitomised by the Family Protection Programme. The initiative rewards women who have children, offering financial and housing support for Hungarian families. Central to the policy is a loan system for married couples, with that loan written off if a woman has three children with her husband. If she has four children, Orbán promised in 2019, she would be excused from paying income tax for life. Again, those children must be the result of her marriage to her husband.

There's nothing inherently wrong with a policy that provides financial support for mothers. In the UK we have child benefit and child tax credits, for example. It becomes problematic only when the driving force behind family policy is not to help women but to promote nationalism. The benefits afforded to families depend very much on a mother's marital status, her and her husband's race and ethnicity, and as a result their class. As such, the programme is essentially a eugenics policy.

Orbán's 2019 speech to the demography conference makes clear the extent to which his government's motivation for the nation's family policy is linked to a white supremacist, pro-birth agenda. Orbán told his eager audience how the Family Protection Programme offers the solution to the 'possible extinction' of white Hungary by incentivising parenthood – to 'ensure that those who decide to have children are guaranteed better living standards than if they decided not to have children'. The Family Protection Programme is therefore a far-right policy that mainstreams and entrenches white supremacy via women's wombs. In this way, Orbán's plans more closely resemble the 1930s Nazi Party medal system, where mothers of large families were rewarded for producing more Aryan babies, than Gordon Brown's child tax-credit policy in the UK.

Through its family policy, contemporary Hungary has reduced women's identity to our wombs. They are tools of reproductive labour put to work for a white nationalist goal. This approach is succinctly summed up by African American abortion doctor Willie Parker, who explains, 'the thing all too many white anti-abortion activists really want, which they can't say out loud, is for white women to have more babies in order to push back against the browning of America'.[23] He's talking about the US, but if you swap 'browning of America' for 'de-Christianising Europe', the same applies to Orbán's Hungary.

Orbán himself characterised his Family Protection Programme as a recognition 'that families and children are ... the precondition for the *biological regeneration* of our national community' (my emphasis). If families, he continued, 'are not functioning, if there are no children, then a national community can simply disappear.'

'In my interpretation,' Katalin Kevehazi, president of the Budapest-based JÓL-LÉT (Well-Being) Foundation told *Balkan Insight*, 'this Family Protection Programme is part of a universal policy agenda that strengthens traditional values, promotes big families, maintains the existing hierarchy in society and enhances the number of Fidesz loyalists ... it's part of a "nation-building" agenda.'[24] This approach is explained by the feminist writers Cinzia Arruzza, Tithi Bhattacharya, and Nancy Fraser in *Feminism For The 99 %: A Manifesto*. They write that by 'incentivising births of the "right" kind, while discouraging those of the "wrong" kind, [governments] have designed education and family policies to produce not just "people" but (for example) "Germans", "Italians" or "Americans"'.[25]

The combination of violently anti-immigration policy, blatant Islamophobia and antisemitism, anti-LGBTIQ laws and natalist approaches to women's rights have won Orbán's Hungary huge support from the far right. Activists such as Rasmussen see the landlocked European nation as a sort of white supremacist El Dorado, a golden land of opportunity where their dystopian vision has come to life. A post on Telegram's 'Opposing the Great Replacement' channel celebrates Orbán's plans: 'this is how you preserve your nation, instead of flooding it with migrants'. Another poster revealed that she and her boyfriend were planning to move to Hungary to have children, where they would be 'safe' from 'invasion'.

To see how successfully this kind of rhetoric and policy has been, we need only to observe the praise for the Family Protection Programme from mainstream politicians and broadcasters. Tim Montgomerie, the influential Conservative activist and founder of the *ConservativeHome* website, tweeted in December 2019 that 'Hungarian family policy is worthy of close study'. In the United States, members of Trump's administration praised Hungary's 'procreation not immigration'.[26] Tucker Carlson added his voice in 2021, describing Hungary as having a government that 'actually cares about making sure their own people thrive, instead of promising the nation's wealth to illegal immigrants from the third world'.[27] Joe Grogan, an aide to President Trump and director of the Domestic Policy Council, lauded Hungary's 'courage and creativity', which he said 'inspired' the Trump administration.[28] At the December 2019 International Conference on Family Policy, Grogan celebrated Hungary's fertility-boosting programmes to affirm the Trump administration's opposition to abortion – explicitly linking anti-abortion with anti-immigration policy.

These comments do not come from extremists on internet forums, or writers of anti-abortion magazines. Rather, these are elected US Republican officials, the TV news presenter rumoured to be a future Republican presidential nominee, and the man once described as the most influential UK Conservative outside of government. They're all praising a racist, sexist and homophobic policy designed by an aspiring autocrat who in 2020 pushed through a vote that allowed him to rule by decree.

At the time of writing, Orbán has become embroiled in another scandal, with his adviser Zsuzsa Hegedüs resigning over what she termed the prime minister's 'Nazi speech'. Orbán had claimed that Hungary was not a 'mixed-race' country, and that countries comprised of 'Europeans and non-Europeans' – by which he means white and non-white people – were 'no longer nations'. Such blatant racism and far-right ideology did not prevent the Hungarian leader from being welcomed to the

Conservative Political Action Conference in Texas a week later, where he was cheered for his comments that white Christian nationalists across Europe and US should unite.[29]

Hungary is a morality tale showing what happens when far-right aims become government policy – the consequences include harm to minority ethnic groups, the LGBTIQ community and women. Since 2011, Hungary's move to the far right has been led from the heart of its (beautiful) parliament palace. The construction of a white supremacist, patriarchal ethno-state via natalism and anti-LGBTIQ policy, the segregation of the minority ethnic Roma community and the denial of entry to people seeking asylum – this is not a fringe fantasy. It has become mainstream government policy.

Vying with Hungary for the title of most far-right EU nation is Poland, which since the end of the Cold War has taken an increasingly illiberal turn. Poland not only helps us to see the deadly and devastating impact of far-right objections to abortion becoming policy, but it also offers an interesting case study in how the far right uses allegations of corruption in order to reach power.

Poland has gone further than Hungary in its attacks on reproductive and sexual rights: in the 1990s it banned abortion except in cases of foetal anomaly, threat to the mother's life or following rape or incest. The move was, in part, a repudiation of the more relaxed Communist laws that had been in place. In January 2021 the ruling far-right Law and Justice Party tightened the ban to include abortions in cases of foetal anomaly, too.

One year after the change was written into law, in January 2022, women in Poland gathered on the streets of major cities, including Warsaw. The mood was sombre, reflective. They laid wreaths and carried candles. Tears were shed and hugs exchanged. Then, as the freezing evening wore on, that sorrow and grief turned to anger. These were women and allies in mourning. That week, a woman had died of sepsis in hospital, having been refused a life-saving abortion. She was the third known death in the year since the tightened ban was introduced. Her name was Agnieszka T.

Pregnant with twins, and with three children at home, one of Agnieszka's twin foetuses had died within the womb. In cases like this, women need a surgical miscarriage to remove the dead foetus, otherwise the decaying foetal tissue can cause sepsis that can, in turn, lead to organ failure. But the family believe that the abortion ban gave the doctors pause: they were concerned that conducting the surgical miscarriage could be construed as aborting the second twin. So they waited, and waited ... until a week later the second twin also died.

By this time Agnieszka was severely ill. In a desperately sad video released by her family, she lies on a hospital bed, her eyes glazed. She has tubes up her nose and is wearing a blue hospital gown. Someone strokes her hair from her face, her skin is sallow and pale. The footage is painful to watch. Agnieszka looks both resigned and afraid. Within days of the film being taken, she was dead. She was thirty-seven years old. In a statement, the family was clear where the blame for Agnieszka T.'s death lay. 'The Polish state has blood on its hands,' they said, before adding the heart-breaking comment: 'She wanted to live.'

A few months before Agnieszka's death, Poland was mourning thirty-year-old Izabela. She was described by her friends as 'strong, brave, resolute', someone whom 'everyone loved'. They shared that she was a woman who loved dogs and who 'always stood up for the weaker'. Izabela, her friends said, was 'afraid of no one – a strong, beautiful, intelligent and influential girl'. She was pregnant with her second child when the foetus developed complications. According to the family's lawyer, the doctors decided not to terminate the pregnancy for fear of 'being held responsible for an illegal abortion'. Izabela knew her life was in danger. She told her friends she was afraid she would die of septic shock, like Savita Halappanaver had in Ireland nine years before. Her worst fear was realised: she died in September, twenty-two weeks pregnant, leaving behind a young daughter.

In the wake of her daughter's death, Izabela's mother said: 'I'll never accept that she's gone. I think this is a dream I wake up from and she will come to me. I'd rather give my life for her. I don't know how I'm going to survive this further'. The hospital was fined for medical malpractice.

The third woman was Ania, who died in similar circumstances to Izabela and Agnieszka, in June 2021, six months after the ban came into force. Less is known about her story, which came to light after Izabela's death.

The protesting in the wake of Izabela's and Agnieszka's deaths was not the first time women in Poland had fought against the rollback of reproductive rights in their country. In October 2020, as the US noisily prepared for the presidential election and the UK went back into a coronavirus lockdown, a feminist revolution swept through the nation as thousands of women and their allies took to the streets in protest at plans to ban abortion in cases of foetal defect.

'In the centre of Warsaw there's a roundabout named after Roman Dmowski,' Warsaw-based journalist Ada Petriczko told me via Zoom.[30] 'He was a politician in the 1930s who is an icon of the alt-right. So all the protesters went there and we renamed it the roundabout of women's rights! We believe that it was the largest protest since the Solidarity movement of the 1980s. We don't know the exact numbers but the city hall of Warsaw estimated it at between 100,00 and 150,000. It was a lot of fun. The language of the protests has been a bit vulgar as we decided it's time to show our anger. At that moment, the main slogan of the movement is simply "FUCK OFF", written in capital letters. That was both criticised and supported. But it makes sense, after thirty years of discussing abortion rights politely, it's time to use a different language.'

Poland's women and their feminist allies weren't only demanding the repeal of the bill, but an end to all restrictions on abortion and contraception (in 2017, the government passed a bill making the morning-after pill prescription only, a move that makes it harder for women to access to it in a timely fashion – enacting a key aim of Agenda Europe), as well as an end to systemic sexism, nationalism and the anti-LGBTIQ sentiments and policies flourishing across the country. A photo of a masked warrior woman, emerging from the smoke, waving a rainbow flag, became the enduring image of the protest.

Not everyone greeted the protests with approval, however. Far-right and nationalist activists also flocked to Poland's streets, shouting abuse and attempting to intimidate the women – and even physically attacking them. On Poland's Independence Day 2020, a far-right march clashed with police as nationalists launched flares at an apartment building flying the Women's Strike flag. And while feminists like me tweeted sisterhood and solidarity to Poland's women, members of extremist misogynistic incel forums praised the 'based' (admirable) Polish government and celebrated the fascist attacks against women.

The fascist backlash against the Women's Strike was predictable. The bill had been enacted by the authoritarian Law and Justice (PiS) Party, which has waged war on democratic and human rights norms for the past decade. The populist far-right party spent the five years leading up to the change undermining the independence of the judiciary and the media, centralising power, and attacking women's and LGBTIQ rights – all while pushing a nationalist agenda that, among other things, included a bill making it illegal to criticise Poland's role in the Holocaust. The backlash against the Women's Strike was intensified by police forces having been given the green light to undermine democratic norms, including arresting journalists and opposition MPs.

As the protests continued, the PiS leadership deliberately riled up its extremist base. The party's chairman, Jarosław Kaczyński, called on his supporters to defend Poland's churches from protesters – warning that the Women's Strikers were part of 'an attack meant to destroy Poland.' He even committed to taking on a shift or two guarding the iconic Holy Cross Church in Warsaw against the protests, stirring up anti-feminist feeling and portraying the activists as bad and immoral women terrorising good Christian Poles. His supporters on the far right claimed feminists were 'destroying' the nation and were determined to 'defend Latin civilisation'. In this narrative, women's role is and should be as the womb of the nation. Patrick Jaki, an MEP and a father of a child with Downs syndrome, spoke of the importance of the family in building a 'strong Poland' – this is irresistable to a far-right base that seeks to 'make Poland great again'.

'It's one of the biggest harms that Kaczyński has done to public life,' Petriczko says. 'People with far-right views have always been there but they were in the niche. And ever since 2015 the ruling party has given voice to these groups. The kind of beliefs and opinions they have, before 2015 they were taboo. These days it's become mundane which is very scary.'

In 2016, PiS's attempt to completely ban abortion, including in cases of rape and threat to the mother's life, was met with Black Friday strikes across the country, as women downed tools and took to the streets to protect their already minimal reproductive rights. The bill was pushed by Ordo Iuris, the Catholic legal organisation linked to Agenda Europe and the far-right Polish leadership. Thankfully, the protests prevented the changes becoming law. In 2018 the government tried again, and women fought back again.

But by 2020, a prolonged attack on Poland's independent judiciary over the previous five years had created the ideal circumstances to impose new restrictions free from democratic oversight. According to Petriczko, since 2015, 'PiS has tried to paralyse the Constitutional Tribunal. Kaczyński knew that the way our law is constructed means that if you control the Constitutional Tribunal, you can pass certain kinds of legislation without actually running it through the Parliament.' What this means is that the government has appointed judges who could be relied on to support the government agenda, and can pass laws without the scrutiny of a parliamentary vote. 'That is exactly what happened with the abortion bill,' explained Petriczko. This is similar to the US system, whereas in the UK all laws go through parliament.

Those early attacks on the independence of the judiciary had brought Polish citizens onto the streets, but PiS ploughed on, packing the tribunal with its own judges who could be trusted to support the party's authoritarian plans. The strategy was then repeated in the nation's Supreme Court where, again, PiS put its own people in charge. 'Kaczyński knew back in 2015 that for a lot of people, changes to the Constitutional Tribunal would be too complicated to understand and that's why they started there,' Petriczko explains. 'If they tried to curb women's rights first, for example, that's bodily. That causes people to go out on the streets immediately. So they started with something less palpable, something smaller, which then grew bigger and bigger and more and more serious.'

The takeover of the Constitutional Tribunal meant that, by 2020, PiS and Kaczyński were set to push through their long-desired attack on abortion. On 22 October 2020 the tribunal met, with very little publicity, to argue whether abortion on grounds of foetal defect was in line with the constitution's commitment to protect all life. PiS had no fears that the judges it had appointed might fail to support the ban and, thanks to the years spent undermining democratic structures, there was no need to put the question before parliament. So – just like that – after five years of trying, a group of (mostly) men managed to take away women's rights.

Kaczyński and his party's far-right goals are backed by the vast wealth of Catholic operatives such as Father Tadeusz Rydzyk's media empire, which uses its considerable clout to spread anti-abortion and anti-LGBTIQ messages across the nation. Rydzyk is the leader of a Catholic organisation called the Redemptorists, and heads up a wealthy foundation: *Fundacja Lux Veritatis*. Right-wing politicians fight to get interviews and coverage on his radio and TV channels that decry feminism, LGBTIQ rights and immigration – as well as echo the Great Replacement conspiracy theory that the three are combining to causes the Islamisation of Europe. The combined income of Rydzyk's empire was estimated to be $82.9 million between 2009 and 2018, a period during which Poland has swung significantly to the right on social issues.[31]

Poland's turn to the far right is similar to the shift experienced in Hungary. Both countries were former communist states that, in the 1990s, were encouraged to embrace the neoliberal western model through the politics of imitation. This worked, for a while. But with increased migration out of Poland, instability across Europe and the global economic collapse, an opportunity emerged for the far right to exploit the chaos by stirring up anti-progressive, anti-gender beliefs in order to win power. In 2015, PiS won an outright majority in the election – the first time since independence that a coalition had not been necessary – and it did so on a raft of populist policies. These included reducing the retirement age, higher taxes on big corporations and more financial help for families and small businesses. But PiS's populism had a far-right, anti-gender slant too, with anti-abortion, anti-LGBTIQ and anti-migrant rhetoric crucial to its winning strategy. Within a year it would try to ban abortion in all circumstances, and within two years it succeeded in making it harder for women to access contraception.

PiS had been in power before, in 2005, when Jarosław Kaczyński, leader of the newly established party, took advantage of a 2001 corruption scandal involving film producer Lew Rywin, who was accused of acting as a middleman between the government and the country's most successful media business, offering amendments to a bill on media ownership in return for $17.5 million. The 2015 election returned PiS to government for four years, and the 2019 elections led to PiS forming a coalition.

That PiS won power in the wake of a corruption scandal in 2005 is crucial to understanding the rise of the far right in Poland. Every far-right, populist leader offers his voters a promise on corruption. Trump promised to 'drain the swamp' of Wall Street by portraying liberal elites and those who make money through finance as corrupt and untrustworthy. In Brazil, Bolsonaro won power by condemning the corruption of the previous regime – although in the end his predecessor Lula Da Silva was cleared of all charges. Never mind that both Trump and Bolsonaro were up to their eyeballs in dodgy dealings and accused of corruption themselves ... they won support by accusing their opponents of being corrupt and supporting big business at the expense of ordinary people. Even in the UK, where accusations of corruption are rare, right-wing populism seeks to create a divide between wealthy, metropolitan elites and the so-called Workington man – a term borrowing its name from a north-west town to describing a working-class white male with traditional values who works in manual labour. The urban middle classes are painted as corrupt and decadent, and the latter as good, salt-of-the-earth people who earn their living through honest work. Never mind the wealthy, metropolitan elite background of populist leaders such as Nigel Farage and Boris Johnson who push this narrative!

Far-right leaders' focus on corruption is manipulative. The far right is not interested in corruption in the usual sense – the financial misbehaviour, cronyism and nepotism that it benefits from. Instead, its understanding of corruption relates to notions of the natural order. According to philosopher Jason Stanley, when the far right mentions corruption, it is alluding to the 'corruption of purity rather than of law' or the 'usurpation of the natural order'.[32] This means that corruption is less to do with wealth on Wall Street, and is rather a matter of women, LGBTIQ and people of colour corrupting white male spaces. Women's bodies are literally, in this mindset, sullying natural male authority – and their ability to do so is directly linked to reproductive freedoms. Stanley explains: 'when women attain positions of political power usually reserved for men – or when Muslims, blacks, Jews, homosexuals, or "cosmopolitans" profit or even share the public goods of a democracy, such as healthcare – that is perceived as corruption'.[33] In other words, the far-right promise to end corruption is predicated on removing progressive forces from power in order to return to the imaginary natural order and the fascist mythic past of white male authority.

In countries such as Poland, Romania and Hungary, corruption has another emotional meaning too, because it is inextricably associated in the public mind with the former communist regimes. Corruption was widespread in Communist Poland, where those in power enriched themselves and ordinary people struggled with everyday shortages. When the Cold War ended, the legacy of corruption continued. Many of the people who had held power during the Communist regime remained in positions of authority. This created the opportunity for a new party to promise voters a break from the corrupt and oppressive past for good. One of PiS's justifications for undermining judicial independence was that it was cleaning the courts of former Communist judges and influences.

Because the corrupt Communist regime is still alive in people's memories, any party presenting itself in opposition to the country's troubled past and promising to sweep away its remnants will be well placed to win support. Parties such as PiS offer the electorate a clean break with the recent left-wing past. But, as Stanley explains, the far-right commitment to tackle corruption is more often than not about restoring the fascistic natural order. This helps explain why, for example, post-communist Poland immediately banned abortion in the 1990s: it was a way of rejecting the previous regime and restoring Poland's traditions. Little surprise, then, that, when PiS won in 2015, it tried to ban abortion completely.

There's another crucial and tragic element to the far-right grip on Poland: the death of President Lech Kaczyński in the 2010 Smolensk air disaster. The event also killed Kaczyński's wife, many of his staff members, eighteen parliamentarians, ten generals and admirals representing Poland's top military leadership, and other political notables.

When the plane crashed, it was travelling to a memorial for the 22,000 Polish military officers captured and murdered by Stalin's regime in 1940. This Second World War incident was an example of Moscow murdering Poland's political and military elite. As news filtered through that the disaster had effectively decapitated Warsaw, many believed they were seeing a repetition of history. It wasn't long before accusations flew around that Russia was responsible for the crash, just like the 1940 massacre.

Lech Kaczyński is the twin brother of the current PiS chairman, Jarosław Kaczyński. Although investigators declared the crash a result of human error, PiS's 2015 electoral campaign fed on populist anger and pledged to get to the bottom of the Smolensk mystery. Defence Minister Antoni Macierewicz took the lead and refuted the recorded account of the disaster, claiming that the previous centre-right Polish government had secretly coordinated with Moscow. Macierewicz promised a fresh look at Smolensk, based on new evidence that he insisted had been suppressed by PiS's predecessors.

This horrific human tragedy contributed to conspiracies and beliefs that Russia – representing the old communist regime – was still trying to undermine and harm an independent Poland, while the previous government with its links to the past was working in partnership with the country's historic enemy. It's easy to see how these suspicions could be whipped up into support for the far right and nationalistic fervour.

Jarosław Kaczyński's PiS attracted its voters by promising to break away from the corrupt regimes of the recent past, justifying the destruction of judicial independence as clearing away old communist judges and claiming that natalist policies would support ordinary working families over business elites. In part due to the terrible loss he has endured, Kaczyński treats politics as a personal crusade, one that performs the fascist understanding of anti-corruption. PiS's attacks on reproductive and sexual rights show that the far right sees progressive rights as a corruption of the natural order: reversing these rights means restoring that order, regardless of the party's own corruption.

Corruption has a long and ignoble history in Italy, another Catholic European country with a growing far right that claims traditional values are under attack by progressive elites. The example of Italy helps us to understand how the far right links nature with nation, as mainstream politicians claim that progressive positions on issues such as abortion and LGBTIQ rights are creating a demographic and existential threat to Italy.

Leading the anti-gender charge in Italy is Lega's Matteo Salvini, another World Congress of Families speaker whose party has been embroiled in corruption scandals of its own. The divorced politician, who once posed for a sexy photo to raise money for the anti-abortion group Movimento per la Vita, has made a name for himself in recent years by taking selfies, kissing rosaries and defending the 'natural family', which he claims is under systematic assault in the West. In doing so, he links family and nation, argues that to be patriotic is to be pro-life and has stoked a culture war designed to help his party consolidate and widen its support.

Two years after Orbán was met with rapturous applause by anti-abortion, anti-LGBTIQ activists at the World Congress of Families, Salvini was welcomed to the congress stage in Verona. The location was deliberate: in 2018 the city's government had declared Verona a 'pro-life city'. The league's Alberto Zelgar put forward the motion to create this designation, saying that 'we defend the social value of giving birth' in a 'country that suffers a heavy demographic crisis'.[34] Verona's pro-life leadership claims that Italy is missing 'six million children ... from its shrinking population as a consequence of abortion'.[35] Such themes were reflected in Salvini's WCF speech: he railed against a perceived 'demographic winter' linked to migration and abortion, and spoke of Europe's 'crisis of empty cribs' in rhetoric that evoked Mussolini's 1922 address.[36]

Journalist Claire Provost, who pioneered feminist investigative journalism as part of *openDemocracy*'s 'Tracking the Backlash' project, reported from the Verona meeting while under cover. She described the speeches as openly mixing 'anti-immigrant and "pro family propaganda" ... [promising] to address their countries' "demographic decline" by getting more (white) women to have babies rather than letting more (non-white) people in. At times, it feels to me as if they're wrapping racism in a "family-friendly" blanket.'[37]

So far, so far right. Salvini, his party and his supporters want to restrict women's access to reproductive justice, incentivise birth, and close the door to people migrating into the country. Lega aims to cement its own power by positioning itself in defence of the family and the nation, all while asserting white male supremacy. It proposes offering financial incentives to encourage women with an unplanned pregnancy to keep the baby and choose adoption – a classic example of natalist policy utilising women's bodies to boost birth rates. Other policies included offering free land to large families, and providing funding to anti-abortion groups. 'Fascism and populism are getting closer and closer here in Italy,' family lawyer Marcelle Pirrone told journalists in the run-up to the 2019 World Congress of Families. 'The laws they are proposing on issues involving family and women use absolutely typical language of fascism. It is promoting pure Italian families. They are giving women money to stay at home and have children.'[38]

Of course, as I mentioned above in the context of Hungary, financial support for mothers and children is not a bad thing. But when combined with rhetoric around 6 million missing

Italian children – a number surely chosen to associate abortion with the Holocaust in people's minds – this financial offering once again reduces women's bodies to vessels. The idea that the state should pay women to continue an unwanted pregnancy before giving the baby up for adoption, as part of a strategy to produce more (white) Italian babies for pure Italian families is reminiscent of Margaret Atwood's dystopian novel *The Handmaid's Tale*. The approach threatens to remove women's autonomy over their bodies, instead putting their wombs at the service of patriarchal families, and, by extension, the patriarchal nation-state.

Salvini's defence of the so-called natural family constitutes an explicit power grab by the far right: its strategy involves the conflation of family and nation, which is a fundamental pillar in the fascist thought architecture. To be pro-life and pro-family is to support the nation and defend the country from decline. By successfully linking the notion of family to the nation, Salvini and his followers can paint pro-abortion, feminist and LGBTIQ people as anti-Italian; and of course, a progressive society can be positioned as a live threat to Italy.

This is only part of the story. The other part is linked to an anti–European Union agenda that really took hold after the 2008 financial crash. The 2008 global financial meltdown hit Italy hard – as did the subsequent economic bruising by the EU. While the EU's punishing austerity programme is normally associated with Greece, it also targeted Italy. Understandably, this caused huge resentment against the EU, and its northern states in particular.

For Salvini, the austerity measures allowed him to position the EU as an enemy of Italy – not only economically, but socially too. As we have explored above, conspiracy theorists and white supremacists believe the EU is engineering the 'Islamisation of the West' by encouraging migration from the Global South, while promoting abortion, LGBTIQ rights and sex education which they perceive as a deliberate attack on the white birth rate. Salvini built on this conspiracy theory, focusing on the EU stance on migration and its progressive politics, and suggested to his electorate that along with its austerity measures, the EU was imposing anti-Italian values on the country. This allowed the far right in Italy to synthesise its family-rights and anti-EU agendas. The austerity that was hurting Italy was attached to another imposition: the progressive politics of a supposedly elitist EU, which, the far right claims, wants to undermine Italian family values, or even commit white genocide.

For feminists, and for women in general, the future looks bleak. According to journalist and activist Giulia Siviero, Italy has become a 'proving ground' for what happens to women's rights when nationalists take power. 'It's common ground in ideology. They come together on immigration issues and on women's bodies – they fit together ideologically,' Siviero said. 'It's as if Lega created a sort of tank where all these parts could come together in one big pot.'[39]

The Italian far right presents its nation as under siege from outside forces intent on imposing immigration, austerity and a progressive agenda. Salvini promised to defend the traditional Italian values of marriage, family, children and Catholicism against invading forces who believe families can have two mothers or two fathers, and who argue that abortion is a human right. Italy, his case ran, had been weakened by this assault on its heritage, exacerbated by increasing migration from the Global South. The far right claimed it could rebuild the nation-state and restore the fascist mythic past – through family, religion, racism and the exploitation of women's reproductive labour. Salvini assured voters that there would be a return to the *natural* family – with abortion and the LGBTIQ community therefore marked out as *unnatural*.

Provost reported that during the Verona Congress Salvini performed 'rhetorical acrobatics in a bid to cast [pro abortion, pro LGBTIQ people] as authoritarians who want to impose their views on others' – a classic move from the Agenda Europe playbook. Salvini praised his supporters and far-right audience: 'You are the vanguard ... that keeps the flame alive for what 99.9 per cent of people want.' Salvini, Lega and its supporters, he argued, represent the real Italy, the *natural* Italy, which is under threat from immigration, abortion, and same-sex families. Its sovereignty could only be defended and protected by Salvini and his League.

In the run-up to the 2019 European elections, Lega official Claudio D'Amico told Provost: 'When we go to vote ... look for candidates that support the family ... we will win!'[40] The party recycled the rhetoric from the congress about demographic decline, an assault on family and the need to increase the Italian birth rate, and scored an electoral victory. World Congress of Families founder Brian Brown took partial credit for the party's European election success.[41]

At the time of writing in 2022, Lega has joined forces with a second far-right party, Brothers of Italy. Its leader Giorgia Meloni has become Italy's first female prime minister, in coalition with Lega and Silvio Berlusconi's Forza Italia, on an anti-immigration, anti-gender platform. Brothers of Italy has roots going back to Mussolini's fascist leadership, and while Meloni denies that she shares Mussolini's ideas, she has also been careful not to condemn his rule. Like Salvini, Meloni has taken an antagonistic stance towards the EU and joined her fellow far-right European leaders in weaponising the debate over gender, saying that no one will take away her identity as a 'woman, a mother, an Italian and a Christian'.[42]

'It is a very strategic and even cynical approach they are taking,' said Datta, explaining why far-right parties including Brothers of Italy, Lega, Fidesz, and PiS are increasingly adopting anti-gender positions to win support. 'They know that there's an electorate for that and that electorate is not being catered to by any other political party since a lot of the mainstream centre-right parties have become more progressive over time. There is a part of the electorate in many countries which is not happy with this. They're not being served by what had been the usual conservative or Christian democratic parties. The far right see an opening in this. By simply shifting their messages a little bit, they're able to rake in a good part of that electorate.'

According to the fascist thought architecture, a patriarchal family structure – with the father/husband holding authority, free from state interference – is crucial to the far right. For this reason, far-right political parties seek to undermine abortion rights, which allows women to take reproductive control. But, as the trad wife subculture demonstrates, such parties also want to restrict women's freedoms even further: conservative support for family values involves attacking divorce laws and protections for women who are experiencing domestic abuse. In the US, Trump undermined protections against domestic abuse in order to meet the demands of his male supremacist base. Putin has effectively decriminalised domestic abuse in Russia, as he seeks to build a society based on the fascist mythic past. Ordo Iuris in Poland drafted an alternative to the Istanbul Convention on Gender-Based Violence, titled the Convention on the Rights of the Family. The document takes a far-right approach to violence within the family – it is 'concerned with attempts to undermine natural notions of the family, sex, marriage and parenthood', and argues that 'the family is the foundation of social order and fundamental group unit of society, primary to the State and autonomous towards public authorities.'

In Spain, the far right has echoed this attack on gender-based violence, with Vox leading the charge against women's safety and security. In a 2018 document titled '100 Urgent Vox Measures for Spain', the party declared itself in favour of repealing the 2004 law on gender-based violence designed to protect women and girls, arguing that the law discriminates against men.[43] Instead, Vox claims, the law should protect *everyone* from violence, including men, children and elderly people. It's laughable: of course there are laws against doing violence to men, children and elderly people in Spain. The law simply recognises that gender and sex are factors in men's violence against women, that women experiencing gendered abuse need specific protections, and that sex should be taken into consideration when preventing and prosecuting cases of male violence against women.

Vox's attack on gender-based violence laws shows how far-right ideas about women's rights can move from the extreme into the mainstream by shifting the Overton window, leading to centre-right parties' adoption of the far-right policies. The more Vox has emphasised the so-called discriminatory nature of gender-based violence laws, the more rival parties started to adopt similar anti-women policies to shore up their own support. This was apparent in the way Spain's conservative People's Party (Partido Popular – also known as the Popular Party) voiced its own opposition to the gender-based violence law. Scrambling for a response to Vox's rising popularity, PP willingly embraced the call for all victims of violence to be protected, no matter their gender or age – a protection that was already in place in the general laws against assault and murder.

Electorally, PP's support had been hit by the rising popularity of Vox among right-wing voters. It was a classic case of what Datta referred to in our conversation, where the far right attracts voters who feel they are no longer served by the 'usual conservative or Christian democratic parties'. If PP wanted to hold onto its vote share and win power, it knew it had to out-right the far right, including on women's issues. This is exactly what the UK's Conservative Party has done on Brexit and immigration: making far-right parties irrelevant by adopting hardline policies, informed by extremist agitation, and attracting a new electoral base. This allowed the Conservatives to neutralise the electoral threat posed by parties such as UKIP, the BNP, and the Brexit/Reform Party in order to hold onto power – with the result that mainstream politics have been pushed towards the hard right.

While PP defended the achievements of the fight against violence against women, feminist journalist Ana Bernal points out that 'its discourse has hardened in the face of Vox's one-upmanship'.[44] Her concerns are shared by sociology professor Maria Silvestre, who worries that the 'biggest danger with Vox is that its discourse might be be legitimised by the right'.[45]

A similar pattern was apparent in the way both PP and Vox attacked abortion rights in Spain. Up until 2010, abortion in Spain was governed by a 1985 law which only allowed terminations in cases of rape or incest, or physical danger to the mother and/or baby. Now elective abortion is allowed up to fourteen weeks. Vox wants to end all public funding for abortions and, eventually, ban the procedure all together. A ban on abortion, it claims, will protect the family and thereby the nation, by making Spain great again. The People's Party was determined not to be outdone in its opposition to abortion. In the run-up to the 2019 April election, representatives from both parties attended anti-abortion protests, while PP leader Pablo Casado advocated returning to Spain's restrictive 1985 abortion laws. Through his attacks on the 2010 abortion law, Casado won the endorsement of Hazte Oír and CitizenGO – despite Vox's traditional alliance with Hazte Oír, and the fact that CitizenGO was credited with revitalising Vox's political fortunes in 2019.[46]

The 2021 Madrid elections demonstrated how interdependent Vox, the PP and Hazte Oír/CitizenGO had become. In the run-up to the vote, CitizenGO ran a petition asking PP mayoral candidate Isabel Díaz Ayuso to 'commit herself' to an anti-LGBTIQ, anti-abortion agenda. It asked supporters to 'sign this campaign and let Isabel Díaz Ayuso know that without a commitment to your values, she will not have your vote'. Petitioners signed up to the statement, 'I do not want to vote for a candidate who does not guarantee that she will defend life and who is lukewarm about abortion … A candidate who does not dare to repeal the trans and LGTBI laws of Madrid.' CitizenGO reminded supporters that the Vox candidate Rocío Monasterio 'has promised in writing to defend what you believe. In fact, we hope that Rocío Monasterio *will push* Ayuso to do the right thing' (my emphasis). The election delivered fragile power to Ayuso, but PP fell short of winning the majority of seats needed for an outright victory. Instead, the party had to turn to Vox for support to form a new coalition government – bringing the far-right agenda closer to power and mainstreaming Vox's anti-gender policies in Madrid's politics.

The Spanish anti-abortion, anti-LGBTIQ knows it does need to put all their political eggs in Vox's basket. They could achieve their anti-women, anti-LGBTIQ aims by encouraging the mainstream right – desperate to protect its own vote share from Vox's insurgency – to adopt far-right positions.

Shifting the Overton window on debates around reproductive rights in order to win mainstream support for anti-abortion measures is precisely what the neo-Nazi L'SNS party has achieved in Slovakia, a country in Eastern Europe that borders Poland, Czechia, Hungary, Ukraine and Austria.

In the 2016 elections, the far-right L'SNS won 8 per cent of the vote and fourteen parliamentary seats, in part thanks to the electoral know-how of its neo-Nazi leader Marian Kotleba. He had transformed the party's image: previously the domain of skinhead thugs, it began to present itself as a choice for concerned citizens who wanted to protect Slovakia's traditional heritage. In 2020, L'SNS did well again, becoming the fourth-biggest party in parliament. The party has spent its time in power normalising far-right attitudes towards abortion, bringing in mainstream support for its anti-abortion agenda and creating a political atmosphere that views women's rights with suspicion and as something that should be curbed.

The rise of L'SNS leader Kotleba was sharp and swift – before a crashing fall. In 2020 he was sentenced to four years in prison over his use of Nazi symbolism in political campaigning.

This included making charity donations in sums that evoked neo-Nazi associations, for example a gift of €1,488, a figure which alludes both to the neo-Nazi slogan Fourteen Words and to 'Heil Hitler'.[47] His party's policy platform was titled 'Fourteen Steps for the Future of Slovakia and Our Children' – another nod to the 'Fourteen Words slogan mentioned in Chapter Two.[48] While his imprisonment effectively ended Kotleba's career, he has successfully managed to shift the abortion debate in Slovakian politics. Slovakia is a perfect example of how a far-right party can mainstream its anti-gender goals through a pincer movement of mob pressure and elite political representation.

When Ľ'SNS first entered Slovakia's parliament in 2016, there was little appetite from mainstream conservatives to work with the party – not least because its neo-Nazi associations were so blatant. While Kotleba had swapped his fascistic green uniform for dapper suits in order to win electoral support, his history of skinhead violence was well known. This is a man who has described the Nazi-occupied Slovak state as 'heaven', and who used to run a shop called KKK where he sold far-right merchandise.[49] He owed his early electoral successes to running anti-Roma campaigns and hosting beauty pageants aimed at 'girls learning to present themselves as ladies, and for them to see that there is still a world that values women's dignity and spiritual beauty'.[50]

But conservatives' traditional reluctance to vote with the far right started to change in 2018, when Ľ'SNS launched its first anti-abortion bill. It did so in a grossly sexist press conference, with party spokesmen claiming women had abortions because they wanted to stay young, slim and 'debauched' – echoing the rhetoric of the Great Replacement/race suicide from white supremacist corners of the web and in incel chat boards. The *Slovak Spectator* reported: 'Of course, it should not surprise anybody that the Ľ'SNS, of all parliamentary parties, would be the one to try and curb the freedom of women, and remain a safe space for men to continue speaking and acting like it is their duty and their right to decide about the bodies and the lives of women.'[51]

Conservatives had made a lot of noise about never working with the far right, but this bill put pressure on them to cosy up to the extremists. Anti-abortion groups, including Slovakia's powerful Catholic Church, allegedly urged right-wing MPs to support the neo-Nazi proposals, arguing that the end of banning abortion justified the means of collaborating with fascists.[52] Mainstream conservative reluctance to vote with the far right started to melt away. 'The proposition was to have a very strong anti-abortion law,' explained women's rights activist Zuzana Kriskova.[53] She has been a leading voice in Slovakia on all kinds of reproductive health issues, including obstetric violence and abortion rights. 'There was a big discussion in society with the conservatives, the so-called classic parties, saying oh, I know it is coming from these neo-fascists but you should support it because it is a very good idea.'

Despite the powerful voices pushing for the mainstream right to support the bill, it did not pass. Many conservative MPs continued to resist allying with Ľ'SNS, even when it came to their shared goal of restricting women's right to abortion, determining instead that Christians did not need to ally with fascists in order to promote 'pro-life' policies. But by 2020, things had taken a different turn: when Ľ'SNS brought a new anti-abortion bill to the table, seventeen mainstream MPs voted with the fascists in favour of a ban. Lending their votes to the far right marked a clear break with the status quo. What had once been unconscionable had become normal over time, with centre-right MPs now happy to align with fascism to deny women their human rights. 'It was quite a lot of them, and I was very surprised,' said Elis, a feminist activist who organised a pro-choice demo in Bratislava in July 2020, as a series of anti-abortion bills were voted on. 'Because they usually don't want to be accused of a connection with a neo-Nazi party.

This is becoming mainstream. Fascism in our country really is becoming mainstream.'[54]

The willingness of some conservative MPs to vote on fascist lines in summer 2020 demonstrated two ways in which far-right anti-abortion views are adopted into mainstream politics. First, L'SNS had successfully used abortion as the gateway to winning parliamentary support for its ideology. Attacking women's rights was now a proven method to bring MPs onto its side, providing the party with greater legitimacy and, it hoped, future support from anti-choice, rebel parliamentarians. Trashing women's rights to bodily autonomy is not simply a far-right aim in and of itself; it's a way for extremists to be accepted into the centre, to consolidate power, and mainstream their influence.

L'SNS had also spent two years attacking women's rights in order to normalise a discourse that treated abortion as inherently evil, a procedure sought by vain, lazy and debauched women, creating the myth that there was an urgent situation in need of legislative intervention.[55] As this view of abortion became more familiar, relatively centrist MPs felt they had to adopt and propose their own anti-women policies: attacks on abortion were no longer beyond the pale of respectable politics.

When L'SNS proposed its draconian ban on abortion, everyone knew it wouldn't pass. Even though Slovakia had elected neo-Nazi minority to parliament, there wasn't enough popular support to mirror neighbouring Poland's strict abortion laws banning terminations in nearly all circumstances. However, L'SNS and its new conservative allies knew that pushing an extreme ban would make any new laws that tried to restrict abortion access more palatable in comparison. By shifting the Overton window to the extreme right, space opened up for restrictive bills – such as extending the cooling-off period or cutting state funding for abortions – to appear as reasonable compromise.

'But what is the compromise?' Kriskova demanded. 'On the one hand, you have people who want to ban abortion. On the other, you have the recognition that women are people. Women have human rights. And those rights include access to healthcare which means access to safe abortion. Women have a right to dignity, to bodily autonomy, a right to privacy, and to informed consent. The compromise in this case means that we will sacrifice the most vulnerable groups of women – including women living with violent partners and women from low-income households.'

With its two-year attack on abortion rights, L'SNS had succeeded in normalising the belief that abortion is a bad thing for women and society, and therefore that Slovakia should endorse new barriers to make it harder for women to access safe, legal terminations. The population was being groomed to see further restrictions as a sensible middle ground between women's human rights, and a total ban. Since that first attempt, conservative parties have continued to introduce new restrictions on abortion. Some have been successful.

The anti-abortion pitch from L'SNS is blatantly fascist, in comparison to far-right leaders in Hungary, Poland, Italy and Spain who lean heavily on religious rhetoric to win support for their anti-gender policies. But a Christian focus only works for some voters. 'People associated with political parties already involved in Agenda Europe, who thought their Christian message was not getting very far needed to create a pagan version of themselves that can still convey the same Christian messages but in a secular fashion,' Neil Datta told me. This was the approach adopted by the Netherlands' far-right party Forum for Democracy, whose leader Thierry Baudet has already appeared above as an example of far-right antagonism towards freedom.

The Forum for Democracy party in the Netherlands became the largest party in the 2019 South Holland, North Holland and Flevoland provincial elections. It won on a far-right policy platform: anti-EU, anti-immigration, pro–high culture and sceptical of the climate crisis. It is against women's and LGBTIQ rights, and promoted a hotline for students to report 'left-wing indoctrination' in universities. In this, it followed the example of the Leadership Institute and far-right youth organisation Turning Point USA, whose *Professor Watchlist* website allows students to denounce left-wing academics.

Its leader Thierry Baudet, who was mentored by late Conservative philosopher Roger Scruton, garnered a reputation for taking nude selfies, and he has posed alongside alt-right provocateur Milo Yiannopoulos. His speeches to the party faithful have included coded terms such as 'cultural Marxism', a reference to antisemitism, and he claims to speak to the 'boreal' world, the fantasy of a white ethno-state of Northern Europeans. Baudet's funding comes from the owner of pornographic websites, real estate moguls, bankers and investment firms, among others. Like Prime Minister Johnson in the UK, Baudet appeals to the idea of elite culture, and quotes Latin and Greek mythology in his speeches – while portraying ordinary Dutch people as being under attack by European, metropolitan elites intent on undermining national culture, pride and tradition.

Baudet also echoes the Great Replacement conspiracy theory in his speeches and his writing. In an essay for the conservative *American Affairs* journal, Baudet criticises the 'individualism' of women pursuing a career and choosing to delay motherhood. Similar to the rhetoric employed by Lauren Southern in her YouTube videos, he claims women's liberation is a con: 'What happens when they hit thirty? If they continue to work full hours, building a family becomes extremely difficult, if not impossible.' In the essay, Baudet accused women's liberation of causing the 'demographic decline of Europe'.[56] When questioned about this by *Politico*, he responded, 'it certainly is the case that when society does not reproduce in sufficient numbers to maintain itself, then either the economy is going to experience a very deep decline, or you're going to have to compensate for that loss in reproduction rates by immigration, which is a very destructive force for your national culture. So either way, you're going to end up in trouble.'[57]

I've covered six case studies here, but the mainstreaming of far-right attacks on women's rights is not confined to Poland, Spain, Italy, Hungary, Slovakia and the Netherlands. When Greece elected the centre-right party New Democracy in 2019, it almost immediately considered a scheme incentivising Greek women to have more children to defeat a perceived 'demographic crisis' of rising immigration and low white birth rates, while also attacking laws that protect women from gender-based violence. Germany's Alternative für Deutschland is another example where an increasingly influential far-right party positions abortion and women's rights as fuelling a demographic crisis. AfD's solution for 'Germany's negative demographic trend ... is to attain a higher birth rate by the native population by stimulating family policies'.[58] To hammer home the message, AfD launched an election poster featuring a pregnant woman captioned: 'New Germans? We make our own.' In France, the far right is increasingly using ideas about gender ideology to push its harmful message, while 2022 presidential hopeful Éric Zemmour pushed the Great Replacement conspiracy theory to win electoral support. All have managed to shift extremist anti-abortion and anti-immigrant rhetoric from the fringes into mainstream parliamentary politics, often using the methods I've described in the case studies above.

The UK, where I live, is not immune from the trend sweeping across Europe. As politics swing ever further to the right on issues from Brexit to deregulation and climate, the UK is in danger of becoming deeply embroiled in a culture war in which women's sexual and reproductive rights will be the main casualty.

The truth is that the UK is already enmeshed in far-right European politics. When it was still a member of the European

Union, the Conservative government's alliance with the European Conservatives and Reformists (ECR) grouping meant it supported Hungary's authoritarian leadership in a crunch vote on Orbán's flouting of EU norms. Since the UK left the EU, the British Conservative Party has maintained far-right alliances across the region by chairing the European Conservatives and Democratic Alliance in the Council of Europe, a supranational body cofounded by Winston Churchill in the wake of the Second World War. Through its membership in this alliance, Britain's Conservative Party is connected to many of the political parties mentioned above: PiS was a cofounder of the group, and its members include representatives from AfD, Vox, Greek Solution, Lega, Brotherhood of Italy and the Freedom Party of Austria. Sitting alongside Conservative MPs are representatives of an Estonian nationalist party whose leader described its immigration policy thus: 'Are you black? Then go back to where you came from.'

The Conservative Party's entanglement with this alliance in the Council of Europe was almost completely ignored by the British press until I broke the story in 2021, in *Byline Times*.[59] The grouping is significant because it reveals what kind of politicians the mainstream British right is willing to sit alongside and ally with: anti-immigrant, anti-abortion, anti-LGBTIQ activists, and proponents of the Great Replacement conspiracy theory. It is clear that there has been a rightward shift in UK politics, away from protecting human rights.

It was a sunny Saturday afternoon in September 2019 when I grasped how the far right had become a mainstream force in British politics. For the fourth time that week I was in Whitehall, joining pro-democracy protests against Prime Minister Johnson's decision to prorogue (shut down) parliament for five weeks, a move that was later found to be unlawful by the Supreme Court. The day is hot and bright; I got moved on by the police who mistook me for an anarchist in my leather jacket; one of my friends gave a great speech; we all sang 'Solidarity

Forever' and 'The Internationale'. Our optimistic mood was threatened, however, as at either end of Whitehall, groups of far-right activists started to gather. One had already broken ranks and squared up to left-wing journalist Owen Jones; another had thrown a glass at a war memorial. An elderly man shook his walking stick at me, yelling 'Scum!' The group, including supporters of far-right activist Stephen Yaxley-Lennon (also known as Tommy Robinson), started chanting, 'We love you, Boris!' How had we got to the point where far-right thugs were declaring their love for the UK prime minister?

The answer takes us back once again to the Brexit vote in 2016. Since the referendum, Britain has moved steadily towards the right, particularly when it comes to immigration and democracy. The Brexit narrative focused on immigration – aided by a hostile-environment policy and the notorious 'Go home' vans driving around multi-ethnic neighbourhoods. The influence of an anti-immigrant focus in the Brexit debate was manifest in the rise in hate crimes against black and minority ethnic people, particularly Muslim women, following the referendum. Populist leaders, including Boris Johnson, Priti Patel and Nigel Farage, promoted a message that Brexit would give Britain control of its borders and end free movement; so did the former prime minister Theresa May, whose obsessive anti-immigration agenda had led to human rights outrages such as the Windrush scandal.[60]

Brexit was never really about immigration though – not, at least, to its biggest backers in Whitehall, the majority of the Leave-supporting Conservative Party and the cluster of think tanks in Westminster and Washington that pushed for a harder and harder EU exit. Instead, Brexit offers an opportunity for mass deregulation of workers' rights and environmental protections, and the removal of barriers to wealth-making. It provides a once-in-a-generation chance to abolish pesky rules such as maternity pay and protections for part-time workers (two regulations that disproportionately impact women), and to turn Britain into an all-singing, all-dancing low-regulation, low-tax, free trade haven. Brexit was sold as a solution to the grievances of a disenchanted white working class, living in left-behind and impoverished towns – in fact, it is a boon to big money and disaster capitalism, and it has the potential to make some very rich and powerful people even richer and even more powerful.

The far-right economic policies associated with a hard Brexit and the steady swing to the right of the modern Conservative Party are promoted by a series of UK and US think tanks. On the UK side, these organisations inhabit Tufton Street in Westminster, and include the Institute for Economic Affairs, the Policy Exchange, Civitas, the Taxpayers Alliance, the Centre for Policy Studies, the Freedom Association, and the Adam Smith Institute. When former Downing Street adviser, Brexit architect and human hand-grenade Dominic Cummings gave an interview to the BBC in 2021, he referred to a group of a 'dozen organisations' working to enact their own agenda on the country: he meant the Tufton Street think tanks. These organisations tended to support a hard Brexit and deregulation, and are against policies such as international aid and workers' rights. ResPublica, one of the leading right-leaning think tanks in this loose grouping, has links to Agenda Europe – its director Phillip Blonde opened the Dublin summit. Many of the Tufton Street think tanks are part of the Atlas Network, a global organisation that brings together nearly 500 'free market organisations' to further the 'cause of liberty'. The network connects US and UK radical-right thinkers and leaders, and its membership includes the Heritage Foundation – an anti-abortion, anti-LGBTIQ, climate crisis–denying and hard-Brexit-supporting US think tank with multiple links to British politicians. 'There's at least a certain faction in the Conservative Party which is in bed with a certain number of think tanks,' said Neil Datta, 'and I think that faction holds quite a bit of influence over the whole Conservative Party at the moment and so they are able to get away with certain things. Whether it is directly influenced by US think tanks or whether there is simply a convergence of views, the UK actors are reinforced in their thinking by what they hear from these think tanks.'

The Heritage Foundation began life in the 1970s, with a huge grant from the right-wing Scaife Family Charitable Trust to set it on its feet. It was 'purposefully political, priding itself on creating, selling and injecting deeply conservative ideas into the American mainstream'.[61] The foundation's remit was to produce research and policy papers promoting a deregulated capitalist economy that would benefit its wealthy sponsors, including Scaife, the Koch brothers, Smith Richardson, Adolph Coors, Lynde and Harry Bradley, and John M. Olin. Alongside its economic remit, the Heritage Foundation is concerned with 'the disintegration of the family'.[62] Like the radical-right billionaires in the previous chapter, it might embrace freedom when it comes to trade and oil – but it is determined to control reproductive and sexual rights.

In the years before and after Brexit, various UK Conservative politicians met with the Heritage Foundation. These included former international trade minister Liam Fox, who delivered the annual 2018 Margaret Thatcher Freedom Lecture at the foundation in Washington D.C. He was addressing some of the best-connected people in US politics: Heritage members are part of the Council for National Policy and provided top personnel for Trump's team. Other Conservative MPs who have addressed the foundation are former home secretary Priti Patel, former environment secretary Owen Paterson and former prime minister Liz Truss. In February 2022, the then Conservative Party chairman Oliver Dowden gave a frankly bizarre speech, in which he claimed that 'social justice warriors' and the 'woke mob' were threatening national security by demanding governments focus on cultural issues such as pronouns and statues, which distracted from tensions with hostile states such as Russia and China. At the 2015 Conservative

Party Conference, the Heritage Foundation participated in a drinks reception organised by the Institute of Economic Affairs; former chancellor Sajid Javid was the guest speaker.

The pro-Brexit Conservative Liam Fox is the constituency MP for the village where I grew up. He's also the founder of an 'educational charity' (think tank) called the Atlantic Bridge, which is supposed to promote US/UK trade relations. Atlantic Bridge was largely funded by Sir Michael Hintze, also donor to Prime Minister Johnson and an alleged funder of Agenda Europe. Fox's initiative made him popular with the radical-right ideologues at the Heritage Foundation, who were keen on the idea that Atlantic Bridge could play 'a key role in building links between British and American libertarians, neoconservatives, Tea Party enthusiasts, and their mutual corporate interests'.[63] Heritage Foundation sponsored Atlantic Bridge events before Fox's think tanks was closed down in 2011 following complaints to the Charity Commission. Robin Simcox is another link between the Heritage Foundation and the UK government: appointed as lead commissioner for the government's Commission for Countering Extremism in 2021 by then home secretary Priti Patel, he was also a former Margaret Thatcher fellow at the Heritage Foundation. An investigation by *Byline Times* journalist Nafeez Ahmed revealed how Simcox 'promoted several racist and anti-Muslim conspiracy theorists, including [being] a proponent of the "Great Replacement" ideology', and that he 'spoke in 2019 at a notorious American anti-immigrant hate group, the Center for Immigration Studies'.[64]

Datta described the US radical-right influence as built on a range of actors, including 'think tanks that produce dangerous ideas and sell them across the world. Their main consumers are libertarian, right-wing political and economic actors. And it looks like the UK may be one where the economic agenda of these think tanks took the greatest foothold. I think that in part is what contributed to Brexit, and especially the hard Brexit, that then became reality.' The Atlantic Bridge wasn't the only

Eurosceptic think tank collaborating with the Heritage Foundation to push a radical right agenda. The Initiative for Free Trade, founded by former MEP, prominent Brexit supporter, and now member of House of Lords Daniel Hannan, worked with the Heritage Foundation to draw up a detailed, 239-page draft legal text for a US–UK free trade deal.[65] Other think tanks from the Atlas Network took part in the consultation process, which was published by the Cato Institute, a radical-right initiative from the Koch brothers. The Cato Institute also funds anti-gender action in Europe.

The relationship between the Heritage Foundation and numerous Eurosceptic MPs and MEPs has helped to influence and dictate a Brexit model that satisfies the needs of the organisation's wealthy backers. The disaster-capitalist fantasies of many Brexit enthusiasts are stoking a regulatory bonfire set alight by UK ministers eager to scrap so-called red tape (otherwise known as workers' rights). What this means is that an agenda set by radical-right think tanks both in the US and the UK, including the Heritage Foundation, the Freedom Association, the Taxpayers Alliance, the IEA and other powerful US players and funders– shared with and led by some prominent UK Conservatives and party donors – has become the defining policy of twenty-first-century Britain.

The influence of these radical-right think tanks on UK government policy demonstrates how seemingly fringe US and UK interests can change the direction of an entire nation. The question we must ask is: What is to stop such think tanks expanding their influence on Conservative Party policy when it comes to other hot agenda items, including abortion and LGBTIQ rights? When special-interest groups gain influence over one issue, such as Brexit, how do we prevent their influence leading political parties on other matters? Can this be prevented? With a global right keen to embark on a culture war that positions liberal progressive politics against traditionalism, white supremacy and family rights, will think tanks pushing anti-abortion, anti-gender ideologies have a chance to bring their policy platforms to the cabinet table?

Worryingly, the answer may soon be *yes*, because the mainstreaming of hard-right interests that go beyond economics is already happening within the Conservative Party. It's in part an issue of funding: with membership in the doldrums, the Conservative Party has become ever more reliant on a small pool of big-money donors whose interests are expressed via reports and research from friendly think tanks (that don't have to disclose their own funding), leading to niche issues (that benefit or interest a small pool of wealthy individuals) becoming policy proposals. According to research published in *Byline Times*, 92 per cent of the highest-value Conservative donors are men, and the majority are white. Most work in finance. 'We should be worried that a major party in Britain is struggling to raise funds,' economist Frances Coppola explained to Peter Geoghegan for his book *Democracy for Sale*. 'As that continues they will have to dance ever more to the tune of the cranks who fund it. This will likely mean growing numbers of policies that benefit particular niche interests. Already there are signs of obscure deregulatory projects making their way onto the political agenda.'[66]

Very few people cared about Brexit back in 2006, when the men's-rights activist MP Philip Davies launched a campaign to leave the EU with right-wing pressure group and Atlas Network member the Freedom Association. Now the issue has changed the global status of the UK while threatening to destroy its union of countries. No one had even heard of free ports at the start of 2019; but because free ports were a key issue for some Conservative donors, this niche policy area was pushed into the spotlight by sympathetic thank tanks. When the December election rolled into town that same year, free ports were suddenly being defended by voters on whom the policy would have no real-life impact, and the subject is regularly raised during the weekly Prime Minister's Questions session in the House of Commons.

The influence of a small pressure group of Tory MPs, donors and sympathetic think tanks have brought a deregulatory, anti-EU, climate change–denying, anti-woke and anti-workers' rights agenda into the heart of UK politics. This has changed the lives of UK citizens forever. These individuals and groups have been pushing the UK ever further towards normalising a far right policy platform, waging a culture war that positions multibillionaire capitalists as the common man, and workers' rights advocates as the 'metropolitan elite. We cannot take it for granted that the people and organisations who hold both hard Brexit and anti-gender beliefs won't also start to push their anti-abortion and anti-LGBTIQ policy design into UK politics. Some of them are already doing so, with ADF International and a network of anti-abortion charities and family-rights think tanks already having the ear MPs. We should not assume their influence is limited, and that a far-right agenda won't eventually be adopted. After all, the years following the 2016 Brexit vote have already demonstrated the dangers of a populist-right government prepared to launch a culture war that seeks to roll back progressive rights and entrench white male supremacy.

When New Labour came to power in 1997, it implemented pro-LGBTIQ, pro-women policies, not least because overnight, the number of women in the House of Commons doubled. Research has shown that when women's representation in a country's parliament is increased, that parliament tends to adopt more policies that advance gender equality. The changes under Labour, which governed the country until 2010, paved the way for the highly reactionary Conservative Party to move from true blue to light pink. Boris Johnson, who had a history of making homophobic comments (such as describing gay men as 'tank-topped bumboys'), adopted the rainbow mantle and wore a pink Stetson to Pride. In 2013, Prime Minister Cameron legalised equal marriage, and shortly afterwards the Conservatives under Theresa May launched a (later cancelled) review of the Gender Recognition Act to investigate how to reduce the burden of legal transition.

After 2016, things started to change. Homophobic hate crimes went up after the Brexit referendum. In 2021, members of the government's LGBTIQ advisory committee resigned *en masse* after promises to ban conversion therapy stalled and were weakened, with Equalities Minister Kemi Badenoch admitting that the government did not 'intend to stop those who wish to seek spiritual counselling as they explore their sexual orientation'. As more and more people marched for Black Lives Matter and demanded social reform, the Conservative government seemed determined to wage a culture war echoing those of authoritarian leaders across Europe. It doubled down on support for racist free speech against so-called cancel culture, condemned acts of anti-racist solidarity, and claimed to stand for an imagined, traditional British citizen who valued colonialism and white male supremacy. Ministers in Johnson's government complained about cultural Marxism and supported racist football fans who booed national players for taking the knee. Downing Street may still be decorated with rainbows during Pride month, but Johnson's pink Stetson seemed very far away.

The more I investigated the reactionary turn in the Vote Leave Conservative government, the more I could pinpoint the cause in its 2019 manifesto promises, when the party was elected with a huge majority on a promise to 'level up' the UK. This commitment involved tackling regional inequality which has seen left-behind towns, particularly in the deindustrialised North and rural South, struggling with poverty, poor health, inadequate housing and few educational opportunities. But the Johnson government had a problem: this inequality that he had promised to sort out was the result of ten years of Conservative-driven austerity.

I'd spent much of the previous half-decade reporting on how the government had ripped the welfare state's safety net to shreds, including by introducing a benefit cap that exacerbated poverty and homelessness, and implementing a benefits system structured so as to push families into debt and rent arrears. It cancelled housing benefits for those under twenty-one (a policy it later reversed), instigated the controversial bedroom tax, so that people living in social housing had to pay extra money for a spare room (including for people with two children under twelve sleeping in their own bedrooms rather than sharing), and brought in a two-child tax credit limit, which meant families with more than two children after 2017 would not receive benefit for their third child or subsequent children (this limit was exempt for women who could prove the child was conceived by rape and that they had subsequently left their abuser). Needless to say, the cost of austerity was disproportionately felt by women – according to Labour Party analysis, 86 per cent of the cuts were financed by women. [67]

At the same time, real-term cuts to education and health services hit the poorest communities hardest, while analysis demonstrated that Labour-run councils were less likely to receive investment from central government. Austerity also undermined the safety net for women escaping violent homes – one in six refuges closed between 2010 and 2016, and changes to the benefits system meant women were often increasingly financially dependent on a controlling partner.[68] The destruction of the welfare state made it harder for women to leave their abusers – enacting a far-right agenda around family rights. This was the context in which Johnson launched his levelling-up electoral promise. As his blue buses roamed the UK, figures published in 2019 by the Trades Union Congress found that the number of children growing up in poverty in working households had increased by 800,000 after nine years of Conservative rule.[69] In 2022, 1.8 million children were growing up in the 'very deepest' poverty, meaning household income could not even cover the most basic essentials such as food and heating.

Of course, Johnson's Conservatives weren't going to blame *themselves* for the problem they promised to solve. Instead, the party had to place the blame for rising inequality on something else – and that something else, I discovered, was equality, also known as *wokeness*. Too much attention had been paid, apparently, to issues of racism and sexism, as opposed to the struggles faced by white, working-class boys and men. Levelling up was to be achieved not by reversing a decade of cuts, but by selling women and minorities down the river.

This plan was revealed in 2020 and 2021 by three significant events. The first was the appointment of David Goodhart and Jessica Butcher as two of four new commissioners to the Equalities and Human Rights Council (EHRC). The second was a speech by the Conservative MP Liz Truss, who was minister for women and equalities at the time. The third was the publication of the *Commission on Race and Ethnic Disparities Report* – otherwise known as the Sewell Report – that underplayed the role systemic racism plays in British society, followed by the publication of a report that blamed discussions of 'white privilege' for a lack of educational attainment in white working-class boys.

Let's take the appointments first: Goodhart had claimed that 'white self-interest' was not the same as racism and criticised what he termed a 'victim-status' among minority groups. He also defended the hostile-environment policies instigated by Theresa May to tackle immigration levels which led to the wrongful deportation of Windrush citizens, discussed in the note above. The EHRC was investigating the Windrush scandal at the time of Goodhart's appointment. Butcher, meanwhile, had attacked feminism as being 'obsessed with victimhood' in common with other forms of 'identity politics'.[70] She argued that women should be 'more resilient' when it came to facing gender discrimination, disputed the existence of the gender pay gap, and claimed the Me Too movement against sexual violence had unfairly ruined men's careers. Butcher also argued that

feminists had denied working-class 'girls' employment opportunities by campaigning to ban Page 3 – the *Sun* newspaper
page that had for years featured a topless young woman. It did
not seem to occur to Butcher that working-class women might
have other aspirations.

At a time when the Black Lives Matter movement was exposing structural racism in the UK, and when the coronavirus
pandemic was sending women's equality into reverse, it was
troubling that a defender of racism and a woman highly critical of feminism were put in charge of equalities and human
rights. It signalled the direction the government planned to
take when it came to equality: the focus would be upon individual self-empowerment, bringing an end to so-called victim
culture, sustained by the conviction that merely *recognising*
intersectionality and the workings of privilege was in itself a
cause of inequality because it harmed and undermined white
male supremacy.

This agenda was laid out more clearly in a speech given by
Liz Truss in her role as minister for women and equalities,
when she introduced the Conservative government's vision for
equalities. She explained, 'our new approach to equality will be
based on the core principles of freedom, choice, opportunity,
and individual humanity and dignity'.[71] This would be achieved,
she went on, by moving 'well beyond the narrow focus of
protected characteristics' as a basis for tackling inequality.
This fails to acknowledge the foundation of equality legislation: protected characteristics exist for the reason that women
and minority groups face oppression and discrimination on a
systemic level. Society is stacked in favour of one group at the
expense of others.

Truss and her Conservative colleagues believe the solution
to inequality does lies not in systemic change, but in individual
character. The layers of social and economic inequality disadvantaged groups face are dismissed and overlooked as challenges
to 'their individual humanity, dignity and agency'. Instead, Truss

prioritised an individualistic approach to empowerment, professing to believe that inequality would end if people were given more agency over their own lives, as opposed to the government coordinating a collective endeavour for systemic change.

There is no doubt that regional inequality and the challenges facing poor, white communities are very real and urgently need tackling. But nowhere in Truss's speech and in subsequent discussion was there a recognition that the people most likely to be poor are women, that white women are poorer than white men, and black or minority ethnic women are more likely to be living in poverty than any other group.[72] Nowhere was there mention of the systemic issues facing black women, who are, among other things, lower paid and disproportionately likely to die in childbirth, or of the fact that people of Bangladeshi heritage earn 20 per cent less than white workers.[73] Of course there are poor white men, and poor white boys' academic (lack of) attainment indeed needs to be addressed. But these problems are not caused by anti-racist movements, LGBTIQ equality, or feminism. Nor are the interests of struggling white men served by ignoring structural inequality in the service of individualism.

Truss's speech represented the victory of the far-right narrative that white men are suffering as a result of women's, black people's and LGBTIQ rights. The claims made in far-right circles that white men are oppressed by feminism and civil rights – that men are the victims of progress – had now entered government policy. By placing the blame on feminism, anti-racism and those fighting for social justice, Truss invoked the cultural-Marxists bogeyman, while refraining from saying the words out loud. Truss is not a far-right politician; she's a libertarian conservative. But in doing so, she allowed a far-right conspiracy theory to dictate government equality policy. That is incredibly dangerous.

The agenda outlined in the speech was never intended to address issues of inequality – nor even to defend the interests of the white working-class boys Truss worries are struggling and falling behind in education. Its purpose was to fan the flames of a culture war that placed the blame for regional and socioeconomic inequality on feminism, anti-racism and the left. It argued that caring about issues of sexism and racism leads to white men losing out.

As has been described in previous chapters, 'cultural Marxism' is a term that echoes the 1930s anti-communism of the Nazi Party. For today's far right, it is an umbrella category for all the groups it hates. The term has become a catch-all for feminists, people of colour, climate crisis activists, refugees, human rights lawyers, LGBTIQ people, left-wing academics, and even those who support wearing masks to stop the spread of coronavirus. These disparate groups have been stigmatised and attacked as cultural Marxists in order to create an enemy in the culture wars.

By 2022, the Conservative Party was having its third leadership contest in six years, after Johnson was forced to resign when it was discovered he had promoted an MP called Chris Pincher despite knowing that he had been accused of sexual harassment on numerous occasions. Almost all the contenders to be the next prime minister launched their own personal wars on woke. The debates between the candidates focused on their hardline stances on equalities – with rows erupting over whether the MPs had previously supported trans rights. One of the contenders, then attorney general Suella Braverman, had previously faced criticism for her use of the term 'cultural Marxists' during a speech about censorship (it's not clear if she knew what it meant).[74] Truss was the favourite to win throughout the contest, her equalities agenda setting the tone of a fractious and ugly race to the bottom. She did eventually win, only to resign as prime minister having spent forty-four days in office, after her announcement of a free market, libertarian economic policy tanked the British pound.

Truss's denial of structural causes of inequality and focus on white working-class boys' attainment were reflected in two subsequent reports: one on racial inequality in the UK known as the Sewell Report after its lead author Professor Tony Sewell, and one on educational attainment compiled by the Education Select Committee.

The Sewell Report dismissed the notion that systemic racism existed in the UK, and claimed instead that racial inequality could be explained by individual factors such as family breakdown. Meanwhile, the 'Left Behind White Pupils from Disadvantaged Backgrounds' report argued that white working-class boys were falling behind in education, in part because discussions of 'white privilege' in the classroom were 'alienating' them. Such discussions have now been made illegal[75] – a hypocritical move from a government that claims to care about freedom of speech, and which quoted Alliance Defending Freedom research on 'cancel culture on campus'.

Both reports are important because they demonstrate the direction and consequences of the culture war being waged over equalities in the UK today and highlight the absolute contradiction inherent in the white supremacist culture wars. When it comes to women and black people, there is a refusal to recognise structural inequality, and we are told inequality should be overcome by individual agency and self-empowerment. There is an exception, however, to the rule that individual agency can overcome inequality – and that exception is white maleness. If the people experiencing disadvantage happen to be white men, the causes are no longer individual but externalised ... and the external forces causing the crisis in white maleness are anti-racist, anti-sexist movements, rhetoric and policies. Similarly, the solution for undermining white male supremacy isn't individual empowerment: it's the systemic rolling back of gains in liberation for women, black and LGBTIQ people.

This is dangerous because it melds traditional Conservative neoliberalism with far-right ideologies in Hannah Arendt's 'alliance of the mob and the elite'. When the elite Conservative Party says that feminism and anti-racism are exacerbating the problems of white men, it signals the mob who actively want to blame the struggles of white men on women and black people. This is the real victim culture: the belief that promoting the rights of women or black people or LGBTIQ people is, in fact, victimising white men. Again, it allows the manufactured fear of cultural Marxism to dictate resolutions to real social problems in a dangerous and frightening way.

The culture war fanned by the Conservatives since 2019, codified in Truss's speech and the two reports, all played out in the 2022 leadership contest, is an alarming example of far-right beliefs about equality infiltrating Westminster. The idea that feminism and anti-racism is the cause of inequality and unfairness, as opposed to the solution, and that a focus on women's and black people's rights is a cause of white male suffering, as opposed to neoliberal capitalism and government-led austerity, is a tenet of far-right ideology.

All of these actions are designed to distract attention: so long as you can blame women for male unemployment – or blame girls and black children for white boys' educational issues, or blame foreigners for housing and hospital bed shortages – you won't be blaming the government. This alliance of the elite and the mob entrenches inequality and privilege, while attacking the most vulnerable and least privileged in society.

The attack on equal rights laws in the guise of pursuing an equalities agenda is deeply troubling, and perhaps the most pernicious example of how far-right ideology has infiltrated mainstream government in the UK. It brings the country much closer to Orbán's Hungary and Salvini's Italy – with populist politicians adopting anti-gender, racist rhetoric that positions the stereotype of a traditional British population as under attack by a liberal, feminist and anti-racist, cultural Marxist elite – even when, as we have seen, women and black and minority ethnic people are more likely to be living in poverty and experiencing systemic disadvantage. This puts us on a dangerous path.

Across Europe over the past ten years, government after government has adopted a far-right narrative that links abortion, immigration and white supremacy. Positions that were once considered extreme, views once confined to hateful screeds on internet forums, are now policy from east to west. The Overton window on abortion has been pushed ever further to the right, as governments stoke a culture war and implement anti-women, anti-immigration policies that stage their leaders as strongman heroes, saviours of the nation and protectors of tradition. Meanwhile, the influence of US and UK far and radical-right lobbyists and donors on British politics has made unimagined futures seem possible.

There is one reason to be cheerful. Having rested on our laurels for so long, the progressive movements in Europe appear to have woken up to the threat coming from far-right anti-gender actors. From Slovakian women banging wooden spoons in protest at anti-abortion laws to the energy of the Black Lives Matter protests, European citizens are standing up and making noise. On the legislative side, progressive politicians in the European Parliament are taking action to protect abortion and LGBTIQ rights on a regional level, adopting the non-binding Matic Report on sexual and reproductive health.

Internationally, the United Nations Human Rights Committee in Geneva is trying to protect women's freedoms by launching a campaign to adopt a policy known as Comment No. 36. The document declares that states must provide access to abortion in cases of rape, incest, danger to the health of the mother and fatal foetal abnormality. This would not change much in Europe, since abortion is legal under those circumstances even in Poland – for now. But in countries such as El Salvador and Paraguay, it would allow women and girls to access safe and legal terminations in limited circumstances. It's a change that does not go far enough – but it is a step in the right direction.

7

The Tipping Point: Which Future Do We Choose?

Why now? Why, after years of progress, are we facing this far-right attack on reproductive and sexual rights? What has happened over the past ten or fifteen years, to push us to this brink?

The attacks on abortion rights over the past fifty years, combined with the collapse of neoliberalism and the 2008 crash, have led us to a tipping point: will capitalism and the far right work together to trap women's bodies in reproductive labour in order to fuel a drive for profits and a fascist, patriarchal worldview? Or do we fight for a world where women's freedoms are not only protected but advanced, in a post-capitalist, equal and fairer society? To make that choice, we first have to realise that we face one, rather than an unstoppable right-wing onslaught. Alerting people to the fact that we have a choice is the purpose of this book.

I have deliberately avoided including much autobiographical detail in this book, but some of my personal history is relevant when thinking about how we reached this tipping point. I was born in 1984, during the miners' strikes and the AIDs epidemic; I started primary school during the first Gulf War, as the Royal Family was imploding. My father is a veteran of the Falklands War, rescued from his bombed ship a month after my parents' wedding. My mother came out the same year the hated Section 28 – a law which banned the promotion of homosexuality and same-sex family relationships – was introduced by UK Conservative Prime Minister Margaret Thatcher, who complained that young people were growing up believing they had the right to be gay. The law had a chilling effect on LGBTIQ people for fifteen years. Throughout my school career, from reception class to A-levels, my gay family was treated as invisible, designated by the law as 'pretend'. For working-class children, for the rare children in gay families, it went without saying that we hated Thatcher and her Tories who had smashed the town where my mum grew up, who had taken away rights from our LGBTIQ community, and who had sent my dad to war.

Then in 1997, when I was twelve, Labour won. I will never forget coming downstairs that May Day morning to my mum saying: 'You should have seen it, on the map, all these places were turning from blue to red.' The influx of new women MPs forced hasty infrastructure redesigns as men's changing rooms were converted into women's toilets and a bar turned into a crèche. The anti-gay laws – from a ban on LGBTIQ people in the military and on LGBTIQ people adopting, to the unequal age of consent and Section 28 – were gone within six years. Labour improved benefits for women and single mothers, and reduced child poverty in a push for gender equality. (For good analysis on the impact of Labour's women – dismissively labelled 'Blair's Babes at the time – read *Labour Women* by Professor Sarah Childs.)

When Labour won, it won in part by promising social progress. If you were coming of age in that moment, as I was, it felt as though progress could only ever go one way. Britain was European, it was gay, it was Britpop, it was multicultural. We were promised that things could only get better and we believed it.

That's not to deny, of course, that the rot was already setting in. Blair ushered in the beginnings of NHS privatisation through the expansion of the PFI scheme. While women's and children's poverty were reduced thanks to new welfare measures such as child tax credits, the demonisation of the poor and those on benefits continued to gain momentum. New Labour opened the door for more migration from Eastern Europe while its Home

Office played to the anti-migration crowd – and when it came to foreign policy, the failed interventions in Iraq and Afghanistan contributed to the destabilisation in the Middle East, causing mass suffering and death. But on that May morning in 1997, it really did feel that the dark days of the previous twenty years had ended and things would now get better. Thanks to the hard work and feminist approach of many women MPs determined to pursue gender mainstreaming in policy – for a while, for some – they did.

As I write this, twenty-five years after that sea-change, across the UK we are embroiled in a culture war triggered by an increasingly far-right authoritarian government attacking Black Lives Matter, LGBTIQ rights and women's access to equality. More children in the UK are living in poverty than ever before, as women's equality slides backwards. In the USA, Biden may have won the popular vote and the Electoral College, but he could not prevent the radical-right forces in his country from ending women's access to safe and legal abortion. In Hungary and Poland, women's and LGBTIQ rights are being shredded by far-right governments – with Greece, Spain, France, Italy and others eager to follow in their footsteps.

Where did it all go wrong? To understand what has fuelled the recent rise of a modern far-right obsessed with migration, the content of women's wombs and a genocidal race war bent on the creation of ethno-states, we need to go back to the 2008 financial crash and the relationship between failing capitalism and rising fascism, which, writes journalist and author Paul Mason, 'is a recurrent symptom of system-failure under capitalism'. He goes on to explain:

> In normal times, capitalism is sustained by a belief system that is passive and pervasive. Simply in order to live our lives we need to believe markets work naturally; that democratic institutions are fair and just; that hard work will be rewarded; that, as technological progress happens, life will get better for ourselves

and our children. These beliefs, taken together, constitute an ideology.[1]

For the forty years leading up to the 2008 crash, the world was governed by the ideology of neoliberal capitalism. It was a capitalism based on the primacy of the individual and the belief that markets – not people or democracy – were in charge. Its proponents would of course deny that neoliberalism is an *ideology*. The pretence of being free from ideology allowed Francis Fukuyama to declare 'the end of history' when the Cold War ended. If the twentieth century was the age of ideology, this new millennium would be all about the self. We were told to trust the markets and we were promised that the markets would self-regulate, as we allowed them in turn to regulate our lives. Neoliberalism prioritised the individual above all, smashing solidarity and collective action in favour of the self. Its creed was individualism, and when it collapsed, it left a gaping hole where society should be.

When the wheels came off the global financial order in 2008, the assumptions and promises that had governed our lives for the previous four decades were smashed to pieces. The neoliberal ideology had failed. But rather than admit this, and seek to fill the hole left by its broken promises, the politicians in charge of our countries simply tried to carry on as if nothing had changed. The governments put the banks on life support with bailouts and quantitative easing. Sure, you can put a financial system on life support. You can't do the same for an ideology.

'The global order [that neoliberalism] established was in ruins post 2008,' Mason explains. 'But ... the psychological impact of it being wrong is immense.' Fascism, he adds, 'is what happens when our faith in this ideology evaporates, and no progressive alternative takes its place'.[2] What happens when ideology breaks? People return to the old certainties: to nature, nation and war.

Much of the progress over the previous forty years began in the 1960s, when capitalism suffered what American economist, educator and US Secretary of the Treasury Janet Yellen has called a 'reproductive shock', with the introduction of the contraceptive pill and the liberalising of abortion laws across the Western world. The medical innovation of the pill and the move towards safe, legal abortion meant centuries of biologically rooted oppression were about to be overturned. The rise of the women's liberation movement gave women in the Global North unprecedented control over their own bodies, fertility and reproduction. The result was that women no longer had to be pinned to reproductive labour. And while it would have been nice if we could have seized this moment of liberation to overthrow the patriarchal capitalist system and become liberated from exploitative and unpaid labour, capitalism had other ideas. Ever adaptable, the system shifted from women's entrapment in reproductive labour and shackled them to productive labour instead. Capitalism gave women a new role, as consumer and worker.

It's not a coincidence that women's increased reproductive freedoms matched a boom period in the Global North, particularly in the United States. In some ways, women gained reproductive rights both because the economy could afford it and because capitalist society urgently needed to grow the labour force and consumer class to continue to fuel its own boom.

It is obviously the case that working-class women had always worked – in service, in factories, as labourers, milliners, seamstresses, teachers – but women's liberation from reproductive labour enabled by this reproductive shock led to an unprecedented number of women entering the workforce. The expansion of women in the workforce also led to a growth of consumers – not least because working women now needed to spend money on goods that gave them space to work, from washing machines and childcare, to the ready meals bemoaned by the trad life followers.

Another reason capitalism was able to adapt and embrace its female workforce was the spectre of an aging population. Older people were living longer, with more complex health conditions, and there were many more of them. If states in the Global North were not going to go bankrupt supporting growing numbers of elderly dependents via pensions and healthcare, they needed more workers paying into the system and securing the state's economic stability. Enter the flexible female worker.

There was just one problem: the exploitation of women's productive labour meant women were no longer providing reproductive labour at the same rate. This was a contradiction at the heart of the preference for women's productive labour over women's reproductive labour. The decline in birth rates, combined with the aging population, created an actual demographic crisis. This is the contradiction for which fascism believes it has a solution, and to which capitalism has so far failed to respond.

As the birth rates in the Global North dropped and the population aged, abortion was no longer a social question but, as far as the state was concerned, an economic question too. I realised, looking at the changing world around me, that the production of children – and who will pay for them – has become a key economic battlefront. This has taken the form of a backlash against abortion rights and women's reproductive agency that began in the Reagan era, as the social justice gains of the 1960s and 1970s screeched into reverse. Fears about demographic crises, women's increased economic autonomy and the impact on capital fuelled the anti-feminist backlash recorded by writer Susan Faludi – a backlash that sowed the seeds for the war against women's rights we are living through today.

In the early stages of this shock, capitalism showed itself to be adaptable, by finding a replacement labour source that it could import and exploit. So long as capitalist societies could import labour from abroad through migration, then they could stave off collapse. Orbán claimed in the speech mentioned in Chapter Six that the European Union believes if 'for every missing child, there should be one coming in and then the numbers will be fine'. His words sum up the solution neoliberal capitalism had chosen – even if Orbán didn't like it. Migrant labour offered capitalism a means to fill the gaps caused by a falling birth rate and have enough workers and wealth to support the aging population and prevent a demographic crisis.

As long as the ideology of neoliberalism held up, the importing of migrant labour and the inclusion of women in the workforce was acceptable. This didn't mean there weren't far-right, racist elements in society who were enraged by migration and women's rights – these forces never went away. But so long as people had jobs, so long as the system was working for them and so long as they had access to endless credit to continue being useful and productive consumers, this solution was acceptable to the majority. Rising female participation in the workforce and a narrowing gender pay gap caused by the reproductive shock was palatable even to the most sexist western man, provided he was also making money and enjoying prosperity – if, in other words, the system was functioning for *him*.

But then it *stopped* working for him. In 2008, that system broke down and all hell broke loose: neoliberalism stopped delivering and the promises capitalism had made were broken. Men saw their prosperity dwindle and their security crumble. They looked around and saw women and migrant people in the workplace, and believed those gains in equality had come at the cost of white male status. It's no wonder, then, that at this point laws promoting women's formal equality at work and in family disputes – along with protections from gender-based violence and the cultural normalisation of female sexual independence – all began to be reframed as an attack on men.

For the previous forty years, those pushing the neoliberal project had dismantled a sense of collective identity and unity in order to shape society around individualism. They sought to persuade us that we could and should exist as atomised, autonomous beings, and set out to destroy universalism and any idea, as Thatcher famously put it, that there was something called 'society'. When the neoliberal project started to collapse, an entire population was stranded. Suddenly, all the certainties promised by neoliberalism fell apart. History was supposed to have ended; it was harder to imagine the end of the world than the end of capitalism ... so what had happened, and what would happen next? Living through the crash – I was on the dole having been made redundant from my job in advertising – it was clear that the social and economic norms of the previous forty years had been smashed to pieces and, crucially, that nothing was there to take its place. The only place left to turn was those old certainties – nation, nature and war.

What the far right was able to do with that moment of chaos was fill it with the (wrong) answers. It told angry white men who felt dispossessed that they had lost their jobs and identity due to globalisation. It told them that migrants were responsible for their loss in status and those migrants were being encouraged to come to the Global North by an elite European Union intent on replacing the white race in order to enrich themselves. Feminism, the far right said, was in cahoots with this plan, deliberately suppressing the birth rate via abortion and sexual autonomy, to enact a white genocide – and, of course, this was all the fault of Jewish people.

To regain their power, the far right told white men, they needed to join a genocidal race war and create individual ethno-states; women's power could instead be found in the womb. All women had to do was take themselves out of the public space, return to the domestic, and exist as a reproductive body so the natural order of male supremacy could be restored. These messages were backed up by authoritarian leaders in the Global North, who over the past decade have all succeeded by promising the same three things to their radicalised, right-wing base and a radical-right global elite.

The first promise is that they will make their nation great again by returning to a fascist mythic past. Vote for us, they say, and you can be the patriarchal authority in your home, the white master, the warrior on horseback. This links to the second promise – to restore the imaginary natural order so beloved by fascism. Some leaders, notably Trump and Orbàn, made this claim through overt racism and the blatant repression of reproductive and sexual rights. In the UK, where leaders have tended to try to hide their racism, the representation of that so-called natural order is more coded. This promise included the slow withdrawing of women's economic equality, security and safety – something that was accelerated by the coronavirus pandemic – alongside a phoney culture war. Both promises sought to persuade white men they were being victimised and silenced by a metropolitan elite, and should blame the problems caused by deindustrialisation and neoliberalism on – yet again – women and minorities.

The final promise is to make it unthinkable that white, straight men and their authoritarian leaders will ever lose power – and therefore to ensure that white male supremacy will reign forever. Achieving that aim requires the cooperation of those who already have power. This is capitalism's dirty secret: the willingness of those benefiting from the system to support far-right beliefs and movements in order to protect their wealth and entrench their supremacy.

Before 2008, right-wing populist and authoritarian leaders, along with business elites, were seen as a kind of firewall against the far right. Governments were prepared to incorporate some anti-immigration policies and anti-welfare rhetoric, for example, to stave off a far-right assault on politics and society – not pleasant, of course, but a way of keeping the ugliest aspects of fascism under control. According to Paul Mason, that 'firewall is now on fire'.[3] As explored in the previous chapter, those right-wing populist leaders are now firmly in the far-right camp, or adopting far-right policy and rhetoric to entrench power.

The pressure pushing the elite towards the fascists is that same crisis facing capitalism: the demographic changes caused by aging populations threaten the economic stability of nations. Unless countries can raise enough money to support their older people, they will go bankrupt and take business and elite wealth down with them. Until recently, as the birth rate started to decrease due to women's reproductive independence, that money was raised via women's productive labour and their consumption, and by importing labour from abroad via migration. But that strategy is no longer working, and migration is no longer filling the gap. Women in the Global South are gaining the same reproductive choices as women in the North, meaning they too are having fewer children and the climate crisis is changing everything anyway.

The elites, then, who want to hold on to their wealth and power, have become increasingly willing to form an alliance with the mob in order to repress human rights. They need progress to end to hold on to their wealth: just like the fascists, they need history to be reversed. All of this is exacerbated of course by the climate crisis which will cause a collapse in the wealth created by the exploitation of the planet and fossil fuels.

It's important to note too, that billionaires back authoritarians and far-right mobs because such alliances are mutually beneficial. Political scientist Lee Drutman has found that increasingly concentrated wealth in the US results in more polarisation and extremism, especially on the right.[4] More polarisation is good for populist leaders, who can exploit those divisions, keep hold of power – and guarantee profits.

It's also no surprise that a big-business elite is OK about working with the far right. Traditionally, fascism has defended capitalism for its inherent anti-Marxism. Further, fascism 'nullifies the potential political action of the [working] class,' according to Neocleous, and therefore 'facilitates the extraction of surplus value for the capitalist class'.[5] Fascist movements also focus on crushing trade unions and workers' unity – useful for those whose money and power comes from financial, productive and reproductive exploitation. As Neocleous explains:

> Industrial capital can come to terms with any political regime so long as that regime does not actually expropriate it, and will willingly and happily come to terms with any regime which solves economic depression, ends political chaos, destroys the revolutionary socialist and communist movements, eliminates workers' institutions and commits itself to industrial (capital) modernisation.[6]

This is why the Nazi regime had big-business backing, for example. Capitalism is happy to adapt to fascism, selling women's and minority rights down the river, so long as its elites can repress workers' rights, entrench their own power and hold on to their wealth.

As neoliberalism collapsed following the financial crash and struggled along on life-support, it exposed a myth about progress and, particularly, a myth about women's status in society. The shock of women's newfound reproductive freedoms in the latter half of the twentieth century was softened by neoliberalism and women's move from the domestic into the public sphere; they became atomised worker/consumers whose productive labour helped keep the machine and its ideology running. As a result, we almost didn't notice the change that was happening. We accepted it as normal – an inevitable part of our lives. We took our rights for granted because those rights suited capitalism and the neoliberal power structures of the time. Similarly, while neoliberalism was in its heyday, it was happy to promote migration and the rights of people to move freely to seek work – work that enriched the elites. This was the thinking behind the Blair/Clinton years during which I came of age: progress in women's and migrants' rights is good because it makes us richer.

But when the system started to fall apart, and people began becoming poorer, it exposed how social progress was premised on that wealth creation. As soon as women's and minority rights stop working for the ruling classes, those rights become vulnerable to reversal. This was the lesson of the 1980s and the satanic panic: those years saw the beginnings of a declining birth rate and aging population that spooked the neoliberal elite and saw the growth of a radical-right backlash against women's reproductive rights. The problem is, the global crisis we face now is far, far worse.

So we are at a tipping point. But we have faced such moments before – and we can learn from them.

The success of capitalism in Early Modern Europe was achieved by pinning women to reproductive labour – by stigmatising women's work, attacking abortion and creating the ideal of a submissive pregnant wife, something explored by Silvia Federici in her seminal book on capitalism and reproductive rights *Caliban and the Witch*. Five centuries later, when women got involved in politics and attempted to live more liberated lives in nineteenth-century America, and rising migration was seen as a threat to the white, Anglo-Saxon population, the response was to impose restrictions on abortion. Then, in the years when European women got a taste for liberation following the First World War, having entered the workforce and won the vote, they were met with a backlash that forced them back to reproductive labour, most noticeably in Nazi Germany and fascist Italy. The pattern was repeated after women entered the workforce *en masse* during the Second World War – in the years that followed they were pushed out of their jobs to make way for returning men, while the cult of the feminine mystique sent a message that women's work was womb work. Progress was met by backlash, every time.

None of those glimpses of freedom matched the women's liberation revolution of the 1960s and 1970s, which, in the Global North at least, dismantled legislative barriers to equality and gave women control over their reproductive labour. Because society was cocooned from the reproductive revolution that had taken place due to the economic need for women's productive and consumptive labour, twinned with capital's ability to fill gaps with migration, there has been neither the need nor the desire to roll back the rights we have won since the 1960s – until now.

The good news is we do not have to lose this fight. We can make a choice to resist – to break out of the siege and demand that women's full humanity is respected.

I wrote this book when working two jobs, during three coronavirus lockdowns and while moving house. Spending hour after hour online every day, I watched as far-right anti-abortion conspiracy theories swirled around the US election, including the myth that abortions are satanic sacrifices designed to de-Christianise the West – a plot aided by (primarily Muslim) migration and fuelled by left-wing elites. Over one horrible weekend I reported on a mass shooting by an incel in my birthplace of Plymouth, UK, and the takeover of Afghanistan by the extremist Islamist Taliban group. On the day the fighters took Afghanistan's capital Kabul, images of women in shopfronts were painted over, while reports came in of girls as young as fifteen being rounded up and forced into marriage. Women were made to leave their jobs, girls were banned from secondary school and female MPs went into hiding. Twenty years of increased gender equality, including girls' education and women's political and judicial representation, swung into reverse. Months earlier, I had written about the 6 January 2021 insurrection in the United States and the presence of conspiracists, anti-abortionists and militias trying to overthrow democracy. I researched the abortion bans coming to Poland and Texas, waiting in horror to see what the Supreme Court would decide for US women – and when the blow came, I reported on what it meant for women in the States, in the Global South and in the UK. From East to West, it was clear that the global war on women was in full swing.

Researching this book made me realise just how deeply

some men hate women and how murderous are the genocidal far-right beliefs are about black and minority ethnic people. I read things that I cannot repeat, saw images and memes that I wish I had not – things you can't even tell your close friends because you don't want to upset them. Barely won rights were chucked away, established rights torn up, and women's lives are now hanging in the balance. Rights are fragile. They can so easily be broken.

Despite descending into some of the ugliest spaces I've ever had the displeasure of hanging around, I also have listened to and read about great efforts of resistance. From LGBTIQ activists in Romania and Hungary, pro-abortion marchers in Slovakia, people providing vulnerable teenagers access to safe abortion in Kenya, and the awesome force of Ireland's Together 4 Yes coalition, the great pleasure of writing this book has been the chance to engage with the bravery, dedication and determination of those resisting the assault of the far right.

The threat to reproductive and sexual freedoms from the far right is real, shown most devastatingly by the overruling of *Roe vs Wade* in the United States. We are at a tipping point thanks to the crisis in capitalism outlined above. This is a movement based on two violent oppressions: that of black and brown bodies of all genders, and that of women's and girls' bodies. It is a movement with a genocidal impulse and a goal of asserting white male supremacy via the exploitation of women's reproductive labour and the killing or forced repatriation of the black and global majority. It is funded by wealthy elite donors who want to goad a mob intent on sparking an ethnic war. It is a movement afraid of freedom – determined to destroy the freedoms that for women include the choice not to have a baby in service of an ethno-state. We do not have to let them, because we are movement too – and we can win.

Back in the nineteenth century, Karl Marx argued that human nature changes to keep pace with human societies. Crucially, Marx believed we have the capacity to change human nature itself by changing society. He argued that humans' biologically given purpose is to set ourselves free by changing *both* our environment *and* ourselves. Marx's theory honours the potential of humans to develop more progressive and equal societies that value women and minorities. Along with this societal change, human nature itself transforms to become more progressive and equal – to become free.

Such claims are anathema to the far right, which is, at its heart, anti-humanist and anti-freedom. But if Marx's theory of human nature is correct, it means the far right is categorically wrong in its claims about humanity. Our nature is not fixed, as fascist ideology claims. Instead we have the freedom to change society and ourselves. We don't have to be afraid of freedom.

We have reached a crossroads between fascism and a new, progressive future with a new economic and societal model that will meet the challenges of climate crisis and the rise of artificial intelligence. This choice is urgent. Go one way, and women's, LGBTIQ and black and minority ethnic people's lives will be blighted by oppression, forced to dodge hate and trying to resist genocide.

Choose the other way, and the future is ours.

Acknowledgements

So many people have been influential and helpful to me writing this book, not least because so much of the research for this book began in journalism projects for a variety of newspapers and magazines.

First, I need to thank the team at Verso – the cover designers, Jeanne Tao in production, and Catherine Smiles and Maya Osborne in marketing. But most of all, a huge thank you to my editor Jessie Kindig, whose passion and vision for women's rights and reproductive rights is so inspiring and vital. From day one, with the proposal, she has pushed my thinking further, made me ask questions of my work, supported me through thinking about structure, argument and framing, and helped me create a book I am proud of. Her insights and care throughout this process have been so invaluable. I am proud to work with an editor who is as determined to fight for reproductive rights as I am, and who is doing such amazing work in this area. Thank you!

I also would like to thank Rosie Warren at Verso for becoming my editor after Jessie left, and helping get the book through its last stages and into readers' hands. I am hugely indebted to the skills and patience of Natalie Hume, who copy-edited the book; I am in awe of her keen eye and sense of narrative.

I am deeply grateful to my agent Kate Johnson at Wolf Literary Services for her support and friendship. She understood what I wanted to achieve and helped me shape my proposal, as well as being a brilliant sounding board throughout the writing process. Thanks also to Rachel Crawford, who was my agent when Kate was on maternity leave and who got the proposal over the line.

I owe a huge debt to my editors at *openDemocracy 50:50*, Claire Provost and Nandini Archer. Their determination in exposing the far right and its backlash against reproductive rights not only opened my eyes to what was happening across Europe and the USA, but they also provided me with amazing reporting opportunities that kickstarted me to write this book. It's thanks to them that I went to Romania to report on what ADF was up to, that I went under cover for the first time, and then a second time ... and it's thanks to their hard work that more people are aware of how the anti-gender movement is acting and evolving.

Big thanks to Sascha Lavin for her friendship and for our brilliant working-partnership, including our investigations into Christian Nationalist influence.

Much of the proposal for this book was written when I was Ben Pimlott writer-in-residence at Birkbeck, University of London. Thank you to the university for providing me with the space and time I needed to do the preliminary research and to Professor Sarah Childs in particular for her support, enthusiasm and friendship. Thanks as well for the lunches. Thank you, Hanna Peltonen, too, for letting me house-sit your flat when you were away so I could finish drafting the proposal.

Thank you to Kaye Mitchell and Joanna Walsh for reading early drafts of the proposal. Thank you to Catherine Allen for reading my draft and for all the excellent conversations. Thank you to Iain Overton for providing feedback on close reading, and for challenging my thinking.

Thank you to everyone who gave up their time to speak to me for my research – including Ailbhe Smyth, Ada Petrizcko, Neil Datta, Seyward Darby, Zuzana Kriskova, Elis and many more, some of whom are anonymous.

A huge thank you to my friends Kayleigh Reed, Rosalind

Harvey and Laura Keeling who have put up with me banging on about abortion rights, trad wives and the far right.

Thank you to Paul Mason for helping me with specific questions about the far right and capitalism.

Finally, thank you to the women who are fighting for abortion rights around the world right now and to all the women who fought before. This book is dedicated to every single one of you.

Notes

Preface

1 Mathew Murphy, 'CPAC Head Suggests Abortion Ban Will Solve Great Replacement', Daily Beast, 19 May 2022.
2 Siân Norris, 'Emboldened Opposition and a Galvanised Movement', *Byline Times*, 29 June 2022.

Introduction

1 Center for Reproductive Rights, 'The World's Abortion Laws', reproductiverights.org.
2 Alvin Chang, Andrew Witherspoon and Jessica Glenza, 'Abortion Deserts: America's New Geography of Access to Care – Mapped', *Guardian*, 24 June 2022.
3 Siân Norris, 'Satanic Conspiracies and Brexiteers: Inside a Bizarre Academy for Anti-Abortionists', openDemocracy, 29 October 2019.
4 Rig Live #WOW with Tomi Arayomi discussing Satanic ritual abuse, 9 September 2020, YouTube.

1. The Ideology

1 Paul Mason, *How to Stop Fascism*, Allen Lane, 2021, p. xxi.
2 Ruth Ben-Ghiat, *Strongmen: From Mussolini to the Present*, Profile Books, 2020, p. 67.
3 Mark Neocleous, *Fascism*, Open University Press, 1997, p. xi.
4 Ibid., pp. 75–6.
5 Ibid., p. 79.
6 The Red Pill (quarantined; thread since deleted), reddit.com.

7 Agenda Europe, *Restoring the Natural Order: An Agenda for Europe*, agendaeurope.files.wordpress.com.
8 J. Noakes and G. Pridham (eds), *Nazism 1919–1945, Vol 1: The Rise to Power*, University of Exeter, 1983.
9 Neocleous, *Fascism*, p. 15. My emphasis.
10 Louie Dean Vallencia Garcia, 'This Is What Peaceful Ethnic Cleansing Looks Like', Centre for Analysis of the Radical Right, 4 October 2019.
11 Ibid.
12 Benito Mussolini, speech 21 April 1922, cited in Emilio Gentile 'Fascism as Political Religion', *Journal of Contemporary History*, vol. 25, no. 3 (1990), pp. 229–51.
13 Alon Confino, *Foundational Pasts: The Holocaust as Historical Understanding*, Cambridge University Press, 2012.
14 Jason Stanley, *How Fascism Works*, Random House, 2018, p. 14.
15 Neocleous, *Fascism*, p. 79.
16 Jacob Mikanowski, 'The Call of the Drums', *Harper's Magazine*, August 2019.
17 Ibid.
18 Paul Mason, *How to Stop Fascism*, Allen Lane, 2021, p. xxi.
19 Thierry Baudet, 'Houellebecq's Unfinished Critique of Liberal Modernity', *American Affairs Journal*, vol. 3, no. 2 (summer 2019).

2. The Extremists

1 Thierry Baudet, 'Houellebecq's Unfinished Critique of Liberal Modernity', *American Affairs Journal*, vol. 3, no. 2 (summer 2019).
2 Census for England and Wales, Office for National Statistics, 2011 and 2021.
3 European Network Against Racism.
4 Brentan Tarrant, 'The Great Replacement', March 2019.
5 Eleanor Penny, 'The Deadly Myth of the Great Replacement', *New Statesman*, 9 August 2019.
6 Cas Mudde, *The Far Right Today*, Polity Press, 2019, p. 43.
7 Ibid.
8 Brian Brady and Jane Merrick, 'BNP Official Ousted after Claims of Coup Bid Against Griffin', *Independent*, 4 April 2010.

9   Simon Murdoch and Joe Mulhall, 'Patriotic Alternative Uniting the Fascist Right?', HOPE not hate, August 2020.

10 Ibid.

11 Mark Collett, *The Fall of the Western Man*, self-published, 2016.

12 *Rescue* (summer 2018), p. 3, thelifeleague.com.

13 Ruth Ben-Ghiat, *Strongmen*, Profile Books, 2020, p. 71.

14 Ibid.

15 'The Great Replacement in Blackpool', Knights Templar Order, 20 November 2019, knightstemplarorder.com. My emphasis.

16 Guardian staff, 'Republican Congressman: Civilisation Threatened by "Somebody Else's Babies"', *Guardian*, 13 March 2017.

17 Brian Naylor, 'Rep Steve King Stands by Controversial Tweet about "Somebody Else's Babies"', NPR, 13 March 2017.

18 Leslie Reagan, *When Abortion Was a Crime*, University of California Press, 1997, p. 9.

19 Ibid., p. 10.

20 Angela Y. Davis, *Women, Race and Class*, Penguin Modern Classics, 1981, p. 4.

21 Reagan, *When Abortion Was a Crime*, p. 11.

22 Ibid.

23 Davis, *Women, Race and Class*, p. 188.

24 Charu Gupta, 'Politics of Gender: Women in Nazi Germany', *Economic and Political Weekly*, 27 April 1991.

25 PRRI Staff, 'Understanding QAnon's Connection to American Politics, Religion and Media Consumption', PRRI, 27 May 2021, PRRI.org.

26 Ali Breland, 'Why Are Right Wing Conspiracies So Obsessed with Paedophilia', *Mother Jones* (July/August 2019).

27 Paul Thomas, 'How QAnon Uses Satanic Rhetoric to Set Up a Narrative of Good Versus Evil', *Conversation*, 20 October 2020.

28 PRRI Staff, 'Understanding QAnon's Connection to American Politics, Religion and Media Consumption'.

29 YoltsEmily01, Twitter, 7 November 2020.

30 ClareNJ_, Twitter, 2 November 2020.

31 Tr1AL11, Twitter, 2 November 2020.

32 Carter Sherman, 'This Convicted Planned Parenthood Bomber Was at the Capitol "Fighting" for Trump', *Vice*, 14 January 2021.

33 Jamie Roberts, *Four Hours at the Capitol*, BBC documentary, 2021.

34 'Read Trump's Jan 6 Speech, A Key Part of Impeachment Trial', NPR, 10 February 2021.

35 Ryan J. Reilly, 'Derrick Evans Has Now Been Sentenced for Storming the Capitol', NBC News, 22 June 2022. Caitlin Nolan, 'For Women Who Say Derrick Evans Harassed Them, West Virginia Law-Maker's Capitol Assault Arrest Is No Surprise', *Inside Edition*, 14 January 2021.

36 Roberts, *Four Hours at the Capitol*.

37 Jack Brewster, 'QAnon-Supporting Marjorie Taylor Greene Wins Congress Seat', *Forbes*, 3 November 2020.

38 Pierce Alexander Dignam and Deana A. Rohlinger, 'Misogynistic Men Online: How the Red Pill Helped Elect Trump', *Signs*, vol. 44, no. 3 (spring 2019).

39 Paul Mason, *Clear Bright Future*, Allen Lane, 2019, p. 87.

40 Paul Mason, *How to Stop Fascism*, Allen Lane, 2021, p. 224.

41 Aja Romano, 'How the Alt-Right's Sexism Lures Men into White Supremacy', *Vox*, 14 December 2016, vox.com.

42 Anti-Defamation League, 'When Women Are the Enemy: The Intersection of Misogyny and White Supremacy', 20 July 2018, adl.org.

43 Dignam and Rohlinger, 'Misogynistic Men Online'.

44 Ibid.

45 Ibid.

46 Ibid.

47 Ben-Ghiat, *Strongmen*, p. 138.

48 Dignam and Rohlinger, 'Misogynistic Men Online'.

49 Ibid.

50 GameDevCel, 'What Pisses Me Off Most Is That Chad's Bastards Are Being Killed', 27 June 2020, incels.net.

51 Uncommon, 'Women Destroying Cultures and Countries', 17 October 2020, incels.net.

52 GameDevCel, 'Remember FOIDs Are More than Willing to Genocide to See Their Rights', 30 July 2020, incels.net.

53 Cofffeee, 'Abortion Topic', 10 February 2020, incels.net. Welcome ToMyDNA, 'Abortion Topic', 10 February 2020, incels.net.

54 GameDevCel, 'Abortion Topic'.

55 Ibid.

56 Tupolev, 'Strengthening Components in the Incel Brain', 22 June 2020, incels.net.

57 Kaczor, 'Confess to Me Boyos', 9 July 2020, incels.net.

58 'War on Men', Knights Templar International, December 2019, knightstemplarorder.com.

59 Peter Thiel, 'The Education of a Libertarian', Cato Institute, 13 April 2009, cato-unbound.org.

60 Kaczor, 'Women Destroying Cultures and Countries', 16 October 2020, incels.net.

61 Rachel Andrews, 'Interview with Silvia Federici', *White Review*, January 2022.

62 Lisa Ko, 'Unwanted Sterilisation and Eugenics Programmes in the United States', PBS, 29 January 2016, pbs.org.

63 Ibid.

64 Davis, *Women, Race and Class*, p. 197.

65 Natasha Lennard, 'The Long, Disgraceful History of American Attacks on Brown and Black Women's Reproductive Systems', *Intercept*, 17 September 2020.

66 Jane Lawrence, 'The Little Known History of the Sterilisation of Native American Women', JStor Daily.

67 Tina Vasquez, 'Exclusive: Georgia Doctor Who Forcibly Sterilised Detained Women Has Been Identified', *Prism*, 15 September 2020.

68 'Romani Women Subjected to Forced Sterilisation in Slovakia', Centre for Reproductive Rights, 28 January 2003, reproductive rights.org.

69 Sian Norris, 'The Quipu Project: Testimonies of Forced Sterilisation in Peru', *openDemocracy 50:50*, 16 December 2015.

70 Edwin M Gold et al., 'Therapeutic Abortions in New York City: A Twenty Year Review', *American Journal of Public Health*, vol. 15 (July 1965).

71 Tobi Thomas and Jessica Elgot, 'Women from Poorer Backgrounds Three Times More Likely to Have Abortions', *Guardian*, 23 March 2021.

72 Davis, *Women, Race and Class*, p. 185.

73 Emily O'Reilly, *Masterminds of the Right*, Attic Press, 1992.

3. The Infiltration

1 Anne Kioko, 'CitizenGO Denounced Cultural Imperialism and the Ideological Colonization at the United Nations', YouTube, March 2021.

2 Neil Datta, *Restoring the Natural Order: The Religious Extremists' Vision to Mobilise European Societies Against Human Right*

on *Sexuality and Reproduction*, European Parliamentary Forum on Population and Development, April 2018.

3 Ellen Rivera, 'Unraveling the Anti-Choice Supergroup Agenda Europe in Spain, *IERES Occasional Papers*, no. 4 (October 2019).

4 Emily O'Reilly, *Masterminds of the Right*, Attic Press, p.11

5 Ibid.

6 Agenda Europe, *Restoring the Natural Order: An Agenda For Europe*, agendaeurope.files.wordpress.com.

7 Ibid.

8 Ibid.

9 Ibid.

10 Ibid.

11 World Health Organization, 'Safe Abortion: Technical and Policy Guidance for Health Systems', 2nd edition (2012).

12 Datta, *Restoring the Natural Order*.

13 Ibid.

14 Samantha Brick, 'Anguish of Men the Whose Babies Were Aborted Against Their Will', *Daily Mail*, 6 January 2022.

15 Agenda Europe, *Restoring the Natural Order*.

16 J. C. Willke and Mrs Wilke, *Abortion: Questions and Answers*, Hayes Publishing Co., 1988.

17 Joseph Scheidler, *Closed: 99 Ways to Stop Abortion*, Tan Books, 1994.

18 Robert Arnakis, *The Real Nature of Politics*, Family Research Council Action webcast, 12 July 2017.

19 Agenda Europe, *Restoring the Natural Order*.

20 Ibid.

21 Ibid.

22 Nina Houben, *A Step in the Right Direction: The Impact of Anti-Rights Group CitizenGO on Minority Groups' Wellbeing in Kenya*, Women's Link Worldwide, 8 June 2020.

23 Agenda Europe, *Restoring the Natural Order*.

24 Adam Ramsay and Claire Provost, 'Revealed: The Trump-Linked Super Pac Working Behind the Scenes to Drive Europe's Voters to the Far-Right', *openDemocracy*, 25 April 2019.

25 Heidi Beirich and Mark Potok, 'The Council for National Policy Behind the Curtain', *SPLC*, 17 May 2016, splcenter.org/hatewatch.

26 Alliance Defending Freedom, 'About Us', adflegal.org/about-us.

27 Ricki Stern and Anne Sundberg, *Reversing Roe*, Netflix, 2018.

28 Stephanie Kirchgaessner and Jessica Glenza, 'Women Can Say

No to Sex if Roe Falls, Says Architect of Texas Abortion Ban', *Guardian*, 17 September 2021.

29 Ibid.

30 Fiona Bruce, speech to Westminster, 3 July 2020, *Hansard*.

31 Ibid.

32 Heartbeat International, *Heartbeat History Brochure*.

33 Ibid.

34 Projects Propublica, 'Non Profit Explorer for Heartbeat International', projects.propublica.org.

35 Sian Norris, 'You Could Die and Turn Your Husband Gay', interview with Mara Clarke, *openDemocracy*, 17 February 2020.

36 I took the 'Talking about Abortion' webinar in September 2019 as part of an investigative article into crisis pregnancy centres for *openDemocracy 50:50*.

37 National Health Service, 'Risks: Abortion', nhs.org.uk.

38 'Abortion and Cancer Risk', American Cancer Association, cancer. org.

39 'Risks: Abortion', National Health Service, nhs.org.uk.

40 Caitlin Shannon, L. Perry Brothers, Neena M. Philip and Beverly Winikoff, 'Ectopic Pregnancy and Medical Abortion', *National Library of Medicine*, July 2004.

41 Heartbeat International, 'Abortion: The Basics', based on research conducted in September 2019.

42 'Evidence You Can Use: TRAP Laws', Guttmacher Institute, guttmacher.org.

43 Email sent to the author, 19 November 2020.

44 Philippa Taylor, 'Mythbusters: Abortion and Mental Health', Christian Medical Fellowship, cmf.org.uk.

45 Christian Concern, Christian Legal Centre, *Abortion: Second Edition*, 2019, archive.christianconcern.com.

46 Katie Forster, 'Anti-Abortion Charity Funded by Tampon Tax Gives Pro Life Talk in 200 Schools Despite Government Guidelines', *Independent*.

47 Life, 'Abortion and Mental Health – Why Society Needs to Think Again', 24 November 2017, lifecharity.org.uk.

48 Marian Knight, 'Saving Lives, Improving Mothers' Care', *MBrace UK*, December 2020.

49 Office of National Statistics, 'Number of Deaths Involving Abortion in England and Wales, Deaths Registered between 2015 and 2019', 15 October 2020.

50 Francesca Visser, 'Inside Italian Public Hospitals, I Saw How

a US-Linked Anti-Abortion Network Is Humiliating Women', *openDemocracy 50:50*, 9 March 2020.

51 Ibid.

4. The Allies

1 Mark Neocleous, *Fascism*, Open University Press, 1997, p. 79.
2 Jason Stanley, *How Fascism Works*, Random House, 2018, p. 13.
3 Wilhelm Reich, *Die Massenpsychologie des Faschismus* [*The Mass Psychology of Fascism*], Farrar, Straus and Giroux, 1933, quoted in David Elkind, 'Wilhelm Reich – The Psychoanalyst as Revolutionary', *New York Times*, 18 April 1971.
4 Jason Köhne, speech to Patriotic Alternative Conference 2020, Radio Albion; radioalbion.com.
5 Author's interview with 'Issy', October 2021.
6 Author's interview with Seyward Darby, for a *Byline Times* article, January 2021.
7 Elizabeth Wurtzel, *Bitch: In Praise of Difficult Women*, Random House, 1998, Part One.
8 Alexandra Minna Stern, 'Alt-Right Women and the White Baby Challenge', *Salon*, 14 July 2019.
9 Seyward Darby, *Sisters in Hate*, Little Brown, July 2020, p. 103.
10 Laura Doyle, *The Surrendered Wife*, St Martin Publishing, 2015 edition (2001), p. 128.
11 Lauren Southern, 'Top 10 Anti-Feminist Moments', Rebel News, 8 March 2017, youtube.com.
12 Ibid.
13 Ruth Ben-Ghiat, *Strongmen*, Profile Books, 2020, p. 121.
14 Darby, *Sisters in Hate*.
15 Angela Y. Davis, *Women, Race and Class*, Penguin Modern Classics, 1981, p. 3.
16 Ibid.
17 Jason Stanley, *How Fascism Works*, Random House, 2018, p. 17. My emphasis.
18 Julia Ebner, *Going Dark*, Bloomsbury UK, 2020, p. 54.
19 Ibid.
20 Andrew Marantz, 'Samantha's Journey into the Alt-Right, and Back', *New Yorker*, 22 November 2019.
21 Laura Doyle, *The Surrendered Wife*, St Martin Publishing, 2015 edition (2001).

22 Form 990 for Alliance Defending Freedom, 2016.
23 Dear Colleague Letter on transgender students, US Department of Justice and US Department of Education, 13 May 2016.
24 William J. Malone, *Gender Resource Guide*, Family Policy Alliance, 2022, genderresourceguide.com.
25 Tony Perkins, speech at Oak Initiative Summit, April 2011, *SPLC*, splcenter.org.
26 Helen Joyce, *Trans*, One World, July 2021, p. 225.
27 Natalie Allen, 'This New Bill Could Mandate Unrestricted Access to Abortion', Alliance Defending Freedom blog, 17 June 2021, adflegal.org.
28 Ariel Levy, *Female Chauvinist Pigs*, Simon & Schuster UK, 2006, p. 117.

5. The Money

1 Author's interview with Neil Datta, May 2021.
2 Neil Datta, *Tip of the Iceberg: Religious Extremist Funders Against Human Rights for Sexuality and Reproductive Health in Europe 2009–18*, European Parliamentary Forum for Sexual and Reproductive Rights, June 2021.
3 Ibid.
4 Lester Feder, 'The Rise of Europe's Religious Right', Buzzfeed, 28 July 2014.
5 'Why Has the Leak of 15,000 HazteOír Documents Gone Virtually Unnoticed?', 12 April 2017, media.cat.
6 Datta, *Tip of the Iceberg*.
7 Ibid.
8 Neil Datta, *Restoring the Natural Order: The Religious Extremists' Vision to Mobilise European Societies Against Human Right on Sexuality and Reproduction*, European Parliamentary Forum on Population and Development, April 2018.
9 Siân Norris, 'How the US Christian Right Lends Support to Europe's Anti-LGBTIQ Movement', *Byline Times*, 24 June 2021.
10 'Tbilisi Pride Cancelled as Mob Violence Continues', *OC Media*, 5 July 2021.
11 Adam Ramsay and Claire Provost, 'Revealed: The Trump-Linked Super Pac Working Behind the Scenes to Drive Europe's Voters to the Far-Right', *openDemocracy*, 25 April 2019.
12 Datta, *Tip of the Iceberg*.

13 Ellen Rivera, 'Unraveling the Anti-Choice Supergroup Agenda Europe in Spain', *IERES Occasional Papers no* 4 October 2019.

14 Datta, *Tip of the Iceberg.*

15 Ibid.

16 Ibid.

17 Neil Datta, *Modern Day Crusaders in Europe*, European Parliamentary Forum for Sexual and Reproductive Rights, June 2020.

18 Ibid.

19 Datta, *Tip of the Iceberg.*

20 Interview with Duke Paul of Oldenburg, Pro Europea Christiana, 10 May 2012, nobility.org.

21 Ibid.

22 Datta, *Tip of the Iceberg.*

23 Rivera, 'Unraveling the Anti-Choice Supergroup Agenda Europe'.

24 Marta Borraz and Raúl Sánchez, 'Cinco de los colectivos antiabortistas más activos recibieron casi dos millones de euros de dinero público de 2014 a 2018' [Five of the most active anti-abortion groups received almost 2 million euros of public money between 2014–2018], *El Diario*, 19 January 2019, eldiario.es.

25 Datta, *Tip of the Iceberg.*

26 Kevin Aqiulina, Austin Bencini, Giovanni Bonello and Tonio Borg, 'Two Steps Forward, Two Back', *Times of Malta*, 5 February 2022.

27 Datta, *Tip of the Iceberg.*

28 Ibid.

29 Ibid.

30 Ibid.

31 J. Lester Feder and Susie Armitage, 'Emails Show Pro-Family Activists Feeding Contacts to Russian Nationalists', Buzzfeed, 8 December 2014.

32 Wikileaks, 'The Intolerance Network', 5 August 2021, wikileaks. org.

33 Ibid.

34 Ibid.

35 Andy Kroll, 'The Dark Money ATM of the Conservative Movement', *Mother Jones*, 5 February 2013.

36 Jane Mayer, *Dark Money*, Doubleday, 2016, p. 312.

37 Anne Nelson, *Shadow Network*, Bloomsbury, 2019, p. 71.

38 Ibid.

39 Datta, *Tip of the Iceberg.*

40 Anne Appelbaum, 'History Will Judge the Complicit', *Atlantic*.

41 Lambda Legal, *Courts, Confirmations and Consequences*, Lambda Legal, January 2021.

42 Jeffrey Toobin, 'The Conservative Pipeline to the Supreme Court', *New Yorker*, 10 April 2017.

43 Andrew Perez and Julia Rock, 'How Dark Money Bought a Supreme Court Seat', *The Lever*, 19 December 2021.

44 Imyoung Choi, 'Koch-Backed Advocacy Group Launched a "Full Scale" Campaign to Push Amy Coney-Barrett's Supreme Court Nomination', *Business Insider*, 27 September 2020.

45 Nancy MacLean, *Democracy in Chains*, Penguin Random House, 2017.

6. The Politicians

1 Peter Geoghegan, *Democracy for Sale*, Apollo, 2020.

2 Author's interview Neil Datta, May 2021.

3 Julia Ebner, *Going Dark*, Bloomsbury UK, 2020, p. 226.

4 Claudia Torrisi, Claire Provost and Mary Fitzgerald, 'A Deep Dive into Dark Money', *Face*, 28 August 2019.

5 Geoghegan, *Democracy for Sale*.

6 'Hungary's Appalling Treatment of Asylum Seekers Condemned', Amnesty International UK blog, 27 September 2016.

7 Ebner, *Going Dark*, p. 46.

8 Cristina Maza, 'Pro-Trump Christian Extremist Prepares Serb Nationalists for New War with Muslims', *Newsweek*, 1 January 2018.

9 Viktor Orbán, 'Speech at 3rd Budapest Demographic Summit,' *About Hungary*, 5 September 2019, abouthungary.hu.

10 'The Government Wants "A Hungarian Hungary and a European Europe"', *About Hungary*, 18 Sep 2017, abouthungary.hu.

11 Ivan Kristen and Stephen Holmes, *The Light That Failed*, Penguin; 2020.

12 Ibid, p. 10.

13 Ibid, p. 14.

14 Adam Withnail, 'Aylan Kurdi's Story: How a Small Syrian Child Came to Be Washed Up on a Beach in Turkey', *Independent*, 3 September 2015.

15 Nikolaus Blome and Christian Stenzel, 'Ihr Wolltet Die Migranten, Wir Nicht', *Das Bild*, 7 January 2017.

16 James Landale, 28 May 2002, twitter.com.

17 Gergely Szacas, 'Orban Offers Financial Incentives to Boost Birth Rate', *Reuters*, 12 February 2019.

18 Dr Ingrid Detter de Frankopan, *The Suicide of Europe*, self-published, 2016.

19 Tucker Carlson, 'Hungary's Government Wants to Help Families Grow', *Fox News*, 30 July 2019.

20 Nikolaus Blome and Christian Stenzel, 'Ihr Wolltet Die Migranten, Wir Nicht', *Das Bild*, 7 January 2017.

21 Miklós Kásler, 'Ethnic and Demographic Changes in Hungary's (more than) 1100 Years Long History', *Polgári Szemle*, vol. 13 (special issue), 2017.

22 Nick Thorpe, 'Hungary Footballers' Row Exposes Gay Rights Split', *BBC News*, 14 April 2021.

23 Dr Willie Parker, *Life's Work: A Moral Argument for Choice*, Simon & Schuster, 2017, p. 164.

24 Edit Inotai, 'Hungary's Family Plan Seeks to "Save the Nation"', *Balkan Insight*, 6 August 2019.

25 Ginzia Arruzza, Tithi Bhattacharya and Nancy Fraser, *Feminism For The 99%: A Manifesto*, Verso, 2019, p. 23.

26 Reva Siegel and Duncan Hosie, 'Trump's Anti-Abortion and Anti-Immigration Plans May Share a Goal', *Time*, 13 December 2019.

27 Tucker Carlson, 'Hungary's Government Wants to Help Families Grow', *Fox News*, 30 July 2019.

28 Siegel and Hosie, 'Trump's Anti-Abortion and Anti-Immigration Plans May Share a Goal'.

29 Siân Norris, 'Nazi Speeches and Fascists Return', *Byline Times*, 8 August 2022.

30 Author's interview with Ada Petrizcko, November 2020.

31 Neil Datta, *Tip of the Iceberg: Religious Extremist Funders Against Human Rights for Sexuality and Reproductive Health in Europe 2009–18*, European Parliamentary Forum for Sexual and Reproductive Rights, June 2021.

32 Jason Stanley, *How Fascism Works*, Random House, 2018, p. 35.

33 Ibid, p. 37.

34 Giada Zampano, 'Italy's Politics Give New Life to Anti-Abortion Campaign', *Politico*, 18 November 2018.

35 Jessica Phelan, 'Verona Defies Italy's Abortion Law and Declares Itself a Pro-Life City', *Local*, 5 October 2018.

36 Geoghegan, *Democracy for Sale*.

37 Claire Provost, 'How the Far Right Is Weaponising "The Family"', *The Face*, 17 April 2019.

38 Maya Oppenheim, 'Verona Protests: Tens of Thousands of Campaigners March Against "Medieval" Anti LGBT+ and Anti-Abortion Conference', *The Independent*, 1 April 2019.

39 Lester Federalists and Giulia Alagna, 'Italy Is Ground Zero for the War on Women – Which Is Why These Far-Right Groups Are Meeting There', Buzzfeed, March 2019.

40 Provost, 'How the Far Right Is Weaponising "The Family"'.

41 Geoghegan, *Democracy for Sale.*

42 Norris, 'Nazi Speeches and Fascists Return'.

43 Vox Party, '100 Urgent Vox Measures for Spain', 2018.

44 Thomas Perroteau, 'Far Right Vox Challenge Spain's Fight Against Gender Based Violence', *Local*, 19 November 2019.

45 Ibid.

46 Deborah Madden, 'Right Wing Parties in Spain Are Pushing Extreme Positions on Abortion Ahead of Sunday's Election', *Independent*, 26 April 2019.

47 Shaun Walker, 'How a Slovakian Neo-Nazi Got Elected', *Guardian*, 14 February 2019.

48 Miroslava German Sirotnikova, 'Kotleba Slovak Extremist Who Made Far Right Fashionable', *Balkan Insight*, 26 February 2020.

49 Michael Colbourne, 'Marian Kotleba Wants to Make Slovakia Fascist Again', *Foreign Policy*, 28 February 2020.

50 Walker, 'How a Slovakian Neo-Nazi Got Elected'.

51 Michaela Terenzani, 'Marching in Step', *Slovak Spectator*, 21 May 2018.

52 Ibid.

53 Author's interview with Zuzanna Kriskova, November 2018.

54 Author's interview with 'Elis', July 2020.

55 Miroslava German Sirotnikova, 'Right Power: Slovakia Mulls New Laws Limiting Abortion', *Balkan Insight*, 13 July 2020.

56 Thierry Baudet, 'Houellebecq's Unfinished Critique of Liberal Modernity', *American Affairs Journal*, vol. 3, no. 2 (summer 2019).

57 Naomi O'Leary, 'New Dutch Far-Right Leader's Staying Power', *Politico*, 22 May 2019.

58 Kathleen Brown, 'The Renaissance of Germany's Anti-Abortion Programme', *Jacobin*, 15 March 2018.

59 Siân Norris, 'Mainstream Conservatism and Far Right Extremism an Increasingly Blurred Distinction', *Byline Times*, 12 April 2021.

60 The Windrush Scandal was the revelation in 2017 that people who had come to the UK with their parents from Caribbean countries

in the post-war period and up until the 1970s were being deported despite having lived in the UK most of their lives. Because they had come to the UK under an outdated set of immigration rules, they did not have the correct paperwork that would have guaranteed their right to live in the country. Their landing cards, which would have proved they had the right to live in the UK, had been destroyed. The Windrush was the name of the ship on which migrant people from the Caribbean travelled to the UK in 1948. The scandal led to the resignation of home secretary Amber Rudd.

61   Jane Mayer, *Dark Money*, Doubleday, 2016, p. 125.
62   Ibid.
63   Geoghegan, *Democracy for Sale*.
64   Nafeez Ahmed, 'New Government Counter-Extremism Chief's Ties to Pro-Donald Trump Hate Groups', *Byline Times*, 13 April 2021.
65   Daniel Ikenson, Simon Lester and Daniel Hannan, eds, *The Ideal U.S.–U.K. Free Trade Agreement: A Free Trader's Perspective*, Cato Institute, 2018.
66   Geoghegan, *Democracy for Sale*.
67   Heather Stewart, 'Women Bearing 86% of Austerity Burden, Commons Figures Reveal', *Guardian*, 9 March 2017.
68   Jon Trickett, 'One in Six Refuges Have Closed since 2010 – the Tories Must Do More to Protect Vulnerable Women', Labour List, 27 March 2017.
69   'Child Poverty in Working Households Up by 800,000 Since 2010, Says TUC', TUC website, 18 November 2019.
70   Chaminda Jayanetti, 'New Equalities Minister Attacked "Modern Feminism" and "Me Too"', *Observer*, 22 November 2020.
71   Liz Truss, 'Dignity and Humanity, Not Quotas and Targets', *ConservativeHome*, 17 December 2020.
72   'Gender and Poverty Briefing', Women's Budget Group, June 2015.
73   'Ethnicity Pay Gaps in Britain', Office for National Statistics, 2018.
74   Peter Walker, 'Tory MP Criticised for Using Antisemitic Term Cultural Marxism', *Guardian*, 26 March 2019.
75   Oliver Dowden, 'Standing Up for Our Values', speech to the Heritage Foundation, 15 February 2022.

7. The Tipping Point

1 Paul Mason, *How to Stop Fascism*, Allen Lane, 2021, p. xiv.
2 Ibid.
3 Ibid, p. xiii.
4 Jane Mayer, *Dark Money*, Doubleday, 2016, p. 364.
5 Mark Neocleous, *Fascism*, Open University Press, 1997, p. 46.
6 Ibid, p. 52.

Index